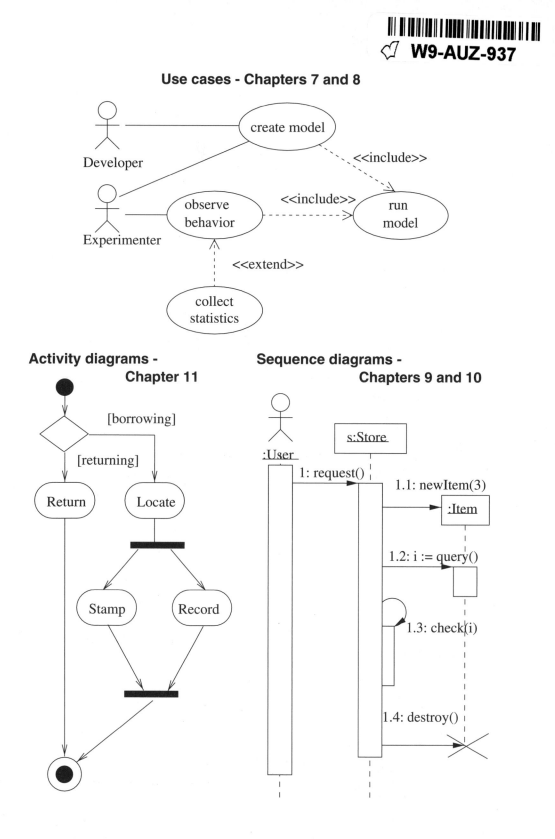

Use cases - Chapters 7 and 8

Developer

create model

<<include>>

Experimenter

observe behavior

<<include>>

run model

<<extend>>

collect statistics

Activity diagrams - Chapter 11

[borrowing]

[returning]

Return

Locate

Stamp

Record

Sequence diagrams - Chapters 9 and 10

:User

s:Store

1: request()

1.1: newItem(3)

:Item

1.2: i := query()

1.3: check(i)

1.4: destroy()

Using UML

Updated Edition

The Addison-Wesley Object Technology Series

Grady Booch, Ivar Jacobson, and James Rumbaugh, Series Editors

For more information check out the series web site [http://www.awl.com/cseng/otseries/] as well as the pages on each book [http://www.awl.com/cseng/I-S-B-N/] (I-S-B-N represents the actual ISBN, including dashes).

David Bellin and Susan Suchman Simone, *The CRC Card Book*, ISBN 0-201-89535-8

Robert V. Binder, *Testing Object-Oriented Systems: Models, Patterns, and Tools*, ISBN 0-201-80938-9

Grady Booch, *Object Solutions: Managing the Object-Oriented Project*, ISBN 0-8053-0594-7

Grady Booch, *Object-Oriented Analysis and Design with Applications, Second Edition*, ISBN 0-8053-5340-2

Grady Booch, James Rumbaugh, and Ivar Jacobson, *The Unified Modeling Language User Guide*, ISBN 0-201-57168-4

Don Box, *Essential COM*, ISBN 0-201-63446-5

Don Box, Keith Brown, Tim Ewald, and Chris Sells, *Effective COM: 50 Ways to Improve Your COM and MTS-based Applications*, ISBN 0-201-37968-6

Alistair Cockburn, *Surviving Object-Oriented Projects: A Manager's Guide*, ISBN 0-201-49834-0

Dave Collins, *Designing Object-Oriented User Interfaces*, ISBN 0-8053-5350-X

Bruce Powel Douglass, *Doing Hard Time: Designing and Implementing Embedded Systems with UML*, ISBN 0-201-49837-5

Bruce Powel Douglass, *Real-Time UML, Second Edition: Developing Efficient Objects for Embedded Systems*, ISBN 0-201-65784-8

Desmond F. D'Souza and Alan Cameron Wills, *Objects, Components, and Frameworks with UML: The Catalysis Approach*, ISBN 0-201-31012-0

Martin Fowler, *Analysis Patterns: Reusable Object Models*, ISBN 0-201-89542-0

Martin Fowler, *Refactoring: Improving the Design of Existing Code*, ISBN 0-201-48567-2

Martin Fowler with Kendall Scott, *UML Distilled, Second Edition: Applying the Stndard Object Modeling Language*, ISBN 0-201-65873-X

Peter Heinckiens, *Building Scalable Database Applications: Object-Oriented Design, Architectures, and Implementations*, ISBN 0-201-31013-9

Christine Hofmeister, Robert Nord, Soni Dilip, *Applied Software Architecture*, ISBN 0-201-32571-3

Ivar Jacobson, Grady Booch, and James Rumbaugh, *The Unified Software Development Process*, ISBN 0-201-57169-2

Ivar Jacobson, Magnus Christerson, Patrik Jonsson, and Gunnar Overgaard, *Object-Oriented Software Engineering: A Use Case Driven Approach*, ISBN 0-201-54435-0

Ivar Jacobson, Maria Ericsson, and Agneta Jacobson, *The Object Advantage: Business Process Reengineering with Object Technology*, ISBN 0-201-42289-1

Ivar Jacobson, Martin Griss, and Patrik Jonsson, *Software Reuse: Architecture, Process and Organization for Business Success*, ISBN 0-201-92476-5

David Jordan, *C++ Object Databases: Programming with the ODMG Standard*, ISBN 0-201-63488-0

Philippe Kruchten, *The Rational Unified Process: An Introduction*, ISBN 0-201-60459-0

Wilf LaLonde, *Discovering Smalltalk*, ISBN 0-8053-2720-7

Dean Leffingwell and Don Widrig, *Managing Software Requirements: A Unified Approach*, ISBN 0-201-61593-2

Chris Marshall, *Enterprise Modeling with UML: Designing Successful Software through Business Analysis*, ISBN 0-201-43313-3

Lockheed Martin, Advanced Concepts Center and Rational Software Corporation, *Succeeding with the Booch and OMT Methods: A Practical Approach*, ISBN 0-8053-2279-5

Thomas Mowbray and William Ruh, *Inside CORBA: Distributed Object Standards and Applications*, ISBN 0-201-89540-4

Bernd Oestereich, *Developing Software with UML: Object-Oriented Analysis and Design in Practice*, ISBN 0-201-39826-5

Ira Pohl, *Object-Oriented Programming Using C++, Second Edition*, ISBN 0-201-89550-1

Terry Quatrani, *Visual Modeling with Rational Rose 2000 and UML*, ISBN 0-201-69961-3

Paul R. Reed, Jr., *Developing Applications with Visual Basic and UML*, ISBN 0-201-61579-7

Brent E. Rector and Chris Sells, *ATL Internals*, ISBN 0-201-69589-8

Doug Rosenberg with Kendall Scott, *Use Case Driven Object Modeling with UML: A Practical Approach*, ISBN 0-201-43289-7

Walker Royce, *Software Project Management: A Unified Framework*, ISBN 0-201-30958-0

William Ruh, Thomas Herron, and Paul Klinker, *IIOP Complete: Middleware Interoperability and Distributed Object Standards*, ISBN 0-201-37925-2

James Rumbaugh, Ivar Jacobson, and Grady Booch, *The Unified Modeling Language Reference Manual*, ISBN 0-201-30998-X

Geri Schneider and Jason P. Winters, *Applying Use Cases: A Practical Guide*, ISBN 0-201-30981-5

Yen-Ping Shan and Ralph H. Earle, *Enterprise Computing with Objects: From Client/Server Environments to the Internet*, ISBN 0-201-32566-7

David N. Smith, *IBM Smalltalk: The Language*, ISBN 0-8053-0908-X

Perdita Stevens with Rob Pooley, *Using UML: Software Engineering with Objects and Components, Updated Edition*, ISBN 0-201-64860-1

Daniel Tkach, Walter Fang, and Andrew So, *Visual Modeling Technique: Object Technology Using Visual Programming*, ISBN 0-8053-2574-3

Daniel Tkach and Richard Puttick, *Object Technology in Application Development, Second Edition*, ISBN 0-201-49833-2

Jos Warmer and Anneke Kleppe, *The Object Constraint Language: Precise Modeling with UML*, ISBN 0-201-37940-6

Using UML
Software engineering
with objects and
components

Updated Edition

Perdita Stevens

University of Edinburgh

with Rob Pooley

Heriot-Watt University

 Addison-Wesley

An imprint of PEARSON EDUCATION

Harlow, England · London · New York · Reading, Massachusetts · San Francisco · Toronto · Don Mills, Ontario · Sydney
Tokyo · Singapore · Hong Kong · Seoul · Taipei · Cape Town · Madrid · Mexico City · Amsterdam · Munich · Paris · Milan

Pearson Education Limited
Edinburgh Gate
Harlow
Essex
CM20 2JE

and Associated Companies around the world

Visit us on the World Wide Web at:
www.pearsoned-ema.com.

First published 1999
Updated edition 2000

ISBN 0-201-64860-1

British Library Cataloguing-in-Publication Data
A catalogue record for this book can be obtained from the British Library.

Library of Congress Cataloging-in-Publication Data
A catalog record for this book can be obtained from the Library of Congress.

10 9 8 7 6 5 4 3 2
04 03 02 01 00

Text designed by Claire Brodmann
Typeset by 56
Typeset in 10/12 pt Times New Roman
Printed in Great Britain by Henry Ling Ltd., at the Dorset Press, Dorchester, Dorset

Contents

List of Figures

Preface

UML, the Unified Modeling Language, has been adopted as standard by the OMG, and familiarity with it seems certain to become a core skill for software engineers. Realizing that students increasingly need to know it, we introduced it as the modeling language for our two redesigned undergraduate courses, for third and fourth year students. Unfortunately we found that there was no suitable textbook; what material there was on UML was principally aimed at experienced developers, not students. So we decided we'd have to write the textbook ourselves, and this book is the result.

The philosophy of the book is to be eclectic. Some readers will be offended that we have not jumped onto one or another bandwagon and declared how object oriented development should be done. This is deliberate. We do not think any one faction has a monopoly on truth; we think most successful OO developments in practice use techniques from several; we think it unfair to students to try to sell them the idea that one way is best.

We have used American spellings throughout, on the advice of our publishers: we crave the indulgence of our British readers.

How to use this book

This book is in four parts. Inevitably they overlap and are interrelated. We describe each part, and then show some paths through the book.

Part I introduces the concepts of software engineering and object oriented development.

Part II covers UML, the language. For most major diagram types there are two chapters. The first chapter covers the basic material that any UML user needs to know. The second covers more advanced or specialized features, which readers will want to know before undertaking serious UML development, but which is better studied after a good understanding of the core material is achieved. In our experience confusion as a result of half understanding too many features is a much more serious problem than ignorance of less central features.

Part III consists of three case studies. These are designed as starting points. The book's Web page has code for the functionality analyzed in the chapters, but the chapters also include hints for possible further extensions.

Part IV discusses quality and quality assurance, verification, validation and testing, software project management, teamwork, etc. We concentrate on the differences between the iterative, component based development model and a traditional waterfall approach. We give many pointers to other parts of this very large field of study.

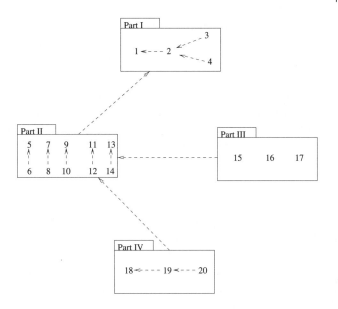

Figure 1   Chapter dependencies, not quite in UML!

There is a Web page for the book (currently `http://www.dcs.ed.ac.uk/home/pxs/Book`) which contains links to relevant information on the Web. This can also be accessed via the publisher's Web site at `http://www.awl-he.com/computing`.

Paths through the book

The diagram of chapter dependencies is a bit misleading: it implies that nothing ever depends on anything that comes later in the book! Of course we have tried to keep these situations to a minimum: but it's impossible to eliminate circular dependencies between, for example, understanding the need for design and what it is, understanding a modeling language, and examples. So, while we encourage you to use the book in whatever way seems most useful, some orders that we suggest are:

- For people new to OO: 1, 2, 3, 4, 5, 7, 9, 11, 15
- For people familiar with OO: 4, 3, then any subsequence of 5–20
- For people with some OO experience particularly interested in applying OO and UML in practice: skim 1–4, then 5, 7, 9, 11, 13, 14, 17, 18, 19, 20.

Special sections

Some special sections need explanation:

- Panels describe topics which are important, but don't completely fit the flow of the rest of the chapter in which they occur. Several design techniques are included in the Part II chapters in this way.

- Technical UML notes will be of interest to readers who want to understand how what we say relates to the primary UML source material, its notation guide and semantics.
- Questions, indicated by the letter Q, are intended to be straightforward; they act as an understanding check.
- Discussion questions, shown in tinted boxes, are more interesting: they require more thought, or research using materials other than this book, such as material pointed to from the book's Web page. We use these questions as the basis for small-group discussion and feedback within lectures; we hope they will also be useful material for tutorials and coursework, or just for provoking thought.

Teaching notes

This book is intended principally as a textbook for higher year (e.g. English second and third year, Scottish third and fourth year) students of Computer Science, Software Engineering and similar courses. Its early chapters are also intended to be readable as background to introductory informatics courses for students in earlier years. Our fourth-year course is also available to MSc students, so this book has been written to be adaptable for use with a wide range of students.

The book has both a publicly available Web page (mentioned above), and a password protected site which is available only to instructors. Contact the publishers at `awlhe.supps@awl.co.uk`, or via the book's catalogue entry at `http://www.awl-he.com/computing` for details of access to the latter, which contains answers to certain exercises, further notes, and, perhaps most helpfully, details of a larger case study than any in this book. (The latter is, however, based on publicly available code, which should be borne in mind if it is to be used for assessment!)

We deliberately do not teach a programming language in this book. There are three reasons.

1. The range of programming languages used in relevant courses is large (even here at Edinburgh, we have not settled the Java/C++ question), and for each possible language there are already many resources available to teach the specifics of the language. We have collected some links to free teaching material for various OOPLs on the book's Web page: please send us more!
2. We wanted to write a short, manageable, affordable book.
3. Most importantly, we feel it is very important for students to realize how much the issues involved in OOA/D and CBD are language-independent.

At Edinburgh, we use the material in this book for two courses. Our third-year course, Software Engineering with Objects and Components 1, covers most of the material in Chapters 1–4, 5, 7, and 9, and also teaches an object oriented programming language (in our case, C++ or Java). By the end of this course we expect students to understand the concepts of object orientation, component based design and software engineering, and to be able to do detailed design. Our fourth-year course, Software Engineering with Objects and Components 2, deepens students' understanding of design and the UML (the remaining chapters of Part II), and explores the harder issues of analysis and architecture. It goes on to deal with the material of Part IV, encouraging a pragmatic, open-minded approach to real-life software engineering. To support this, in SEOC2 we make heavy use of open-ended questions and we encourage students to use other resources, especially the Web. (We think this is an important habit to establish, given the speed at which the field of software engineering is likely to continue to move during these students' careers.) Many of the Discussion Questions in Part IV of the book require students to use other resources to investigate questions. To help with this, the book's public home page includes a collection of links to relevant papers and useful starting points. Some of these links are mentioned specifically in the text. Of course we can not guarantee that the owners of these pieces of material will continue to keep them available, but we will do our best to maintain the links: please let us know of any problems, and send us further links that may be useful to readers.

Tools

We had planned an appendix comparing the CASE (Computer Aided Software Engineering) tools available that support UML; at the time, that seemed a reasonable aim. However, the number of CASE tools supporting UML has grown tremendously since then, and it now seems invidious to list some tools without listing all the ones we know about. The book's home page contains a link to the Cetus links Web site which includes a regularly updated collection of links to tools which support UML.

We have used Rational Rose to support our courses that use UML, and have found the experience positive. Compared with previous courses where all modeling was done with pencil and paper, we find that students reach a higher level of competence more quickly when they have a tool available. This seems to be because the tool gives quick feedback on elementary mistakes like syntactically incorrect diagrams. The downside is that it is easy to create models which are unnecessarily large and complicated.

About the revised edition

This edition has been updated to describe UML 1.3, which was adopted by the OMG on June 25, 1999. For details of the changes, see the book's Web page.

Acknowledgments

We thank our families for their support during the writing of this book.

We thank everyone at Addison Wesley Longman, especially Sally Mortimore and Keith Mansfield, who have been helpful and encouraging throughout.

This book has benefited greatly from comments from anonymous reviewers. Many of our friends and colleagues have also helped by commenting on drafts, discussing ideas and answering questions. We thank in particular: Stuart Anderson, Adam Atkinson, Alan Gauld, Martin Hofmann, Bernd Kahlbrandt, Scott Keir, Ben Kleinman, Lindsay Marshall, Benjamin Pierce, Ian Redfern, Peter Thanisch, Pauline Wilcox and Alan Wills.

Most of all we thank all our students, both at Edinburgh and at the Open University.

July 1999

The publishers wish to thank the following for permission to reproduce the following copyright material.

Pearson Education Limited, UK

Text from p. 427, Jacobson: Software Reuse, 1997, ISBN: 0201 924765 Reprinted with permission

John Wiley & Sons Limited, UK

Text from Buschmann: Pattern-Oriented Software Architecture, ISBN: 0471 958697, 1998 Reproduced with permission

Perdita Stevens
Division of Informatics
University of Edinburgh
JCMB, King's Buildings
Mayfield Road
EDINBURGH EH9 3JZ
Scotland, UK
Perdita.Stevens@dcs.ed.ac.uk

Rob Pooley
Department of Computing and EE
Heriot-Watt University
EDINBURGH EH14 4AS
Scotland, UK
rjp@cee.hw.ac.uk

PART I

Conceptual background

Software engineering with components

This chapter begins to address the following questions:

- What is a good system?
- Do we have good systems?
- What are good systems like?
- How can good systems be built?

We must say 'begins' since the whole of this book, and indeed the whole of the discipline of software engineering, can be seen as an attempt to answer these questions more fully. Our aim in this chapter is to set the scene for the rest of the book, and provide pointers to more information to come.

Before we proceed, we should decide what we're talking about. This book is concerned primarily with *software engineering*. We will consider how software is deployed on hardware; but we do not, for example, usually consider the special needs of embedded systems. This is a book about *object oriented software engineering* so we are thinking principally of the kinds of systems that are often built with object oriented technology.

1.1 What is a good system?

Ultimately a good (or *high quality*) system is one which meets its users' needs. That is, it must be:

- **useful and usable**: good software makes people's lives easier or better.
- **reliable**: good software has few *bugs*.
- **flexible**: users' needs change over time, even while software is being developed, so it is important to be able to make changes to the software later. Moreover it must be possible to fix the bugs! All changes made to software after it has been released are traditionally called *maintenance*.

- **affordable**: both to buy and to maintain. Labor costs are the most significant element of software costs, so what this comes down to is that it must be reasonably easy and quick to develop and maintain.
- **available** – otherwise it doesn't matter how good it is! We'll consider two aspects of availability.

  — Software must be able to run on available hardware, with an available operating system, etc. This implies, for example, that a system must be sufficiently portable, and also brings us back to maintainability, since it must be practicable to make any changes which are necessitated by changes to the software's environment.
  — The software must exist in the first place! So a software project must complete successfully, and deliver the software promised.

1.2   Do we have good systems?

Before we launch into all the problems of modern software systems, let us take a moment to realize how much software *does* satisfactorily do for us. Advances in software have revolutionized book preparation, banking, and information finding (think of library catalogs, or the Web), to give just a few examples. We are doing some things right.

1.2.1   Problems...

Unfortunately you will, doubtless, know of failures too. You will know of many systems which don't meet their users' requirements and/or have technical failings. Systems are usually out of date even as they are being designed. Users' needs are often missed during requirements capture. Even if their needs are captured correctly at the beginning of a project, they may change while the system is being developed, so that the delivered system doesn't meet the users' needs by the time it is delivered. Companies still commonly give 'computer error' as an excuse for poor service to their customers. Most business PC users expect their applications and even operating system to crash, hang or otherwise misbehave fairly regularly. Software is not always usable, useful, reliable, or available.

Q: Consider a piece of software that you enjoy using. In what respects is it a high quality system? Are there aspects of it that make it not a high quality system in the sense presented here? Which features are most important in influencing how you feel about it? Are there important features that we haven't considered here?

Q: Consider a piece of software which is very successful but which you personally do not enjoy using. Answer the same questions.

Discussion Question 1
What are the best and worst experiences you or people you know have had recently which have involved software?

> **Discussion Question 2**
> How might the delivery of a new system *itself* affect users' requirements?

Flexibility too is lacking. Consider the millennium problem! As you probably know, developers of early software were unwilling to use more space for storing a date than was necessary, so their date formats didn't specify the century. Instead they used just the two-digit year, which was understood to be in the 20th century. This was in many cases reasonable and understandable; for example, secondary storage, such as disks, used to be much more expensive than it is now, and it wasn't to be wasted. But at the time of writing (mid 1998) there is great concern about getting these systems updated to be able to cope with dates in the 21st century. Many systems are being abandoned altogether because it would be too expensive to make this change! At least one company is reported to have decided to shut itself down, invest the money for five years, and start up again when the new century is safely underway. The real reason why this is interesting from our point of view is that, conceptually, it's hard to imagine a simpler change to a system than this change to date formats. When you consider the fact that users of software actually want much more far-reaching changes, to allow their changing business processes to be properly supported by software, you see why we have a problem with *legacy systems*. We need techniques for building more flexible software, for not all inflexible systems are old. We're still building them.

Finally let us consider affordability. This turns out to be intimately connected with re-liability and flexibility, since the cost of bug-fixing and maintenance is the largest cost in providing high quality systems. Complexity, interdependence of components and introduc-tion of new errors are all factors in this. If software is in use over a long period of time, the need for new staff to understand the whole of an old system to look after it makes the problem worse. Often the best staff are not attracted to such work and it has to be given to less able people. Even though maintenance can require as much skill and ingenuity as other development, many people find it more rewarding to produce something new than to improve something old.

1.2.2 ... even drastic failures

Sometimes failures of these desirable attributes have more dramatic effects than we have so far considered. You may be aware of some of these infamous examples:

Ariane 5 whose maiden flight on June 4, 1996 ended in the launcher being exploded because of a chain of software failures.

Taurus A planned automated transaction settlement system for the London Stock Ex-change. The project was canceled in 1993 after having lasted more than five years. The project cost was around £75m; the estimated loss to customers was around £450m; and the damage to the reputation of the London Stock Exchange was incalculable.

Denver baggage handling system where a complex planned system, involving around 300 computers, overran so badly as to prevent the airport opening on time, and then turned out to be extremely buggy and cost almost another 50% of its original budget of nearly $200m to make it work.

London Ambulance System   where because of a succession of software engineering failures, especially defects in project management, a system was introduced that failed twice in the autumn of 1992. Although the monetary cost, at 'only' about £9m, was small by comparison with the other examples, it is believed that people died who would not have died if ambulances had reached them as promptly as they would have done without this software failure.

Therac-25   where between 1985 and 1987 six people (at least) suffered serious radiation overdoses because of software-related malfunctions of the Therac-25 radiation therapy machine. Three of them are thought to have died of the overdoses. An important root cause was a lack of quality assurance, which led to an over-complex, inadequately tested, under-documented system being developed, and subsequently to the failure to take adequate corrective action.

> **Discussion Question 3**
> Which of our desirable attributes failed, in each case? Are any causes of failure not covered?

> **Discussion Question 4**
> In both the Ariane 5 and Therac-25 cases, a contributory factor was that software which had previously been used without apparent problems was reused, sometimes with modifications, in a new context where it did give rise to serious problems. Find out in more detail what happened (there are some Web links from the book's home page), and consider the implications of these cases for reuse.

Nor are these isolated examples. Returning to the economic perspective, consider the following much-quoted statistics from an article by W. Wayt Gibbs [25]:

- On average, large projects take 50% longer than they were planned to do;
- Three-quarters of large projects are operational failures;
- One-quarter of large projects are canceled.

(The article is not always credited, but even if these are significant overestimates, the scale of the problem is enormous.)

The RISKS mailing list and digest (see the book's home page) is a good source of contemporary problems with software projects, particularly when failures cause dangers to lives, businesses, or integrity and security of information.

1.2.3   Promises, promises

Every new technology promises to reduce development times and increase success rates of projects, but experienced software engineers tend to be justifiably skeptical of such claims. One of the fundamental problems that a technique for dealing with large projects has to handle is Fred Brooks' 'mythical man-month' [10]. The larger the project, the higher the proportion of the project's costs and time which is eaten up by communication between people on the project, because each person has more people with whom to communicate. One effect of this is that the natural reaction to a project which starts to slip behind schedule, namely to put more people to work on the project, often fails. If you double the number of people on a project, you cannot expect to halve the time it takes. You may even increase the time it takes! It takes time and effort for a large group of people working together on a system to communicate all the information they need in order to keep their work consistent; and if they fail, the result can be parts of a system that don't plug together. The effects are especially devastating if such a mismatch is discovered late in the project. For this reason, large projects are both more expensive and more risky than small ones.

It was in an attempt to solve the software crisis that the US Department of Defense commissioned the design of the language Ada, which was standardized in 1983. Ada was intended to support the 'best practice' concepts of structured analysis, design and programming. *Modularity* and *encapsulation* were key concepts in the language design. Even this huge investment has failed to solve the software crisis. More recent efforts have concentrated on improving methodologies for software engineering.

1.3 What are good systems like?

Over the last few decades we have gained a gradually deeper understanding of which systems are most likely to be good. Much remains to be understood. The fundamental problem is that

> There is a limit to how much a human can understand at any one time.

Small systems, in which category we include almost everything university students normally build, can be built by 'heroic programming' in which a single person does attempt to have in mind everything relevant about the system; but in general it is impossible for a developer or a maintainer to understand everything about the system all at once. This means that it is essential to be able to undertake a development or maintenance task without understanding everything about the system.

To see how understanding of the problem evolved, consider a maintainer who wants to make a small change to a large system, perhaps changing three lines of code. What else does the maintainer have to understand, to see whether it may be affected by the change? Naturally the first guess is that you have to understand the code which is close to those three lines, but not code which is further away. Very early in the history of programming, people realized that the wrongness of this guess was a major cause of bugs in programs; for example, a go to statement in a remote piece of code which directed the flow of control close to the change could mean that remote parts of the program were affected by the change. Identifying which remote pieces of code could be affected was not always easy. The term 'spaghetti code' was coined[1] to describe systems in which the flow of control and dependency was too complex to understand. Edsger Dijkstra's short note 'GoTo statement considered harmful' [15] of 1968 was a famous early step in the direction of controlling the complexity of systems so that they could be understood by humans.

The next step is to think of a system as a collection of *modules* and to identify dependencies between modules. In the most general sense of the word, a module might be any identifiable

---

[1] seemingly by W.G.R. Stevens, father of P., in the early 1960s!

'bit' of a system which it makes sense to consider separately. For example, modules might be:

- files
- subroutines
- library functions
- classes, in an object oriented language
- other constructs known as module or similar
- independent or semi-independent programs or subsystems

Of course not all modules are equal: taking a monolithic program and splitting it randomly into files is not optimal. The rest of this section considers what characteristics modules should have in order to make development and maintenance of systems as easy, cheap and reliable as possible. We must consider the related concepts of *dependency*, *coupling*, *cohesion*, *interface*, *encapsulation* and *abstraction*. (Different authors use slightly different definitions of these terms, so the ones we use here are our favorites rather than the only possible.) Having identified what it is to be a good module, we can contemplate reusing a good module as a *component*.

Module A *depends on* Module B if it is possible for some change to Module B to mean that Module A also needs to be changed.

We sometimes say that Module A is a *client* of Module B, or that Module B acts as a *server* to Module A. (However, the terms client and server are also used in more specific ways: in a 'client–server architecture' for example, the client and server are generally separate processes on different machines.) In general, it is normal for the same module to be both a client and a server. That is, it depends on some modules, whilst other modules depend on it. It is even possible for a pair of modules each to have the other as a client; however, this is an example of a *circular dependency*, which should be avoided where possible because it hampers *reuse*.

Dependency is sometimes known as *coupling*. A system with many dependencies has *high coupling*. Good systems have *low coupling*, because then changes to one part of a system are less likely to propagate throughout the system.

Discussion Question 5

How can coupling be identified? Measured? Reduced? Consider: if you take a system with two coupled modules, and merge the two modules into one, does this reduce coupling in the system?

1.3.1 Encapsulation: low coupling

So other things being equal we want to minimize the number of cases in which a change to one module necessitates a change to another module. This means we have to know which changes inside a module may affect the rest of the system. However, in order to be able to take advantage of the low coupling of a system, it is just as important to be able to *identify* which modules are coupled; otherwise we may have to spend effort checking whether changes are needed to a module, which is expensive even if the conclusion is that no changes are needed. We would like to know with certainty which modules of a system might be affected by a change to a given module.

In summary, once the boundaries between our system's modules are settled, there are two kinds of information that may be useful.

1. What *assumptions* may clients of a given module make about it? For example, what services is it assumed to provide? Answering this should enable us to know what kinds of changes to a module *may* be dangerous.
2. Which modules are clients of a given module? Answering this tells us which modules we may have to change, if we do make a dangerous change to a module.

We'll address these questions in turn.

Interfaces

An *interface* to a module defines some features of the module on which its clients may rely. The rest of the system can only use the module in ways permitted by the interface(s); that is, an interface *encapsulates* knowledge about the module. Parnas writes 'The connections between modules are the assumptions which the modules make about each other'. Any assumption that a client makes about a server runs the risk of being wrong: so we should *document* such assumptions in interfaces and *check* their correctness. If we successfully document all the assumptions in the interface we will be able to say:

If a module changes internally without changing its interface, this change will not necessitate any changes[2] anywhere else in the system.

So far an interface could be, for example, a comment section at the head of a file which, by convention, is kept up to date by everyone who changes or uses the file. The problem with this is that there is no way to guarantee that everyone respects the conventions. Ideally, there should be automatic checks that no other module makes any assumption about this module that isn't documented in its interface, and also that the module always justifies the assumptions that are documented there. The more a programming language allows these checks to be automatic, the more it is said to support modularity and encapsulation.

What information can be recorded in an interface and automatically checked depends of course on the programming language.[3] Typically there will be some functions which can be called, possibly some names of data values or objects which can be used; some languages permit types or exceptions to be named in an interface. Client modules will not be permitted to mention anything defined in the server module that isn't in the interface. In many languages some checks will also be done on how client modules use the names of things in the interface, for example, to check their assumptions about what *types* things have. Using a name not in an interface or using it on the assumption that it has a type different from the one documented results in an error, at compile, link or run time. This deals well with the *syntactic* aspects of dependency.

---

[2] code changes, anyway: unfortunately, depending on the environment, even interface-preserving changes to source code components may make recompilation necessary.

[3] As we shall see in Chapter 6, UML also has a notion of interface, whereby an interface can only include operations. Here we consider more general notions.

Discussion Question 6

Consider the examples of modules we listed above, and any others you know, in any languages. What can be documented in interfaces to the modules, and how much checking is automatic? Which checks happen when?

Ideally we'd like more: we'd like to be able to check *semantic* dependency. That is, if an interface is truly to document the assumptions that may be made about modules, it should be a real *specification* of the module, explaining what clients can assume about the behavior of the module, not just the syntax of how they can interact with it. Unfortunately present-day programming languages do not provide this information (with a few partial exceptions). The main reason for this is that theoretical computer science has not yet advanced far enough to make such features technically possible. This is a very active area of research; you may expect future programming languages to have more powerful notions of interface.

Context dependencies

There are several reasons for wanting to know not only what dependencies could exist – that is, what features are documented in the interfaces of the system's modules – but also what dependencies really do exist. We've mentioned the situation in which you make a change to a module that may affect its clients; its clients are (by definition) the modules which may need to change, so it's important to be able to tell which they are. Next suppose you're considering reusing a module. You need to know not only what services it will provide – what its interface is – but also what services it requires in order to work. The services a module requires are sometimes called its context dependencies. They may themselves be expressed in terms of interfaces; the module may guarantee that if certain interfaces are provided to it, then it in turn will provide its own interface.

Between them, the context dependencies of a module and the module's own interface constitute a contract describing the module's responsibilities. If the context provides the things the module needs, then the module guarantees to provide the services described in its interface.

Benefits of modularity with defined interfaces

Even a very poor interface to a badly chosen module can make a system easier to understand and modify. Why is this? The fundamental reason is that anything that reduces what has to be known about a module by someone using it is beneficial in a number of ways.

- In a team development, people developing code that uses a module should only have to understand the module's interface, not how it works, so they can be *more productive*.
- Because developers can safely ignore some aspects of the system, they are more likely to thoroughly understand the aspects they *do* need, so *fewer bugs should be introduced*.
- Bugs should be easier to *find* (both during development and during maintenance), because it should be possible to avoid examining irrelevant modules.
- Once a module exists, with documentation of what it provides and what it requires, it is at least possible to consider reusing it.

The real challenge, however, is to define good modules with the right things in their interfaces. Only then can the full benefits be achieved.

Discussion Question 7

What are the results of badly chosen modules or poor interfaces? What makes an interface 'too big' or 'too small'? Have you encountered examples?

A module may have several interfaces

If we know Module A can sometimes be affected by changes to Module B, we also want to be able to identify as easily as possible what changes are required, if any, in our particular case. Sometimes it is convenient to document the services that a module provides as several different interfaces, so that we can be more precise about what services a given client needs. Again, this is useful both for maintenance and for reuse.

We now have a partial answer to the question 'what are good systems like?'

A good system consists of encapsulated modules.

1.3.2 Abstraction: high cohesion

Good modules often have the property that their interfaces provide an *abstraction* of some intuitively understood thing which may nevertheless be complex to implement. Such modules are said to have high *cohesion*.

The interface *abstracts away* from things the client developer does not have to understand in order to use the module, leaving an uncluttered, coherent picture of what the user of a module does want to know. The module does a sensible collection of things, but as far as possible the client developer is shielded from irrelevant information about how the module does what it does. This concern to *allow* the developer to concentrate on essentials is subtly different from the concern of encapsulation to achieve low coupling, which is concerned with *preventing* the developer from using hidden information.

As a simple concrete example, suppose a module provides an interface to a point in 2D space, and that the interface allows clients to get and set the position of the point using either its Cartesian co-ordinates (x, y) or its polar co-ordinates (r, θ), whichever is most convenient to the client. Does the module store both sets of co-ordinates and keep them consistent, or does it store one set and use that one to calculate the other on demand? This information is of no interest to client programmers; the module interface should abstract away from it, and encapsulate the data structure inside the module. This kind of combination of abstraction and encapsulation is often referred to as *information hiding*, but we repeat the warning that there's no firm consensus on exactly what each of the three terms covers. We prefer to summarize:

Abstraction is when a client of a module doesn't need to know more than is in the interface.
Encapsulation is when a client of a module isn't able to know more than is in the interface.

The situation in which the interface provides means of interacting with some data, but reveals nothing about the internal format of the data, is typical of both object oriented and abstract data type style development. Some authors restrict their use of the word encapsulation to cover only this kind of encapsulated module.

If a module, of whatever size and complexity, is a good abstraction – it has high cohesion and low coupling – it may be feasible to *reuse* it in later systems, or to *replace* it in the existing system. That is, it may be possible to regard it as a pluggable *component*. However, whether this is possible also depends on the *architecture* in which the component is developed and in which it is to be used. We are led to consider *architecture-centric component based development* (CBD).[4] The meanings of these terms, which are more recent buzzwords than those we've addressed so far, are even more controversial! In the next subsection we will explain what we mean in this book by these terms. In Panel 18.1, we will return to this controversy in the light of the rest of the book.

1.3.3   Architecture and components

In the 1980s and early 1990s, *object orientation* (which we will discuss in detail in Chapter 2) was the fashionable technology which was going to solve the software crisis. If your project used object orientation, you would automatically deliver a high-quality product, on time and to budget, and your organization would experience phenomenal and ever-increasing levels of reuse because classes developed for one project would be usable on the next, and the next, and the next . . . .

That was the hype. As you will have guessed from the litany of failed projects, from this same era, that we gave earlier, reality was slightly different. The best comprehensive definition we can come up with for the word *component* is 'thing we will be able to reuse or replace' – the cynical view is that component based development (CBD) achieves high levels of reuse by definition, since if it doesn't, it isn't really CBD!

For now we consider a component to be a *unit of reuse and replacement*. A component may be a module with properties that make it reusable and replaceable. There are many other forms of reuse, which we will discuss in more depth in Chapter 18; we will also discuss the controversial question of what the definition of component should really be. Many people regard *late composition* as an important feature of component based development: the point is that it is easier to replace a module if you can do so without needing to recompile the system. However, opinions differ, especially about how late is late, and we prefer not to impose this restriction. (Unfortunately, UML also uses the term 'component' for a related but different concept which we will discuss in Chapter 13.)

What determines whether a module is reusable? It should not be a surprise that a reusable module is good according to the criteria discussed above: it has high cohesion, low coupling with the rest of the system, a well-defined interface, and is an encapsulated abstraction of a well-understood thing. What may be more surprising is that whether a module is reusable depends on the context in which it was developed and in which it is to be reused. The context includes a wide variety of technical and non-technical factors, which we will return to in Chapter 18. As an illustrative example of a non-technical factor, in

---

[4] You may also see the term *component oriented programming* (COP) – it's a synonym for CBD.

an organization which rewards programmers according to the number of lines of code they write, no module is reusable, since no programmer has any incentive to reuse anything! This is an extreme example, but such social and organizational factors are arguably more important than technical factors.

To see the importance of the technical context, consider an organization which produces a sequence of systems which have much in common; this is sometimes known as *product-line* development, for obvious reasons. If the high-level structure of two successive systems is the same, it is far more likely that it will be possible to take a module developed for one system and plug it unchanged into the other – black box reuse – than if the two systems have different *architecture*. The architecture of the system includes high-level decisions about what the overall structure of the system should be, which apply to more than one system and are taken in order to achieve repeatable benefits such as component reuse. It may also include other decisions covering how the system is to be built. A low-level example is that a decision always to handle unexpected errors in a certain way is an architectural decision; a high-level example is a decision to use a certain manufacturer's database or a certain programming language. Part of the motivation for making these decisions is the same as the motivation for identifying suitable modules: to reduce the burden on the developer or maintainer. If certain things are reliably done in the same way throughout a system, and better still from system to system, the developer or maintainer can expect things to be this way and is spared the trouble of working out how they are in this particular instance. A component developed in the context of a set of architectural decisions is most likely to be reusable in a new context if the two contexts share architectural decisions. (In this case the architecture *itself* is being reused: but it is also increasing our chances of reusing components. We will briefly consider reusing architecture in Chapter 18.) Thus, just as any interface is better than no interface at all, a suboptimal architectural decision can be better than no architectural decision at all. Just as with interfaces, the real challenge is to identify good architectural decisions.

1.3.4 Component-based design: pluggability

The ideal way to build a new system is to take some existing components and plug them together. *Pluggability* is of course the property of something that lets you do this. The metaphor suggests correctly that this is only partly a property of the things being plugged. The components do have to be bits which fulfill needs in the whole system. More than that, though, they have to be compatible with one another, and that depends on the presence of a suitable architecture.

Consider an electrical appliance which plugs into the mains using a standard plug. We have not told you what the functionality of the appliance is. That it is to be powered by mains electricity and use a standard plug, though, are architectural decisions, with obvious advantages. An alternative possible architectural decision might have been to make the appliance battery powered using readily available batteries. Which of these two architectures is most appropriate is an important decision which depends on things about the project which we haven't detailed. Such a decision should probably be taken very early in the project, since it will have an important influence on the design of the appliance. This is characteristic of architectural decisions. An almost certainly poor architectural decision would have been to design the appliance with a non-standard plug. More interestingly, if the appliance is to be sold exclusively in the UK it would be a bad decision to design the appliance with a standard US plug, even though this would have been a perfectly sensible decision if the appliance were to be sold exclusively in the US. Architectural decisions:

- need to be taken early in a project
- are affected by the nature of the components in the architecture
- may be influenced by the environment of the project.

In summary, development is architecture-centric and component-based if it gives high priority to following (and making) good architectural decisions, and to using (and developing) good components.

Object orientation, as we shall see, is a (but not the only) suitable paradigm in which to do architecture-centric CBD.

1.4 How are good systems built?

We will return to the *development process* in Chapter 4. Here let us set the background by considering the term *software engineering*, whose adoption suggests that systems might be built by analogy with engineered artifacts, e.g. engines or bridges. An engineering approach:

- uses a defined *process* with clear *phases*, each of which has an *end-product* (maybe a document, maybe something built)
- is concerned with meeting a clear set of requirements, carefully defined as early as possible, so
- regards forms of verification and validation, such as testing and sometimes proofs, as just as essential as building the product itself
- uses a store of relevant *knowledge*, *architectures* and *components*
- makes sensible use of tools

We have already identified that software systems should make use of a considered modular architecture reusing components, as do engineered artifacts.

Discussion Question 8
What are the differences, and the other similarities, between software engineering and other forms of engineering?

SUMMARY

This chapter was a whistle-stop motivation for and introduction to the kind of software engineering this book is about. We considered what a high-quality software system is, and the extent to which we have high-quality systems today. We discussed the need for modularity, and covered the characteristics of good modules. We considered how to go beyond engineering good modules in isolation towards engineering systems based on good reusable architectures with endemic component reuse. Finally, we mentioned process.

CHAPTER 2

Object concepts

In this chapter we continue to explore the question 'what are good systems like?' by describing the object oriented paradigm, whose popularity is due partly to the fact that it supports the development of good systems. Using object orientation is neither necessary nor sufficient for building good systems, however! We shall answer these questions:

- What is an object?
- How do objects communicate?
- How is an object's interface defined?
- What have objects to do with components?

Finally we consider inheritance, polymorphism and dynamic binding.

This chapter applies to standard modern class-based object oriented languages such as Java and C++. Most of it also applies to Smalltalk, Eiffel, CLOS, Perl5 and other object oriented languages you may meet: but a detailed comparison of object oriented programming languages (OOPLs) is outside the scope of this book.

This chapter includes questions about how the programming language *you* are using provides the object oriented features we discuss. If you already know the language, you should be able to answer the questions as you go. If you do not, you may prefer to read this chapter to the end, then study the basics of your chosen language, and then return to the questions to check that you have understood the way in which the language provides object orientation. (We refer to any language you are considering using as 'your language' for short.)

2.1   What is an object?

Conceptually, an *object* is a thing you can interact with: you can send it various *messages* and it will react. How it *behaves* depends on the current internal *state* of the object, which may change, for example, as part of the object's reaction to receiving a message. It matters which object you interact with, and you usually address an object by name; that is, an object has an *identity* which distinguishes it from all other objects. So an object is a thing which has behavior, state and identity: this characterization is due to Grady Booch [7]. Let us consider these aspects in a little more detail.

Thing This is more interesting than might at first appear. Not only is an object a thing in the system; it is also the system representation of a conceptual thing. For example, an object may represent a physical thing such as a customer, a board, or a clock. In fact the first time objects arose explicitly was in Simula, where they did represent real-world objects, the objects being simulated. Clearly, however, if general purpose software systems are to be built using objects, an object need not represent a physical thing. We will return to the question of how to identify objects in Chapter 5.

Q: Which of these might be objects: hammer, sphere, chemical process, love, fog, river, anger, cat, grayness, gray cat?

State The *state* of the object is all the data which it currently encapsulates. An object normally has a number of named *attributes* (or *instance variables* or *data members*) each of which has a value. Some attributes can be mutable; that is, their values can be changed. For example, an object representing a customer might have an attribute `address` whose value must change if the customer moves house. Other attributes may be immutable or constant; for example, our customer object might have an attribute for the customer's unique identifying number, which might have to be the same throughout the life of the object. In most present-day object oriented languages the set of attributes that an object has cannot change during the life of the object, even though the values of those attributes can change.

Behavior The way an object acts and reacts, in terms of its state changes and message passing. An object *understands* certain *messages*, which is to say that it can receive the messages and act on them. The set of messages that the object understands, like the set of attributes it has, is normally fixed. The way in which an object reacts to a message may depend on the current values of its attributes: in this way, even when (as usual) the outside world is not granted direct access to the attributes, it may be indirectly affected by their values. This is the sense in which the values of the attributes are the *state* of the object.

Identity is a little more slippery. The idea is that objects are not defined just by the current values of their attributes. An object has a continuing existence. For example the values of this object's attributes could change, perhaps in response to a message, but it would still be the same object. An object is normally referred to by a *name* (the value of a variable in a client program, perhaps `aCustomer`) but the name of the object is not the same thing as the object, because the same object may have several different names. (This is probably only surprising if you are a pure functional programmer; and there are some distinguished ones who say you can do OO in a purely functional way, but we will not consider the question in this book.)

2.1.1 Example

Consider an object which we'll call `myClock`, which understands the messages `reportTime` and `resetTimeTo(07:43)`, `resetTimeTo(12:30)`, indeed more generally `resetTimeTo(newTime)` for any sensible value of `newTime`. It may advertise this by giving an *interface* which says that it accepts messages of the form `reportTime()` and `resetTimeTo(newTime: Time)` where `Time` is a type[1] whose elements are the sensible values of `newTime` we mentioned.

How does it implement this functionality? The outside world doesn't need to know – the information should be hidden – but perhaps it has an attribute `time`, the value of which is returned by the object in response to message `reportTime`, and which is reset to `newTime` when the object receives the message `resetTimeTo(newTime)`. Or perhaps it passes these messages on to some other object, which it knows about, and has the other object deal with the messages.

2.1.2 Messages

From this example we see some things about messages. A message includes a keyword called a *selector*; here we've seen the selectors `reportTime` and `resetTimeTo`. A message may, but need not, include one or more arguments, which are values being given to the object just as values are passed into a function in a normal function call. In the example, `07:43` is an argument forming part of the message `resetTimeTo(07:43)`. Usually, for a given selector there is a single 'correct' number of arguments which should be present in a message which starts with that selector; we will not expect `myClock` to understand `resetTimeTo` with no argument, or `resetTimeTo(4, 12:30)` etc. The acceptable values of arguments are also laid down[2] in the interface of the object.

Q: What is the syntax for message sending in the language(s) you're using?

Notice that values – for example, values of attributes of an object, or values of arguments sent as part of messages – do not have to be members of basic types (characters, integers, etc. – exactly what's a basic type is language-dependent). They can also be objects in their own right.

Q: What are the basic types in your language?

One of the things that an object might do in response to a message is to send a message to another object. If it wants to do this it has to have some way of knowing a name for the object. Perhaps, for example, it has the object as the value of one of its attributes, in which case it can send the message by using the attribute as the name.

Q: Suppose o is an object. Apart from any objects which o may have as values of its attributes, to what objects might o be able to send messages?

Note that when you send a message to an object, you do not in general know what code will be executed as a result, because that information is encapsulated. This will be important at the end of this chapter when we talk about dynamic binding.

---

[1] or a class: classes are discussed in 2.1.4 below.

[2] by giving the class (see 2.1.4 below) or sometimes just the interface, which the object passed as an argument should have, or its type if it should belong to a basic type like `int` or `bool` – the details here are language dependent.

2.1.3 Interfaces

The object's *public* interface defines which messages it will accept regardless of where they come from. Typically the interface records the selectors of these messages together with some information about what arguments are required and what if anything will be returned. As we remarked in Chapter 1, we would probably prefer the interface to include some kind of specification of what the effect of sending a message to the object will be, but these specifications are normally given only in comments and accompanying documentation. In most languages there can be attributes in the public interface of an object as well; putting attribute x in the interface is equivalent to declaring that this object has a piece of data x, which the outside world can inspect and alter.

> **Discussion Question 9**
>
> If you are using a language which does not permit attributes in the public interface, how can you achieve the same effects using messages to access the data? Are there any advantages of using this style even in a language that does permit attributes in interfaces? Disadvantages?

Often, it isn't appropriate for everything in the system to be allowed to send every message to an object that the object could possibly understand. So an object is typically capable of understanding some messages that are not in the public interface. For example, we explained in Chapter 1 that the data structures used by a module should normally be encapsulated; here, this corresponds to the idea that an object's public interface should normally not include attributes.

An object can always send *to itself* any message which it is capable of understanding. It may seem odd or over-complicated to think of an object sending messages to itself: the reason for thinking this way will become clearer when we discuss dynamic binding later in the chapter.

So typically an object has at least two interfaces: the public interface, which any part of the system can use, and the larger private interface which the object itself and other privileged parts of the system can use. Sometimes another intermediate interface, providing more capabilities than the public interface but fewer than the private interface, is useful. Sometimes only part of an object's public interface is needed in a given context; this increases the number of objects which could potentially be used as replacements, so it can be useful to record which features are really necessary in a smaller interface than the whole public interface of the object. Because of this, an object can have (or *realize*) more than one interface. Conversely, many different objects may realize the same interface.

If not otherwise specified, 'interface' will mean public interface.

2.1.4 Classes

So far we have been talking about objects as though each object were separately defined, with its own interface and its own individual way of controlling which other objects could send it which messages. Of course this is not a sensible way to build a typical system, because objects have a lot in common with one another. If my company has 10 000 customers and I want to build a system with an object representing each of these people, the objects which represent customers have a great deal in common! I will want them to behave consistently, so that developers and maintainers of the system can understand it. We will have a *class* of objects which represent customers. A class describes a set of objects with an equivalent role or roles in a system.

In class-based object oriented languages, every object belongs to a class, and the class of an object determines its interface.[3] For example, perhaps myClock belongs to class Clock whose public interface specifies that each object of class Clock will provide the operation resetTimeTo(newTime: Time); that is, it will understand messages with selector resetTimeTo and a single argument which is an object of class (or type) Time.

In fact even the way in which an object reacts to a message is determined by the object's class, together with the values of the object's attributes. A *method* is a specific piece of code which implements the operation. Only the fact that the object provides the operation is visible in the object's interface; the method that implements the capability is hidden.

Similarly the set of attributes which an object has is determined by its class, although of course the values taken by those attributes are not determined by the class, but may vary. For example, perhaps objects belonging to class Clock have a private attribute called time. If you send identical messages to two objects with the same class, the same method is executed in both cases, although the effect of executing the method may be very different if the objects have different values of their attributes.

In summary, objects from the same class have the same interfaces. We could describe the public and private interfaces for the Clock class like this:

```
- time : Time
+ reportTime() : Time
+ resetTimeTo(newTime: Time)
```

The public interface consists of the lines marked with +; the private interface includes the lines marked – as well.

Q: In your language, how does the programmer define a class such as Clock? Are the interface and the implementation defined separately? What are the public and private interfaces called? (Probably public and private!) Are there any other possibilities? What do the possibilities mean?

We call the process of creating a new object belonging to class Clock *instantiating* class Clock, and we call the resulting object an *instance* of class Clock – this, of course, is why the variables whose values belong to the object and may vary over its lifetime are sometimes called instance variables. Creating an object involves creating a new thing with its own state and its own identity, which will behave consistently with all other objects of the class. The creation process normally involves setting the values of the attributes; the values may be specified in the creation request, or may be specified as default initial values by the class of the object. In languages such as C++ and Java the class has a direct role in the creation of new objects – it actually does the work, rather than just acting as a template. That is, a class can often be seen as an *object factory*.

---

[3] Actually an object can belong to more than one class, and the *most specific* class to which it belongs determines its interface.

Q: In your language, how is a new object of a given class created?

Most languages allow a class to behave as though it were an object in its own right, having attributes and understanding messages itself. For example, the *class* Customer might have an attribute numberOfInstances which might be an integer incremented each time a new Customer *object* is created. Smalltalk takes this view particularly consistently, but C++ and Java also have traces of it. In Smalltalk, for example, you'd create a new Customer object by sending a message (e.g. new) to the Customer *class*. The class's reaction would be to create a new object and return it to the caller.

> **Discussion Question 10**
> Consider what happens if you try to apply this idea consistently. We said that every object has a class; so when you regard a class C as an object, what is the class of C? And the class of that?

Q: Does your language have features like this? Exactly what?

Digression: why have classes?

Why not just have objects, which have state, behavior and identity as we require?

Classes in object oriented languages serve two purposes. First, they are a convenient way of describing a collection (a class) of objects which have the same properties. Object oriented programming languages can use classes essentially just as a convenience. For example, there is no need to store a copy of the code representing an object's behavior in every object, even though conceptually we think of every object as encapsulating its own code. Instead, developers write the definition of a class once, and compilers create a single representation of a class, and allow objects of that class to access the class representation to get the code they need.

Remember that convenience is not a triviality. Our overall aim was to make systems easier to understand, so that developing and maintaining them is as easy, cheap and reliable as possible. Making similar objects share the same design and implementation is an important step towards this.

This is an important occurrence of a principle[4] which is so important in software engineering, and not only in code, that we will shout it:

WRITE ONCE!

We mean that if two copies of the same software engineering artifact – piece of any sort of code, piece of a diagram, piece of text from a document – must always stay consistent, then there shouldn't *be* two copies. Any time you record the same information in more than one place, you not only spend effort on repetition that might be better spent on doing something new, but also you set yourself up for maintenance problems, since the two versions will not stay synchronized without effort. The skill in applying the principle is in spotting whether or not you really do have two copies of the same information, or two potentially different

---

[4] emphasized by Kent Beck, in particular.

pieces of information that just happen to be the same at the moment. In the latter case, copy and paste is appropriate. In the former case, an attitude of resentment to duplicating the information in more than one place is actually an asset: you should agree to do so only for good reason.

Discussion Question 11
Does this principle mean that we think duplication of data in a distributed database is a bad idea? Why?

You can see that there are other ways to get the capability to create arbitrarily many similar objects whilst writing their code just once; for example, we could define a prototypical object, and then define other objects as being 'like that one, but with these differences'. Again, we would need to keep only one copy of the code. This is roughly what the elegant prototype-based language Self does. However, class-based languages dominate object orientation today and will probably continue to do so.

Secondly, in most modern OO languages, classes are used in the same way that types are used in many other languages, to specify what values are acceptable in given contexts, and thus to allow the compiler – and, at least equally importantly, the human reader – to understand the programmer's intention and to check that certain kinds of errors do not occur in the program.

Often people think of classes and types as being the same thing – indeed it's convenient, and not often misleading, to do so. However, it's wrong. Remember that a class defines not only what messages an object understands – which is really all you should need to know in order to check whether it is acceptable in some context. It also defines what the object does in response to the messages.

2.2 How does this relate to the aims of the previous chapter?

We are looking for modules, ideally for the reusable replaceable modules which may make good components. Where will we find them in an object oriented system?

Individual objects could be considered as modules, but they would not be good modules, because there are usually many different objects in a system which are very closely related conceptually. If each object were considered as a separate module, then either there would be confusing inconsistencies between conceptually related modules, or the need to maintain consistency would create high coupling.

Classes are intended to be loosely coupled, highly cohesive modules. Therefore we may hope (maybe still in vain, as we shall discuss in the next subsection) to obtain the benefits advertised in Chapter 1, namely, reduced development time and cost, ease of maintenance and high reliability. These benefits are not specific to OO, though OO is the best-known path to them at present.

Another claimed major benefit of object orientation doesn't fall into this category. It is that it is inherently natural to look at the world in terms of objects. Recall that a major requirement on a good system was that it should do what the users need, and that we cited the difficulty of capturing this accurately and tracking changes in it as among the hardest things about systems. It is important that the system's model (of the problem domain and the processes to be carried out) is compatible with the user's model. It seems that the domain objects change less frequently and less dramatically than the exact functionality that the user requires. So if a system is structured on the basis of these objects, changes to the system are likely to require less major upheaval than if the system were based on the more volatile functional aspects. In summary, we hope that our system can match the users' model of the world, so we can

- capture requirements more easily and accurately
- follow changes in user requirements better
- allow for more naturally interacting systems. For example, it is easier to implement a user interface that allows the user to interact with a file, a clock or a printer as a whole – which is sensible from the user's point of view, because these things are like real-world objects – if they are coherent objects from the system's point of view too. For this reason, user interfaces were one of the first major areas where object orientation became popular.

Notice, however, that we have to be tentative in claiming these benefits. There are cases (say, order processing systems) in which an object oriented approach seems very natural, and others (say, compilers) in which the argument looks much less compelling.

In any case, when OO achieves its aims, it is usually *not* because of any of the things that are specific to OO. It's because

- the object oriented approach takes modularity, encapsulation and abstraction as fundamental
- and OOPLs make them (comparatively!) easy, so that there is a reasonable likelihood that the obvious way to do something is also a good way to do it.

OO is a religion: it's the *people* who become oriented towards objects.

Discussion Question 12
What effects, good and bad, does the statement 'OO is a religion' suggest might exist?

2.2.1 What have objects to do with components?

The hype surrounding object orientation sometimes suggests that any class is automatically a reusable component. This, of course, is not true. In Chapter 1 we discussed the reasons why the reusability of a component is not simply a fact about the component itself, but depends on the context of development and proposed reuse. Another important factor is that the class structure often turns out to be too fine-grained for effective reuse. For example, in order to reuse a single class effectively and easily you have to be writing in the same programming language and using a compatible architecture. This is not always impracticable; successful, widely used class libraries exist and their classes can sensibly be regarded as reusable components. Often, however, a group of related classes is a more appropriate component. The greater the effort of plugging the component into a context, the greater the benefit provided by the component has to be before the effort is worthwhile.

We've deliberately blurred the question of whether components are built from objects or from classes: we have not yet made a clear type/instance distinction. The reason is that, given our wide definition of component, either or both can be the case. A class or collection of classes can be a component at the source code level; the context in which the component is used then makes use of the language's facilities to create objects of the classes. In other cases a component might provide access to a particular ready-made object of some class, with or without also providing access to the capability of making more objects of the class. Remember that a component itself has a well-defined interface. If the component is made of objects and/or classes, the component's interface does not normally allow access to everything that is in the interfaces of the objects and classes inside. The component itself is trying to be an encapsulated abstraction, and it is probably appropriate for it to hide some or all of its own internal structure; for example, whether and how it is composed of objects and classes.

Discussion Question 13

Use the Web and any other resources available to you to research a popular component architecture such as JavaBeans, CORBA or DCOM. What is the architecture? What internal structure can a component have, and how is the interface of the component defined?

2.3   Inheritance

So far, in fact, we have only discussed the conceptual basis of what's sometimes called *object-based design*. In this section we consider *inheritance*, which is the icing on the cake, and the remaining conceptual element underlying object *oriented* design. The metaphor indicates that it's nice, and that people often think it important, but that in fact it's less nutritious than what we've already covered!

In this section we will consider inheritance as a technical feature of object oriented languages, useful (in a limited way) for low-level reuse. Chapter 5 will consider how it is used in modeling.

Our example here is drawn from the case study in Chapter 15. We consider a system in which there is a class whose objects represent Lecturers and a class whose objects represent Directors of Studies. Now a director of studies is a kind of lecturer: specifically, a director of studies is a lecturer who, in addition to the normal duties of a lecturer, is responsible for overseeing the progress of particular students. Within our system, let us suppose that a `DirectorOfStudies` object ought to understand the same messages as a `Lecturer` does, and in addition ought to be able to respond to the message `directees` by returning a collection of `Student` objects.

Suppose we've already implemented the `Lecturer` class, and that we now have to develop `DirectorOfStudies`. Suppose (just for concreteness) that we're using a language like C++ where the interface of a class and its implementation are stored in different files. What do we need to do to implement the new class as easily as possible? We could cut and paste the code that defines the interface of `Lecturer` into a new interface file, and type the description of the extra message into the bottom. Similarly, we could copy the code that implements the reaction of `Lecturers` to messages into the implementation file for our new class, and then make any changes and additions. However, as we have already mentioned, such code reuse by cut and paste has disadvantages. The most important is that if a change has to be made to some of the duplicate code – for example, if a bug is discovered – we now have to make the changes in two places instead of one. This is a nuisance, and is likely to lead to errors.

Instead, object oriented programming languages allow us to define the new class `DirectorOfStudies` in terms of the old class `Lecturer`. We simply specify that `DirectorOfStudies` *is a subclass of* `Lecturer`, and then type only what pertains to the extra attributes or operations of `DirectorOfStudies`.[5]

More interestingly, because in object orientation knowledge of which code an object executes when it receives a message is encapsulated, it is possible for class `DirectorOfStudies` to implement different behavior, on receipt of some message, from what `Lecturer` implements. That is, we can *override* some of `Lecturer`'s methods in `DirectorOfStudies`: as well as inheriting the methods of `Lecturer`, `DirectorOfStudies` can include a new method implementing the same operation for which `Lecturer` already had a method. When an object of class `DirectorOfStudies` receives a message requesting it to perform the operation, the method to be invoked will be the specialized version provided by the class `DirectorOfStudies`.

> A subclass is an extended, specialized version of its superclass. It includes the operations and attributes of the superclass, and possibly some more.

Q: How is a subclass defined in your language? Can a class be a direct subclass of more than one class (multiple inheritance) or not?

Terminology   We say that

- `DirectorOfStudies` *inherits from* `Lecturer`
- `DirectorOfStudies` *is a subclass (or derived class) of* `Lecturer`
- `DirectorOfStudies` *is a specialization of* `Lecturer`
- `DirectorOfStudies` *is more specialized than* `Lecturer`
- `Lecturer` *is a superclass (or base class) of* `DirectorOfStudies`
- `Lecturer` *is a generalization of* `DirectorOfStudies`

These all mean almost the same. Often people use subclass/superclass as a description of a concrete relationship between classes, and specialization/generalization as a description of a relationship between the concepts represented by the classes. Usually the two coincide. The conceptual relationship need not necessarily show in the class structure, though. Conversely, sometimes people use inheritance in a class structure in cases where the conceptual relationship of generalization between the classes does not hold. (We do not recommend this: it can be convenient in the short term but you almost always pay in confusion in the long run.)

Do we say that an object of class `DirectorOfStudies` belongs to class `Lecturer`? We should, if we are thinking about classes as sets of objects. When we talk about 'an object of class `Lecturer`' we will certainly want to include the objects which also belong to class

---

[5] A few languages, notably Eiffel, also permit subclasses to delete attributes or operations of a superclass – but this is now normally considered a bad idea.

`DirectorOfStudies` – it's just too clumsy to write 'class `Lecturer` or any subclass' the whole time, and moreover the idea that an object of a subclass should be *substitutable* for an object of the superclass is fundamental. Therefore whenever we talk about objects belonging to a class we will include objects belonging to subclasses. On the other hand, it's extremely convenient to be able to talk about 'the class of this object' as though the object belonged to only one class. By 'the class' of an object we will mean the *most specialized* class to which the object belongs. This means that it remains true that an object's behavior is determined by its class!

2.4   Polymorphism and dynamic binding

These terms are often used interchangeably by the object oriented community. Actually they are quite distinct concepts – in general, languages can have either without having the other – but in OO they are related, both having to do with inheritance.

First of all notice that the simple fact that we can define one class in terms of another, getting code reuse, does not have to have any implications for the way client code treats objects of those classes. It would be quite possible to have a language in which inheritance was *just* a device for code reuse. You could define `DirectorOfStudies` in terms of `Lecturer`, but all client code (and the compiler) would have to be sure of the exact class of any object with which it interacted. Technically, this says you could have a language with a form of inheritance that had only *monomorphic* types. Object oriented languages, however, do better.

Polymorphism   This term, derived from Greek, is to do with *having many shapes*. In programming languages, it refers to a situation in which an entity could have any one of several types. In an object oriented situation, a polymorphic variable could refer (at different times) to objects of several different classes. A polymorphic function can take arguments of different types. Now, we said that an object of a subclass is supposed to be usable anywhere an object of the superclass could be used. This should mean, in particular, that a subclass object should be acceptable as the value of a variable, if an object of the base class is. In other words, in an object oriented language *any* variable is polymorphic, at least in this limited sense! Similarly, if some function (e.g., method) can take an argument of class B it should also be able to take an argument of any class C which is a subclass of B; so any function is polymorphic in this limited sense. For example, a function which expects a `Lecturer` object as argument should not break if it is given a `DirectorOfStudies` object instead.

Discussion Question 14
Consider whatever programming languages you know (C, perhaps, or a typed functional programming language). Do they have polymorphism? Is it more or less restrictive than the OO polymorphism described here? (How) is it useful?

Thus polymorphism saves us a great deal of duplication of code. It really comes into its own, however, when combined with *dynamic binding*.

Dynamic binding The term 'binding' in *dynamic binding* (or late binding – the two are usually used interchangeably) refers to the process of identifying what code should be executed as the result of some message. To understand this, let us consider a couple of examples.

Suppose that the `Lecturer` interface includes the operation `canDo(duty: Duty)`, which takes something representing an administrative duty as argument, and that the `Lecturer` is supposed to return a boolean value, which is `true` if the lecturer is able to do the duty. Suppose further (slightly unrealistically!) that a `DirectorOfStudies` is expected to be able to do anything, so should always return `true`. That is, the subclass `DirectorOfStudies` has reimplemented – overridden – the operation `canDo`, presumably replacing some complex code that examines information about the lecturer's interests or experience with some simple code that simply returns `true`.

Now suppose that `lecturers` is a variable which refers to a collection of `Lecturer` objects. This collection may of course include some `DirectorOfStudies` objects, since if we can add a `Lecturer` to `lecturers` we can add a `DirectorOfStudies`. Suppose some client – a task trying to find someone to do seminar organization – performs something like:

```
for each o in lecturers
    o.canDo(seminarOrganization)
```

(Notice the dot notation for message sending, which is common to many languages. The expression `o.canDo(seminarOrganization)` indicates that the message `canDo` `(seminarOrganization)` is sent to object o. It can also be used to represent the value which o returns to the sender after acting on the message.)

The most we can assume, looking at this code, is that o is a `Lecturer`. Remember our original idea that an object encapsulates its own behavior, and that classes were introduced only as a shortcut. If o is in class `Lecturer` only, the `Lecturer` code for `canDo` should be executed: that is its behaviour on receipt of that message. What should happen when the `for` loop reaches an object o which is in fact in class `DirectorOfStudies`? Clearly, in this case the `DirectorOfStudies` code should be executed. (If the object o really were carrying its own code around with it, this would happen automatically – and the fact that it doesn't is supposed just to be an optimization.) That is, the same piece of syntax should cause two different pieces of code to be executed at different times. The message-send is *dynamically bound* to the appropriate code.[6]

Finally let us consider another very simple example of dynamic binding, which also illustrates why we may want to think about an object sending a message to itself.

Suppose that the `Lecturer` interface includes the message `abilities`, in response to which the `Lecturer` object is supposed to return a collection of the duties that the lecturer is able to undertake. Perhaps the `Lecturer` code implements this by something like the following pseudocode (in which `self.canDo(duty)` represents the result returned after the message with selector `canDo` and argument `duty` is sent to this very object):

---

[6] This can most simply be done by checking at runtime what the type of the object is, although current research is making progress in allowing the compiler to do more of the work, which is more efficient.

```
thingsICanDo := emptyCollection
for each duty in globalDutiesList
  if (self.canDo(duty)) then add duty to thingsICanDo
  else do nothing
return thingsICanDo
```

We could override this operation, too, in the new class `DirectorOfStudies`. But why should we? (Performance is most unlikely to be important.) Suppose we leave it in place, so that this code is inherited unchanged by `DirectorOfStudies` objects. Recall, though, that `DirectorOfStudies` did override the operation `canDo`. What should happen when a `DirectorOfStudies` object receives the message `abilities`? It will execute the code above – there's nothing more specific. This makes it send message `canDo` to itself. It's a `DirectorOfStudies` object, so when it receives the message `canDo` it will execute the specialized version of the code defined in the `DirectorOfStudies` class.

If you use a pure object oriented language, this behavior should quickly become second nature. If you're using C++ beware: only virtual methods have this behavior. Some people (including me[7]) feel strongly that when you begin object oriented programming in C++ you should get into the habit of making all methods virtual[8] and learn about non-virtual methods later.

SUMMARY

This chapter was a whistle-stop motivation for and introduction to object orientation. We considered what an object is and how messages are sent between objects. We showed that the objects in a system can usefully be divided into classes, rather than being considered individually, and we began to consider the connection between objects and components. We discussed how a class can be defined using another class's definition by inheritance. Finally we discussed the other feature of inheritance in object oriented languages, its ability to provide polymorphism and dynamic binding.

In the next chapter, we will introduce the main topic of the book, the Unified Modeling Language, which can be used to express the specification and design of systems which take advantage of object orientation.

---

[7] Stevens.

[8] including (especially) destructors, but never constructors. Why?

CHAPTER 3

Introductory case study

In this chapter we introduce UML, the Unified Modeling Language. We aim to demonstrate just enough of UML, and the way it is used to specify and design systems, to put the more detailed chapters which follow into context. In the next chapter we will discuss the origins of UML and its role in the development process. In Part II we will discuss UML in greater depth, often drawing on the very simple case study used here.

3.1 The problem

The most difficult part of any design project is understanding the task you are attempting. In this example we assume the following situation.

> You have been contracted to develop a computer system for a university library. The library currently uses a 1960s program, written in an obsolete language, for some simple bookkeeping tasks, and a card index, for user browsing. You are asked to build an interactive system which handles both of these aspects online.

3.1.1 Clarifying the requirements

The problem statement given above is very vague, but is typical of the sort of initial requests received when projects are first discussed. Before even agreeing whether to tackle a design, a more detailed analysis of the requirements of the users is needed. This task of *requirements engineering* is complex for a variety of reasons.

- Different users will have different, sometimes conflicting, priorities.

- Users are not likely to have clear, easily expressed views of what they want: for example, they will find it hard to distinguish between what an existing system does and what any suitable system *must* do.

- It is hard to imagine working with a system of which you've only seen a description, so users may think a description of the system sounds OK when in fact it misses something vital.

- The managers who talk most to the developers may not have direct experience of doing the jobs that users of the system do.

Discussion Question 15

How can you as the developer help to overcome any of these problems?

A full treatment of requirements engineering is outside the scope of this book: one good treatment is [44].

After some careful investigation, the following facts emerge about the requirements that an ideal system would satisfy:

- **Books and journals** The library contains books and journals. It may have several copies of a given book. Some of the books are for short term loans only. All other books may be borrowed by any library member for three weeks. Only members of staff may borrow journals. Members of the library can normally borrow up to six items at a time, but members of staff may borrow up to 12 items at one time. New books and journals arrive regularly, and old ones are sometimes disposed of. The current year's journals are sent away to be bound into volumes at the end of each year.

- **Borrowing** It is essential that the system keeps track of when books and journals are borrowed and returned, since the current system already does that. The new system should produce reminders when a book is overdue. There may in future be a requirement for users to be able to extend the loan of a book if it is not reserved.

- **Browsing** The system should allow users to search for a book on a particular topic, by a particular author, etc., to check whether a copy of the book is available for loan and, if not, to reserve the book. Anybody can browse in the library.

This is better, but it's still not clear what the different tasks are or who needs what.

Discussion Question 16

What further questions would you need to ask?

Discussion Question 17

What are the disadvantages of designing a system to meet the requirements above, without further analysis?

3.1.2 Use case model

If a system is to be seen as having high quality, it must meet the needs of its users.[1] So we take a *user-oriented* approach to systems analysis. We identify the users of the system and the tasks they must undertake with the system. We also seek information about which tasks are most important, so that we can plan the development accordingly.

What do we mean by 'users' and 'tasks'? UML in fact uses as technical terms *actors* and *use cases*. An actor is a user of the system *in a particular role*. (In fact an actor can also be an external system which is like a user from the point of view of our system: the crucial point is that it's someone or something external to the system we're designing, which interacts with our system and can place demands on our system.) For example, our system will have an actor BookBorrower representing the person who interacts with the system to borrow a book. It's not clear to us whether this is a library member, or a librarian acting on behalf of a library member, but for our present purposes we don't need to know. A *use case* is a task which an actor needs to perform with the help of the system, such as Borrow copy of book. Notice that the simple name can hide quite complex behavior with a variety of outcomes: borrowing a copy of a book will require checking that the borrower is a member of the library and that s/he doesn't already have the maximum number of books on loan, for example. It's possible that the use case may end without the user having successfully borrowed a book, but we name the use case after what happens in the normal, successful case.

The detail of each use case should be documented, usually in third-person, active-voice English.[2] For example:

- **Borrow copy of book** A BookBorrower presents a book. The system checks that the potential borrower is a member of the library, and that s/he does not already have the maximum permitted number of books on loan. This maximum is six unless the member is a staff member, in which case it is 12. If both checks succeed, the system records that this library member has this copy of the book on loan. Otherwise it refuses the loan.

Discussion Question 18

The library system considered in this chapter is simplified. By considering libraries you know, suggest what else a full system might have to do or check to carry out this use case. Amend the use case description as appropriate, remembering that it should only include requirements, not design.

Remark on user interfaces User interface design is a vast and extremely interesting field, outside the scope of this book. To the user interface designer, it may matter a great deal whether a book is borrowed by a library member or a librarian. We assume here, though, that our task is to build the underlying system, providing functionality which will be invoked by the user interface which is being built by somebody else. This is not an unreasonable assumption: user interfaces are more prone to change than the rest of the system will be,

---

[1] Some authorities prefer to talk about the needs of customers, on the grounds that he who pays the piper calls the tune; but the customer is likely to get feedback from the users, and it is a strong-minded customer who retains the idea that a system is high quality when the users curse it!

[2] 'The system checks' rather than 'Check' or '... is checked by the system'.

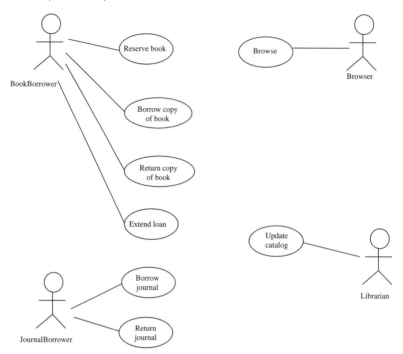

Figure 3.1   Use case diagram for the library.

and a separation between the user interface and the underlying system makes modification
or replacement of the UI more feasible. Moreover it makes sense to have user interface
designs done by expert user interface designers. For more on user interface design see, for
example, [48] or [16].

At this point we can record the information pictorially, in a *use case diagram* for the
system, as shown in Figure 3.1. The notation is self-explanatory: stick figures represent
actors, ovals represent use cases, and there is a line between an actor and a use case if the
actor may take part in the use case.

Managing UML diagrams – drawing them, sharing them, keeping them consistent –
can be made easier by using a CASE (Computer Aided Software Engineering) tool which
supports UML.[3] However, for small systems a piece of paper or the back of the proverbial
envelope will suffice. Beware of making diagrams very complex, which is easy with a
powerful tool. If a diagram is too complex to draw by hand, it's probably also too complex
to think about clearly. In this case it should probably be split, or drawn at a higher level of
abstraction, or both. In this case, we collapsed all the Librarian's adding and removing
of books, sending away of journals, etc., into one use case Update catalog. When we
considered this functionality in detail, we might want to separate this out into separate use
cases.

At this stage each use case should be documented, at least in outline. We emphasize that

---

[3] We use Rational Rose, but there are many others. There are some links from this book's home page.

you have to decide only what the system should do, not how it should do it. For example, in `Borrow copy of book`, we did not mention in what form the system should record the information about the loan; we just said what had to be recorded.

Q: Write short use case descriptions for some of the use cases in Figure 3.1.

Do not invent requirements.

This may sound obvious – but as you examine use cases you will probably think of many things the system could usefully do. It's essential to avoid confusing things you know the system must do because the customer told you so, with things you think the system could or should do. You may find it useful to make a list of questions and possibilities with each use case, for discussion with the customer: but do not incorporate dubious features into the use case descriptions themselves.

3.2 Scope and iterations

Now we have a reasonably clear idea of what an ideal system would do. However, experience has shown that the 'big bang' single-release approach to systems building, in which the developers aim to deliver an ideal system in their first and only delivery, is extremely risky. To limit the risks, it is better to aim to get to the ideal system in several steps or *iterations*. The first iteration results in the delivery of a system with only the most basic and essential functionality; later iterations enhance the system. We will discuss this topic in more detail in the next chapter, but you might like to discuss it now:

> **Discussion Question 19**
> What advantages and disadvantages can you see in adopting an iterative approach to the development of this system?

One of the main purposes of use cases is to help identify suitable dividing lines between iterations: an iteration can deliver enough of the system to allow certain use cases to be carried out, but not others.

In this case, let us suppose that after discussing priorities with the customer we decide that the first iteration of the system should provide the use cases:

- `Borrow copy of book`
- `Return copy of book`
- `Borrow journal`
- `Return journal`

The limited use case diagram for the first iteration of our system is shown in Figure 3.2.

The following is a brief restatement of the requirements of the first iteration, discarding irrelevancies. In a real project you might have to prepare a document like this that describes all the use cases to be provided in the first iteration (for example, to be part of a contractual document) or you might be able to use the use case descriptions and just list the names of the use cases to be provided.

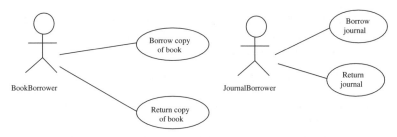

Figure 3.2 Use case diagram for the first iteration.

- **Books and journals** The library contains books and journals. It may have several copies of a given book. Some of the books are for short term loans only. All other books may be borrowed by any library member for three weeks. Members of the library can normally borrow up to six items at a time, but members of staff may borrow up to 12 items at one time. Only members of staff may borrow journals.
- **Borrowing** The system must keep track of when books and journals are borrowed and returned, enforcing the rules described above.

In a real project you would at some stage look at resource issues, including the choice of suitable languages, tools and applications. For the purposes of this book, we will assume that the outcome of this review is that the system is to be implemented in an object oriented language, and so you will develop the design in UML. We will ignore database issues: see Panel 3.2 on Persistence, toward the end of this chapter.

Discussion Question 20
Our choice of the first iteration for this system was, we confess, influenced by our aim in this book of introducing interesting OO techniques without spending much time discussing things outside the scope of the book. Ignoring these constraints, what other options for first iterations of the system do you see? Do you think any of these are better?

3.3 Identifying classes

In the standard jargon of analysis we often talk about the *key domain abstractions*. The term *domain* covers the application area we are working with, i.e. the library. We could refer to the key domain classes; we use the term *abstraction* instead of class to emphasize that we describe only the aspects of the domain which are important to the application. (Remember, though, that we have argued in Chapter 2 that all good modules, including classes, are abstractions.) Therefore, put more simply, we are looking for the features and facts about the library, which matter in the system we are building to support it.

Identifying the right *classes* is one of the main skills of OO development. It is crucial for building genuinely extensible software with reuse. We start the process of identifying the key domain abstractions using the following approach, which is (rather long-windedly) known as the *noun identification technique*:

Books and journals The <u>library</u> contains <u>books</u> and <u>journals</u>. It may have several <u>copies of a given book</u>. Some of the books are for <u>short term loans</u> only. All other books may be borrowed by any <u>library member</u> for three <u>weeks</u>. <u>Members of the library</u> can normally borrow up to six <u>items</u> at a <u>time</u>, but <u>members of staff</u> may borrow up to 12 items at one time. Only members of staff may borrow journals.

Borrowing The <u>system</u> must keep track of when books and journals are borrowed and returned, enforcing the <u>rules</u> described above.

Figure 3.3 Nouns and noun phrases in the library.

Take a coherent, concise statement of the requirements of the system and underline its *nouns* and *noun phrases*; that is, identify the words and phrases that denote *things*. This gives a list of *candidate classes*, which we can then whittle down and modify to get an initial class list for the system.

This is only one technique among several that you will use to identify classes. In Chapter 5 we will introduce several more techniques which can be used to select classes and validate choices. At this stage we are just trying to get a rough list of possible candidates.

We take the sentences given in subsection 3.1.1 and we underline the nouns and noun phrases, giving the result in Figure 3.3. (You could also use the use case descriptions, of course.)

Next we discard those which are 'obviously' not good candidate classes for any one of a variety of reasons. (When you're familiar with the technique, of course, you will simply not underline those things that are obviously unsuitable.) We consider each in the singular. We will make this more general and systematic in Chapter 5. In this particular case we discard:

- library, because it is outside the scope of our system;[4]
- short term loan, because a loan (short term or otherwise) is really an event, the lending of a book to a user, which so far as we know is not a useful object in this system;
- member of the library, which is redundant: it means the same as library member, which we keep;
- week, because it is a measure of time, not a thing;
- item, because it is vague: when we clarify it we see that it means book or journal;
- time, because it is outside the scope of the system;
- system, because it is part of the meta-language of requirements description, not part of the domain;
- rule, for the same reason.

This leaves:

- book
- journal
- copy (of book)

---

[4] The question of whether there is a 'main' system object is discussed in Chapter 5.

- library member

- member of staff

as our first-cut list of probable classes. At this point you might start to use CRC cards to record the provisional responsibilities of the classes and to identify improvements in the list, but we postpone discussion of that to Chapter 5.

Notice that library members and members of staff are people who use the system. Of course a system's users don't always have to be represented inside the system (and in fact in this case, we have not represented the librarians), so one has to consider in each case whether it's desirable to do so. In this case, there are limits on how many books a library member or member of staff can borrow, so it's clear that the system has to keep some data about these users. It is less obvious what behavior the object representing a user should have. Here we will use a technique which is often useful, though it isn't appropriate for every system. We make the system objects representing actors responsible for carrying out actions on behalf of those actors. For example, when the library member Jo Bloggs is borrowing a copy of a book, the message `borrow(theCopy)` will be sent to the `LibraryMember` object which represents Jo Bloggs. (The message is sent by the user interface, which we do not model in this chapter.) This `LibraryMember` object will then be responsible for carrying out whatever has to be done to record (or deny) the loan, by sending messages to other system objects.

Of course this process of identifying objects and classes is not an exact science. We could have discarded the same candidates for different reasons. In fact we do not have to get it absolutely right at this stage and we are *not* trying to design the system: we *are* trying to identify the important real-world objects within the domain of the system.

Discussion Question 21
Do you disagree with any of the decisions we made? Why?

It is important to be clear about what is meant by each term (classname, etc.). Some methodologies dictate that at this stage you draft a *data dictionary entry* to define each term. In our experience, most projects neither support nor need this bureaucratic overhead. We assume that whatever document you are using to keep track of your design (maybe a whiteboard or back of an envelope, maybe a 'real' document or a computer supported design document) includes whatever notes or further specifications may be necessary to ensure that everyone on the project has the same understanding of the common terms. In the early stages of a project you may have to settle for everyone agreeing that a term has not been fully defined yet. That's OK. What we must avoid is misunderstandings where people have different ideas about what is meant.

3.4 Relations between classes

Next we identify and name important real-world relationships or *associations* between our classes. We do this for two reasons:

- to *clarify our understanding* of the domain, by describing our objects in terms of how they work together;
- to *sanity-check the coupling* in our end system, i.e. make sure that we are following good principles in modularizing our design, as described in Chapter 1.

The second of these requires some explanation. If one object is believed to be closely related to another, it is probably fairly harmless for the class that implements the one to depend on the class that implements the other, i.e. for them to be closely coupled.

There are at least two justifications for this:

1. If domain objects are conceptually related, then a human maintainer who recognizes this relation will be alerted to expect a dependency between the corresponding classes; so s/he is likely to take the possibility of a dependency into account when modifying one of the classes. The likelihood of an unexpected problem arising because of the dependency is thus comparatively low.

2. If the domain objects are conceptually related, it is likely that an application which can reuse one of the classes can also reuse the other; so although any coupling in a system complicates reuse, the effect will be comparatively benign.

Recall that we said a major argument for OO is that the structure of an OO system reflects the structure of reality: here is a concrete instance of that benefit.

In this case we can see that:

- a copy *is a copy of* a book
- a library member *borrows/returns* a copy
- a member of staff *borrows/returns* a copy
- a member of staff *borrows/returns* a journal

We can record the information pictorially in the UML class model in Figure 3.4.

This class model in fact records a little more information than we have mentioned so far: it also shows the *multiplicities* of the associations. For example, each copy is a copy of just one, uniquely defined, book, so the figure 1 appears at the Book end of the association between Book and Copy. On the other hand there may be one or many copies of a given book (presumably if there are no copies the system isn't concerned with the book, but that is a presumption that might have to be revised), so 1..* appears at the other end of that association. We will treat this in detail in Chapter 5.

Notice that the diagram does *not* say whether a Copy object knows about (depends on) the corresponding Book, or vice versa, or both: that is, it says nothing about the navigability of the associations we have shown.

Discussion Question 22
In which direction(s) do you think the associations should be navigable, bearing in mind that we should not introduce unnecessary coupling? Consider this again at the end of the chapter.

Finally, we may notice that MemberOfStaff shares in all the same associations that LibraryMember does, and that this agrees with our intuition that a member of staff is a kind of library member. Recording this in the class diagram will clarify our understanding

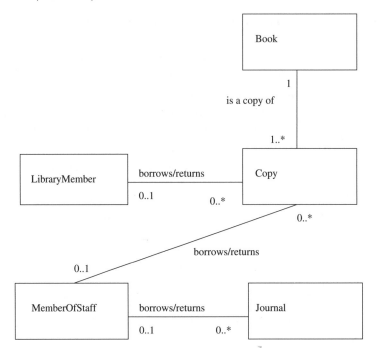

Figure 3.4 Initial class model of the library.

of the situation, that there is a generalization relationship between LibraryMember and MemberOfStaff. We may or may not choose to implement this generalization relationship using inheritance (that is, by making MemberOfStaff a subclass of LibraryMember) – that design decision will depend on a deeper understanding of the system than we currently have. Recording the generalization in UML notation, we get the rather neater-looking class model shown in Figure 3.5.

3.5   The system in action

So far we have sketched the static structure of the system, but we have not yet described its dynamic behavior: for example, we have yet to record how the objects in the system work together to allow a user to borrow a copy of a book. There is no active connection between the use cases we started with and the objects we have decided make up the system.

In UML we can use *interaction diagrams* to show how messages pass between objects of the system to carry out some task – for example, to realize a particular use case. We need not do this for every use case, and some projects will do it for none: you should use an interaction diagram when you think there is sufficient benefit to outweigh the costs. For example, if a use case is particularly complicated, or if there is doubt about which of two realizations is better, then interaction diagrams may be an aid to clear thought.

As an example let us consider in more detail what happens when a library member borrows

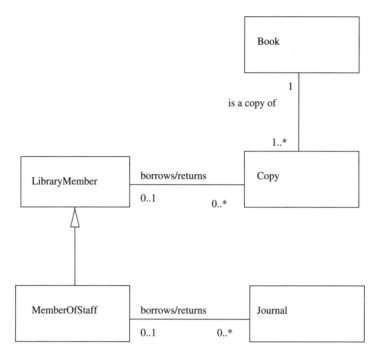

Figure 3.5 Revised library class model.

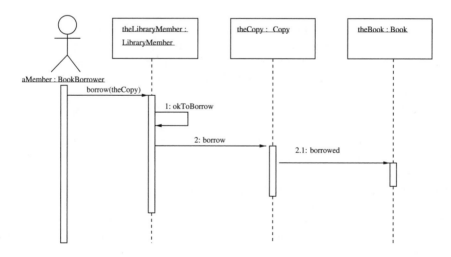

Figure 3.6 Interaction shown on a sequence diagram.

a copy of a book. In the physical world, a human library member will presumably come to the issuing desk with a physical copy of a book, and via the system user interface there will be some means of identifying the library member and copy concerned. (This may be by means of a card reader and a barcode scanner, or by a person entering identification details into a GUI: whatever.) So we can start from the position of having a certain `LibraryMember` object (call it `theLibraryMember`) and a certain `Copy` object (call it `theCopy`).

Recall that we said above that we would let the `LibraryMember` objects act on behalf of the library members, so this interaction begins by a `BookBorrower` actor sending a message to `theLibraryMember`. The message will specify what service is required: in this case, to borrow `theCopy`. Let us call the message `borrow(theCopy)`. The system has to check that it's permitted for `theLibraryMember` to borrow another book: one of the duties of `theLibraryMember` will be to perform this check. (This will probably be implemented simply by comparing the number of items the user currently has on loan, which may be recorded as an attribute of the class `LibraryMember`, with the maximum permitted number of items: but we deliberately don't decide this in detail at this stage.) We should probably represent this by having `theLibraryMember` send itself a message, say `okToBorrow`.

Next we want to update the system's information about how many copies of this book are in the library, since there's now one fewer. This involves whatever `Book` object is associated with `theCopy` by the association 'is a copy of': call this object `theBook`. Let us suppose that `theLibraryMember` informs `theCopy` that it is being borrowed by sending it the message `borrow`, and that `theCopy` then sends `theBook` a message to say that a copy of the book is being borrowed, say `borrowed()`. Nothing else needs to be done: all these messages receive replies signaling no error. The user interface will somehow signal to the human borrower that all is well, and the human borrower will take the physical book away.

Q: How else could we have implemented this behavior? Do you think any of the alternatives are better? Why?

One way – much more readable than the words above – to describe this in UML is by the *sequence diagram* in Figure 3.6. A sequence diagram describes some piece of system behavior – typically a use case or part of one – by showing which messages are passed between objects and in what order they must occur (read the messages from top to bottom of the page).

In a real project you probably wouldn't feel the need to develop a sequence diagram for an interaction as simple as this one. Sequence diagrams can be much more expressive than we've yet shown; details are in Chapters 9 and 10. For example, in this example the messages have to occur in a fixed order: there is only one *thread* of activity and activities cannot proceed in parallel. Moreover, we were concerned only with the order in which things happened. By attaching times to the various activities it is also possible to deal with questions resulting in real-time problems.

There are other ways of looking at this sort of interaction. In Chapters 9 and 10 we see how to record the same information in a *collaboration diagram*: each way has its own advantages.

Q: Develop a sequence diagram for the alternative scenario in which `okToBorrow` returns false, because the library member already has the maximum number of books.

PANEL 3.1 Design by Contract I

In this panel we consider how we can record decisions about what the behavior of an operation should be, in more detail than just its name and the types of its arguments and return values.

Pre- and postconditions   A fundamental problem is that the types in a programming language are only a very rough way to describe the properties which an object's attributes and operations should have. For example, the okToBorrow message takes no arguments and returns a boolean value. This is true of the implementation which always returns the value false; however, the library system won't work correctly with such an implementation, because it will never allow a library member to borrow a book! The problem is that, although we definitely do want the value returned from the method to be a boolean, that isn't all we want: we also want it to have some particular connection with the state of the object.

We can express extra conditions, or constraints, on operations using *preconditions* and *postconditions*.

A precondition describes something that must be true when an operation is invoked; it is a bug to invoke the operation otherwise. The precondition could involve the current state of the object (values of its attributes) and/or the arguments to the operation. That is, the precondition describes what the operation demands.

A postcondition describes something that must be true when the operation returns; the implementation of the operation is buggy if its postcondition ever turns out to be false after it was invoked with its precondition true. The postcondition could involve the value returned by the operation, the arguments to the operation, and the state of the object both before and after the operation. That is, the postcondition describes what the operation promises.

Consider the operation okToBorrow on LibraryMember again. The return value should be true if the member has fewer than the member's maximum permitted number of books on loan, otherwise false. We may also want to say that an implementation of the operation is allowed to assume that the member had no more than the maximum allowed number of books out to start with. Suppose LibraryMember has attributes numberOfBooksOnLoan : integer and maxBooksOnLoan : integer. We could document the intended behavior of the okToBorrow operation using a precondition and a postcondition in English like this:

> okToBorrow
>   pre: numberOfBooksOnLoan is less than or equal to maxBooksOnLoan
>   post: return value is true if numberOfBooksOnLoan is less than
>   maxBooksOnLoan, otherwise false. State of the object is unchanged.

Of course if you plan to write a lot of pre- and postconditions you will certainly want a more concise notation than this! Options include boolean expressions of a programming language, or statements in a special purpose language; Chapter 6, which also discusses recording constraints in UML, has a panel on the special purpose Object Constraint Language, OCL, which is designed to work well with UML.

Discussion Question 23

If the arguments to an operation or the return value from it are (as is often the case) objects themselves, rather than being values of a base type like integer or boolean, then what should the pre- and postcondition of the operation be allowed to say about these objects?

Class invariants   In the example, the precondition wasn't really specific to this operation. It would *always* be a bug for a `LibraryMember` to have on loan more books than the permitted maximum number. Rather than put this as a precondition on every operation, we can more simply let it be a class invariant. That is, we put it as documentation of the `LibraryMember` class that a valid object of the class always has the value of the attribute `numberOfBooksOnLoan` no greater than the value of the attribute `maxBooksOnLoan`. Conceivably this condition could be violated by the object when it's in the middle of processing a message, but it has to be restored by the time the processing is complete, so that it always holds at the time any message is sent to the object.

Q: How would you check that the class invariant always holds?

Type, or constraint?   There is no gulf in meaning between something's type and a constraint that should hold on it. Both type and constraint are there to tell you something about what the thing can be. The type of an object describes what attributes and operations it has, and *their* types. (Because a class definition also gives this information, we will often confuse the type of an object with its class – but remember that the object's class specifies its implementation as well.) A constraint – in this case a class invariant – tells you something extra; for example, it may tell you something about the connection between different attributes.

Similarly, the type of an operation tells you what the types of the arguments are and what the type of the result is. A constraint on an operation takes the form of a precondition and a postcondition. Just as an operation is expected to work only if it is given arguments of the right type, it is expected to work only if its precondition is satisfied. Just as it is expected to return a value of the right type, it is expected to return a value that satisfies the postcondition.

So when you try to describe what things are permitted in some context – as objects of a class, or as implementations of an operation – you first tie them down loosely, using the type system of your programming language. If this isn't precise enough for your needs, you just add a constraint to express the rest of what you want to say. At the extreme – a language like Smalltalk which has no static typing – everything you want to say about what are suitable values for an expression has to go into a constraint. Languages like Java and C++, which have static typing, allow you to let some of the more routine checking be done by the compiler. You write constraints only for the more interesting bits.

The disadvantage of constraints compared to types is that usually there is no automatic checking that the constraints are satisfied, though an exception to this is Eiffel.

In several languages you can use *assertions*: boolean expressions of your programming language which can be checked at runtime, perhaps only when debugging is turned on.

3.5.1 Changes in the system: state diagrams

You will probably have noticed that the state of the book object may change when a copy of the book is successfully borrowed: the book may change from being borrowable (there is a copy of it in the library) to not borrowable (all copies are out on loan or reserved). (In fact this isn't very important in this iteration, but it will be important when we implement browsing or reservations in future iterations of the development.) We can record this using a *state diagram* as shown in Figure 3.7.

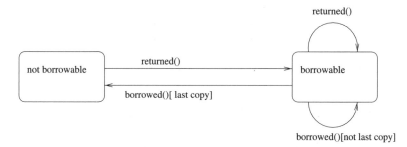

Figure 3.7   State diagram for class Book.

This notation shows that whether or not the borrowing of a copy causes a state change in the book depends on whether there are any other copies still in the library. We've used informal English to express the condition in this case.

> **Discussion Question 24**
> Have we recorded enough information? Do you think we might want to know *how many* copies of the book are available for borrowing? What issues would arise if we tried to model that?

3.5.2 Further work

In developing the sequence and state diagrams, we have identified certain messages which our objects have to understand; that is, certain operations on our classes. We have, of course, to carry this further by considering the other interactions of the system. We can also identify the data which is encapsulated in the objects, including the data which implements the associations we have shown, such as references to other objects. All of this information can be added to the class model: we can list the attributes and operations of a class in the class icon. However, we postpone discussion of how to show this in UML to Chapter 5.

Once we have identified how all the use cases are realized, down to the level of what messages are passed and in what order, it is rather straightforward to implement the classes.

This gives us the first iteration of our system, which can then be tested by developers and users to identify any misunderstandings or other failings. Further iterations of development should produce a system which is closer to ideal.

PANEL 3.2 Persistence

So far we have not considered the very important issue of object persistence. Of course it must be possible to shut down the system and restart it without losing the information about library members, books and journals in the library, etc. Objects which must last longer than the lifetime of a running instance of the program are called *persistent*. Persistent objects can also potentially be used by different programs, but that is not the issue here.

In very simple cases, objects can simply be stored 'raw' in files: an object can write itself into a file, and an object can be reconstructed by reading the file. The details of how this is done are language dependent: many, but not all, object oriented languages provide standard mechanisms, in which case the developer does not have to worry about such issues as file formats. However, this mechanism is not suitable for systems which need non-trivial object persistence; it is inflexible and inefficient.

Q: How can this kind of storage be done in your language? (Hint: in Java, look at the `Serializable` interface; in Smalltalk80, look at the `storeOn:aStream` method; in C++, look in your class libraries.) Write a simple program that lets you create an object and change its state, then write it to a file, then reconstruct the object from the file.

Q: What disadvantages does this method have? Consider, for example, how you can deal with objects which have links to other objects.

A more serious option is to use a *database*, which provides much more than just persistence. For example, a database will provide support for *transactions* – sets of updates which must succeed or fail together. The most common course is to use a *relational* database. This is by no means straightforward, since there is an *impedance mismatch* between SQL and the object oriented programming language. Data is stored as tables and must be translated between them and the object form which is useful in the object oriented system: the developer cannot simply classify certain objects as persistent and expect changes to them to be permanent. However, tool support is increasingly available, and recent developments in RDBMSs (in particular, SQL3) aim to ease these problems. An alternative is to use an object oriented database. OODBs explicitly support object orientation, including inheritance, and they usually also allow more flexible interaction with the data than RDBMSs have done. However, they still have only a small share of the market.

The study of object oriented databases is outside the scope of this book; one good and readable book on the subject is [31].

Q: If you have access to any databases, consider how they might be used to support the application described here.

Discussion Question 25

What factors would affect whether it is desirable to integrate the library system with other university systems, such as the student registration system?

SUMMARY

This chapter described a simple case study. It introduced the main features of UML in a necessarily sketchy way; Part II of the book covers each diagram type in detail, but since the diagrams are designed to be used together in an iterative development it is important to have an overview of what UML is before going on to discuss details.

We described a single *iteration* of the development of this system, and we did not justify the techniques we used. In the next chapter we discuss the development process.

DISCUSSION QUESTIONS

1. We concentrated on just one use case – borrowing – in this chapter. Can you develop similar diagrams for the other use cases?
2. How worthwhile do you think the effort of creating this model has been? Try to remember how you would have approached the same problem before you read this chapter and consider whether you have benefited from the understanding gained.
3. Librarians are seen as existing merely to service the use cases of the library members. How could we model their own use cases, which include the need to add and remove new books and new copies of existing books? How far would their addition to our design require us to change our existing model?
4. What do you think about the way we treated journals?
5. We've modeled the actors members of staff as kinds of library members, but members of staff are allowed to borrow more books than normal library members. Is this a problem?
6. How will or should the system cope with books which consist of multiple volumes, books with associated CDs or audiotapes, etc.? List some options, and consider what pros and cons you would want to discuss with your customer.

CHAPTER 4

The development process

This chapter addresses the question 'How can good systems be built?'.

In our simple case study, it was possible to imagine that we just sat down and did the work, beginning at the beginning, going on until the end, and then stopping. For more complex systems, however, the development process must be managed. It must be possible to plan the development and to tell how much it has achieved and whether it is on schedule. We must have an appropriate toolkit of techniques for developing a system. We must have an understandable way of documenting and controlling what is done, for example so that people can safely leave and join the project as it proceeds.

Many different *development processes* or *methodologies* have been used. This book does not propose any one of them; at the end of the chapter we shall return to the question of why not. In this chapter we shall briefly discuss some aspects of process, and give some pointers to more information.

4.1 Defining terms

The terms 'process', 'methodology' and 'method' (with or without the prefixes 'development' or 'design') are used in different ways by different people, often without definition. We shall mean, by a *development process*, a set of rules which define how a development project should generally be carried out. This may include a description of what documents, design models and other artifacts should be produced and in what order.

The terms *methodology* and *method* are also used in similar ways; there is a tendency for these terms to be used for things which specify techniques for developing particular design artifacts, such as the class model we saw in Chapter 3. Sometimes this is emphasized by talking about a *design methodology*. If there is a difference between 'method' and 'methodology' it tends to be, as the length of the words suggests, that a methodology is a bigger thing with broader scope. The distinctions between these words are not absolute, however, and it is not always possible to be definite about whether something is a process or 'just' a methodology. Neither is the question particularly interesting!

A [design] method[ology] normally specifies what *modeling language* should be used in describing the analysis and design work. It also tells you something about how you should produce these things, for example by giving a list of steps to go through in order to capture the users' requirements. In this book we will discuss many such techniques that may form part of a methodology, but we leave the choice of methodology open. Sometimes this collection of techniques is itself called the process, but we will try to avoid this use.

Since we've mentioned the modeling language, let us discuss this before returning to the other aspects of the development process.

4.1.1 Models and modeling languages

A *model* is an abstract representation of a specification, a design or a system, from a particular point of view. It is often represented visually by one or more diagrams. It aims to express the essentials of some aspect of what we're doing, without giving unnecessary detail. Its purpose is to enable people involved in the development to think about and discuss problems and solutions without getting sidetracked. If it is to be useful, a model must have a precise and well understood meaning: abstract does not mean woolly!

A *modeling language* is a way of expressing the various models produced during the development process. A modeling language defines a collection of *model elements*, which are roughly analogous to the utterances (words, sentences, television sit-com scripts) in a spoken language; a model is made up of model elements, as a sentence is made up of words. UML, the Unified Modeling Language, is of course an example of a modeling language. A modeling language is normally diagrammatic, but could be text based. It has

- *syntax* – in a diagram-based modeling language, the rules that determine which diagrams are legal;
- *semantics* – the rules that determine what a legal diagram means.

Both syntax and semantics can be given more or less formally. Most modeling languages have both syntax and semantics given informally in everyday English. Our explanations of UML in this book can be seen as an informal way of giving syntax and semantics of UML – that is, by the time you've read the book you should have a good understanding of whether a diagram is legal UML and if so, what it means, though you would not be able to express your understanding in mathematics. UML's official Notation Guide [49] describes the notation[1] informally, and explains the semantics, again informally. UML's official semantics document [50] expresses the abstract syntax of UML in a structured and semi-formal or *rigorous* way, and describes the semantics in terse English. Documents such as [50] are generally (and deliberately) more useful to tool (and book!) writers than to developers. At the opposite extreme from informal English, it's possible (but very hard work) to give a completely formal, mathematical description of the syntax and semantics of a language. To cite one of the few complete examples, [40] defines the syntax and semantics of the programming language Standard ML. A formal definition of a language is developed if it is necessary to eliminate any possibility of ambiguity. It is not likely ever to be done for the whole of UML, since the benefit is not likely to match the cost.

---

[1] that is, the concrete syntax, in terms of lines and characters, as distinct from the abstract syntax, which describes the underlying structure.

As well as being used to support the development of a particular system, a modeling language may be used to document a reusable artifact such as a component or a framework.

UML is unusual in being a modeling language not tied to any particular process. In the past each design methodology has had its own notation, that is, its own modeling language. This distinction is the root of a great deal of confusion. People often consider themselves to be using a methodology if they draw their diagrams in that methodology's notation, whether or not they use any of the techniques recommended by the methodology or follow its rules. You are likely to hear people talking about 'the UML methodology' and comparing its supposed merits and demerits against their favorite methodology. This is bogus: it's comparing apples and oranges. A more sensible question might be 'How easy or sensible is it to follow my favorite methodology using UML as my notation?'.

Why a *unified* modeling language?

Given that developers need a modeling language to help them to discuss the problems and solutions involved in building a system, what should determine which language they use? The chosen language should be:

1. expressive enough, so that it is possible to express the aspects of the design that it will be necessary to discuss, and meaningfully to reflect changes in the design which are made during the development as changes in the models;

2. easy enough to use, so that the modeling language aids clear thought rather than getting in the way;

3. unambiguous, so that the modeling language helps to resolve misunderstandings rather than introducing more;

4. supported by suitable tools, so that developers' effort can be spent on work that requires their skills, not on routine work such as making a diagram using a drawing tool;

5. widely used, for a variety of reasons. Of course the more widely used a language is the more likely it is that the four points above will be satisfied. Also,

   - when new people join the project, it's an advantage if they already know the modeling language instead of having to learn it then;
   - to do component based design you have to be able to read the descriptions of components, and the more easily and quickly you can do so the cheaper it is to consider a component. The more widely used your modeling language, the greater the chance that it's the same one the component writer chose to use.

> **Discussion Question 26**
> What other advantages can you see to having a unified modeling language? Disadvantages?

We'll discuss the history of UML and the overall nature of its models toward the end of this chapter.

4.1.2 Process and quality

As we shall see in Chapter 20, there is a significant overlap between the concerns of a development process and those of a *quality management system*. The ultimate aim of both

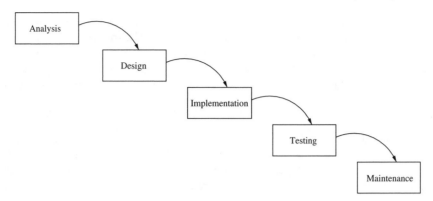

Figure 4.1   A simple waterfall process.

is to insure that the process (and hence, it is to be hoped, the product) has high quality. In general, the development process will specify more technical aspects of the process and the quality management system the more managerial ones; but the terms do overlap.

It is important to remember that no process or methodology, however good, can *ensure* the success of a project. It can at best support the people involved in the project in producing a good outcome. DeMarco and Lister's excellent book *Peopleware* [14] rightly emphasizes this fact.

4.2   The development process

In this section we consider the overall, high level process of developing a system. You have almost certainly seen the famous and now at least partly discredited *waterfall process*,[2] shown in Figure 4.1.

The process has a fairly small number of identifiable bits, in this case the five *phases* of the lifecycle. Some sort of division into parts is an essential part of any process, because the process aims to help humans to understand something, and humans like to identify parts of things! In this case the process is divided into parts on the basis of the activity which is being performed; however, there is also an implication that the activities are being done one after the other, time proceeding down the page.

Figure 4.1 shows a simple version of the waterfall process sometimes called the 'throw it over the wall process', since it incorporates the assumption (or restriction) that once a phase is supposed to have finished, it's never re-entered. If it were possible to make perfect decisions all the time it might be the way things worked. Unfortunately it isn't possible, for example because new information is constantly becoming available. In practice, it is necessary to revise earlier decisions in the light of later experience: for example, to revise the requirements specification when you find that the customer doesn't like the implemented

---

[2] More often known as the waterfall *model* (of the lifecycle), but the overloading of 'model' seems unnecessarily confusing in this context.

system. Refusal to revise decisions can easily result in the complete failure of the project. The waterfall process is often drawn with additional backward arrows, to reflect this reality. However, the criteria for deciding to return to an earlier phase are often left implicit. The implication is that the normal, correct situation is that we proceed from one phase to the next: first we do all the requirements analysis, then we start system and software design, and so on.

Discussion Question 27

Given its rather obvious disadvantages, why is the 'throw it over the wall' process so difficult to give up? What advantages does it have, and to whom? Under what circumstances might you be right to decide to live with the disadvantages?

Now, though, it is recognized that for almost all systems it is right and necessary to have some kind of *iterative* process. Modern development processes take iteration as fundamental, and try to provide ways of managing, rather than ignoring, the risks.

Risk management is a large and extremely important topic. Let us consider just two aspects here:

1. Any time you make a decision, you run the risk that it is wrong. More importantly, the later an error is discovered, the harder it is likely to be to put right. Therefore we may try to control risk by discovering errors as soon as possible. One way is to have evaluation steps frequently and explicitly defined by the process.

2. A major risk is that the developers may misunderstand the requirements. Anything which increases confidence that the stated requirements are correct reduces risk. It is often easier to criticize a system than to describe it, so *prototyping* a system may be a good way to firm up the requirements.

Discussion Question 28

You will encounter the view (maybe unstated) that in order to manage the risk of making a wrong decision it is best to put off making the decision as long as possible. Is this a good idea? Does it depend on the type of decision? How and why?

Boehm's *spiral process* [4] incorporated both of these ideas, and many variants of the spiral process have appeared since. A simple variant is illustrated in Figure 4.2. Starting from the centre of the spiral, a project following the process goes through successive risk analysis and planning, requirements analysis, engineering and evaluation phases. The engineering phase of the spiral process involves design, implementation and testing. The number of iterations is arbitrary.

Notice what the spiral process as shown here doesn't say. It doesn't prescribe how each phase is done. Indeed, it doesn't even specify what the outcome of an implementation phase is: is it a running system with more functionality each time, or is it a more detailed set of models of a system, which becomes a running system only in the final iteration? This ambiguity about what is meant by an iteration is one of the main differences between modern methodologies, which have their own versions of the basic spiral.

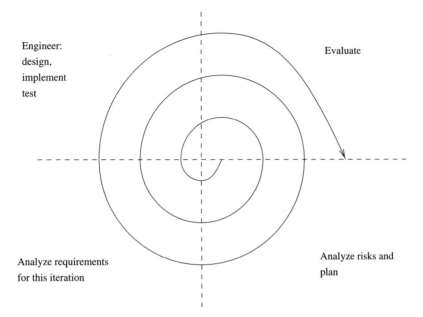

Engineer:
design,
implement
test

Evaluate

Analyze requirements
for this iteration

Analyze risks and
plan

Figure 4.2 A simple spiral process.

4.2.1 A unified methodology?

As object orientation has become fashionable, and now has moved through from being fashionable into the mainstream of software development, a plethora of *object oriented development methods* has naturally been put forward, each with ideas and notations which overlap, but are not identical. Three of the most popular – although there were and are many others – were:

1. Grady Booch's method, occasionally called OOD [7]
2. James Rumbaugh's OMT [41]
3. Ivar Jacobson's OOSE and Objectory [29]

(Each had a major book which appeared in the early 1990s.) As you see, each method is championed by a single inventor, who in each case is a highly experienced and respected expert in the field of OO development. Like most people, the authors expected that for the foreseeable future we would have more or less this situation, the *methods war*, with each method having its proponents. (After all, we haven't settled on one programming language yet!)

The methods war is over: we won   However, it isn't turning out quite that way. Booch was and is in charge of Rational Software (the developers of Rose). In 1994 Rumbaugh also joined Rational, and the two of them declared that they intended to merge their methods. In 1995 Rational bought Ivar Jacobson's company Objectory, and it was all over bar the shouting. Booch, Rumbaugh and Jacobson became known as the Three Amigos.[3] An early draft of documentation for the so-called *Unified Method* was produced, and seemed likely to take over the world. (Needless to say, not everybody was happy about this, and the development by the OPEN consortium of OML, the Open Modeling Language [8] was one reaction. However UML, as it now is, does seem set to dominate, and has now been adopted by the main standardization body for object oriented matters, the Object Management Group (OMG).)

Later the focus was shifted away from developing a unified method toward developing a unified modeling language, and so we have UML. The authors believe that this, doubtless pragmatic, decision was correct. We have already given some reasons for wanting a unified modeling language; however, we do not believe that there are such compelling reasons for having a unified methodology. We think it will always be the case that different methodologies suit different organizations with different kinds of projects. Indeed, we think that the variety of methodologies that organizations have used has up until now been concealed behind the different notations. In our experience, when someone claimed to be using 'OMT' or 'the Booch method' they often meant little more than that they were using that method's *notation*. Different organizations 'using OMT' could in fact be following quite different processes. It may be that settling on a single notation will make it easier in future to identify the real differences between processes.

Of course, methodologies include techniques which can often be transplanted between methodologies. We will discuss many such techniques that you might like to import into your methodology.

4.2.2 Processes to use with UML

We will take as agreed that a development process should

- take risk management as a central concept, and in particular
- allow iteration as a means of controlling risk;
- be architecture-centric and component-based: that is, as discussed in Chapter 1, it should have as high-priority activities the following and making of good architectural decisions, and the use and development of good components.

The final characteristic which the developers of UML believe any development process should have is that it be *use case driven*. We postpone discussion of this until Chapter 7: without a detailed discussion of use cases, it is not possible to define what this means without being dangerously misleading.

Unified Process

In this section we will briefly discuss the so-called Unified Process, which incorporates ideas from all the Three Amigos and from many other sources.

---

[3] After the 1986 John Landis film of that name?

We started to discuss iterative methods above. However, this isn't the end of the story. An *ad hoc* iterative approach works well for small, fast developments, but even there, there will be a stage before the project is definitely decided on, and a stage after it has been 'finally' delivered, which it's sensible to separate out. It's also normally essential, for management and political reasons, to have a plan for what the iterations will be and what will be covered by each, rather than simply taking as many as are required. The Unified Process puts its main spiral inside its Construction phase:

- **Inception** ends with commitment from the project sponsor to go ahead: business case for the project and its basic feasibility and scope known.
- **Elaboration** ends with

  — basic architecture of the system in place,
  — a plan for construction agreed,
  — all significant risks identified,
  — major risks understood enough not to be too worried;

- **Construction** (definitely iterative) ends with a beta-release system;
- **Transition** is the process of introducing the system to its users.

These phases may differ wildly between projects in how long they take and what their deliverables are. For example, for a small or straightforward project (or one with a laid-back sponsor!) the inception phase might even be a development manager having a short chat with the project sponsor. At the other extreme, it might require a series of high-level board meetings and a formally signed-off business case.

Other processes

In fact, UML is so expressive that it is unlikely to be impossible to use it with any object oriented development methodology or process. For example, any of the original Three Amigos' methods can still be used with UML.

Catalysis [17] is a particularly interesting development methodology which has adopted UML as its modeling language. It is mostly concerned with the technical aspects of systems development, and explicitly embraces the idea that there is no one correct process that works for all software projects. It emphasizes the rigor with which a system is developed, and especially the role of frameworks; a framework can be seen as a reusable chunk of architecture, which defines how a group of objects or components interact. We will cover frameworks briefly in Chapter 18, after developing a simple example in Chapter 16.

Discussion Question 29

Use whatever means are available to you (the Web will be useful, and there are some start-ing points on the book's home page) to find out about some of the following development processes and methods:

- The Rational Unified process
- Catalysis
- OPEN
- Extreme Programming, pioneered by Kent Beck
- Fusion, developed at Hewlett Packard
- The Bazaar, most famous as the process used for developing the free operating system Linux
- SCRUM
- DSDM, the Dynamic Systems Development Method
- SSADM, for contrast
- ...

Consider what its scope is, and whether it either enforces or is compatible with an architecture-centric, component-based approach. Compare and contrast.

4.3 System, design, model, diagram

Any development process aims to produce, probably after several iterations, an implemented *system*. This is a program or collection of programs which work in an appropriate environment to fulfill users' needs, including implicit needs such as maintainability. The *design* and (especially) the *architecture* of the system embody the important decisions about how the system is built, abstracting away from many details. A language for describing a design should almost certainly be diagram-based, since experience suggests that's how we naturally think about systems. It's inconceivable that a single diagram could capture everything about our design; and indeed that might not be desirable, since we will be interested in different aspects of the design at different times. We will build different models of our design, reflecting these different aspects, and will express each model using diagrams in a modeling language.

We will want to distinguish models on several axes:

- The *use case* model describes the required system from the users' points of view.
- A *static* model describes the elements of the system and their relationships.
- A *dynamic* model describes the behavior of the system over time.

We may take a

- *logical* view: which parts notionally belong together? For example, what are the classes and how are they related? We model this principally to check that the functional require-ments are met.
- *process* view: what threads of control are there? For example, which things can happen concurrently, and what synchronization must happen? Modeling this helps to insure the non-functional requirements such as performance and availability are met.

- *development* view: which parts can sensibly be developed by the same team of people, and what can be reused? Modeling this helps to manage the project.
- *physical* view: which parts will run on the same computer? Modeling this helps to ensure non-functional requirements are met; it takes a more concrete view than the process view.

These are the four models in Philippe Kruchten's '4 + 1 view model of architecture' [32].

> The diagram is not the design: the diagram is a representation of (part of) a *model* of the design, which captures an aspect of the design in a form which can be discussed.

There can be several diagrams of one model, which must of course be consistent. Similarly, the models must be consistent. This is common sense: the whole set of diagrams, describing various parts and aspects of the design, are all supposed to be descriptions of aspects of a single system, so they must not contradict one another. For example, if your static structure diagram shows that class Foo has no relationship with class Bar, your dynamic diagram had better not show an object of class Foo sending a message to an object of class Bar. Some of this consistency checking can be automated by a suitable tool.

SUMMARY

We discussed development methods in general, and the need for modeling languages. We briefly discussed the history of UML, and the question of what development methodologies can be used with UML. Finally we discussed the role of design, models, and diagrams. A system has a design. There can be several models of a design, focusing on different aspects, which must all be consistent. A model can be represented by some diagrams, which must all be consistent.

PART II

The Unified Modeling Language

CHAPTER 5

Essentials of class models

This chapter introduces UML class diagrams, which are used to document the static structure of the system; that is, what classes there are and how they are related, but not how they interact to achieve particular behaviors. A class diagram can also show other aspects of static structure such as packages, which are discussed in Chapters 6 and 14.

In UML, a class is shown in a class diagram as a rectangle giving its name. Figure 5.1 is a class icon for the class Book.

Later in this chapter we will see how to represent more information about the data and behavior encapsulated by a class, but for now we will concentrate on identifying classes and the associations between them.

5.1 Identifying objects and classes

Building a class model involves identifying the classes that should exist in our system: this is a major part of the work of designing an object oriented system. Before we discuss how to identify objects and classes, let's discuss the criteria for success.

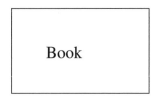

Figure 5.1 A very simple class model.

5.1.1 What makes a class model good?

Ultimately, we have two objectives which we aim to meet:

- Build, as quickly and cheaply as possible, a system which satisfies our current requirements;
- Build a system which will be easy to maintain and adapt to future requirements.

These aims are often seen as being in conflict; a reason for the success of object oriented and especially component-based design techniques is that they take us a long way toward reconciling them.

In order to meet the first objective:

> Every piece of behavior which is required of the system must be able to be provided, in a sensible way, by objects of the classes we choose.

We have already seen in Chapter 1 that in order to meet the second objective we should build a system composed of encapsulated modules, with low coupling and high cohesion. In addition:

> A good class model consists (as far as possible) of classes which represent enduring classes of domain objects, which don't depend on the particular functionality required today.

For example, any library system will involve books, so it's reasonable to have a class Book. (Notice that names are important: it would not be so clear to call the class LiteraryPaperArtifact or B.)

Discussion Question 30
Why is there a conflict between the two aims above? What considerations might determine whether an organization considered one more significant than the other?

5.1.2 How to build a good class model

Let us first emphasize that you can use any technique you like to get your classes: anything, including divine inspiration, is fine, if it leads to a class model which is good by the criteria we've given. Conversely, if you produce a bad class model (one that does not meet the criteria) nobody will care what wonderful method you used to get it!

In practice you will not be likely to get it right first time. The collection of classes in your design model is one of the things that will probably change over and within the iterations of development. You will usually identify the most important classes of *domain* objects – i.e. those belonging obviously to the *problem* rather than those you have introduced to solve it – first and most easily; the other classes, which correspond less clearly to domain objects, are harder to identify with confidence.

What drives?   OO experts tend to fall into one of two camps, those who advocate *data driven design* and those who advocate *responsibility driven design*. As we have seen in Chapters 2 and 3, classes have both data and responsibilities. A caricature of data driven design (DDD) is that it involves identifying all the data in the system and then dividing it up into classes, before considering the classes' responsibilities; the noun identification technique, which we used in Chapter 3 and will consider further here, is a central part of DDD. A caricature of responsibility driven design (RDD) is that it involves identifying all the responsibilities in the system and dividing them up into classes, before considering the classes' data.

Of course both caricatures describe extreme approaches which could not work: nobody seriously proposes anything so extreme. We feel that the distinction between RDD and DDD is not a useful one in the context of this book. It is much easier to use a mixed approach on a project than to describe it in a book: for clarity, we will present techniques separately, but the nature of a successful object oriented project is that a variety of techniques will be used, often simultaneously. Noun identification, which we describe next, is a technique associated with DDD; CRC cards, which we describe at the end of the chapter, is more an RDD technique.

One technique: noun identification   In Chapter 3 we saw one example of how to identify objects and classes. We proceeded in two stages:

1. Identify candidate classes by picking all the nouns and noun phrases out of a requirements specification of the system. (Consider them in the singular form, and do not include phrases containing 'or' as single candidates.)

2. Discard candidates which are inappropriate for any reason, renaming the remaining classes if necessary.

The reasons (some of which we saw in Chapter 3) why we might decide that a candidate is an inappropriate class include that it is:[1]

- **redundant**, where the same class is given more than one name. It is, however, important to remember that similar objects may not be entirely identical: whether things are different enough to merit different classes is one of the things you have to decide. For example, we include under this heading pairs like 'loan' and 'short term loan': they are different, but probably only in the value of attributes. Choose a name for the class that encompasses all the descriptions you mean to include.

- **vague**, where you can't tell unambiguously what is meant by a noun. Obviously you have to clear up the ambiguity before you can tell whether the noun represents a class.

- **an event or an operation**, where the noun refers to something which is done to, by or in the system. Sometimes such a thing *is* well modeled by a class, but this is not the usual case. Recalling the discussion in Chapter 2, ask yourself whether an instance of the event or operation has state, behavior and identity. If not, discard it.

- **meta-language**, where the noun forms part of the way we define things. We use the nouns *requirements* and *system*, for instance, as part of our language of modeling, rather than to represent objects in the problem domain.

---

[1] This list is inspired by, but not identical to, one described by Rumbaugh *et al.* in [41], and adapted in the Open University course M868 [47].

- **outside the scope of the system**, where the noun is relevant to describing how the system works but does not refer to something inside the system, e.g. *library* in the example of Chapter 3. Names of actors are often discarded by this rule, when there's no need to model them in the system. We could also use this rule to justify the discarding of *week* in Chapter 3, though this is an example of where it's much more obvious that something isn't a class than why.

- **an attribute**, where it is clear that a noun refers to something simple with no interesting behavior, which is an attribute of another class. ('Name' of library member might be an example.)

Discussion Question 31

In general, if you are in doubt about whether to keep a class, do you think it is better to keep it in (possibly throwing it out later) or to throw it out (possibly reinstating it later)?

This is a question on which experienced people disagree: there is probably an element of individual psychology. Some people keep two lists, one for strong candidates and one for weaker ones, and this is a useful technique to avoid losing information while still distinguishing between things you're sure about and things that have yet to be settled. For example, in the library example of Chapter 3, you might not be sure about discarding loan or rule, so these might go on your 'possibles' list. (We'll discuss association classes, of which loan might turn out to be an example, in Chapter 6. Rule is not a very likely class in this particular system, but it can be useful to code so-called *business rules* as classes, especially in cases where the rules are complex and prone to change.) Once you begin identifying associations among classes the question of what classes belong in a conceptual level class model will usually resolve itself quite quickly.

This rather simple technique is a remarkably useful way to get started. That's all it is: for example, the list of reasons for discarding candidate classes isn't exhaustive, and there may be more than one reason for discarding the same candidate. When you have more experience, you will probably use it in your head as a check to find any domain abstractions you may have forgotten. You will probably identify classes and associations in parallel, although, for clarity, we present these as separate procedures here. Beginning to use CRC cards at this stage is also useful: we discuss CRC cards at the end of this chapter.

Discussion Question 32

Is the list of reasons for discarding reasonable? Can you think of cases where it might be too selective or too permissive? Do you want to alter the list?

5.1.3 What kinds of things are classes?

A class describes a set of objects with an equivalent role or roles in a system.

Objects and their division into classes often derive from one of the following sources (originally given by Shlaer and Mellor [43] and later paraphrased by Booch [7] and adapted further here):

- Tangible or 'real-world' things: book, copy, course
- Roles: library member, student, director of studies

- Events: arrival, leaving, request
- Interactions: meeting, intersection

These categories overlap, and the first two are much more common sources of objects and classes than the last two. On the other hand, if we have identified objects which fall into the first two categories, the other two may help us to find and name associations between them.

5.1.4 Real world objects vs their system representation

It is important to remember that objects are really things inside a computer program – that when we talk about 'books' and 'copies', for example, we really mean the representation of these things within our system. The consequences of this are that we must be careful

- not to record information that is definitely irrelevant to our system;
- not to lose sight of the fact that the objects *are* the system!

The latter point is particularly interesting. A classic error for people not yet steeped in OO is to invent a class, often called [Something]System, which implements all the system's interesting behavior. But in OO the whole caboodle is the system – that's the point! It's easy to drift into *monolithic* design in which there is just one object that knows and does everything. This is bad because such designs are very hard to maintain: they tend to have assumptions built into them about how the system will be used. (There is a quite different way of having a class which encapsulates the system: it is often useful, and in some languages obligatory, for there to be a main class, which is instantiated just once in each running instance of the system, and which provides the entry point of the program. Starting the program automatically creates this main object, which in turn creates the other objects in the system. The main object does not, however, have any complex behavior of its own. At the very most, it might forward messages arriving from outside to the appropriate object. This is related to the *Façade pattern*, which we will consider in Chapter 18.)

In Chapter 7 we will return to the question of how participants from outside our computer system (known in UML as *actors*) are represented in our design. This (it will turn out) is an essential part of what we've been discussing here. We've already touched on this in Chapter 3.

Q: Revisit the requirements description for the library system in Chapter 3. Apart from the classes identified for the first iteration, what classes should be in the final system?

5.2 Associations

In the same sense that classes correspond to nouns, associations correspond to verbs. They express the relationship between classes. In the example in Chapter 3, we saw associations like is a copy of and borrows/returns.

There are instances of associations, just as there are instances of classes. (Instances of classes are called objects; instances of associations are called *links* in UML, though this term is rarely used at the moment.) An instance of an association relates a pair[2] of objects.

---

[2] We discuss only binary associations in this book, though in fact UML does have associations of other arities.

We can look at associations conceptually or from an implementation point of view. Conceptually, we record an association if there is a real-world association described by a short sentence like 'a library member borrows a book' and the sentence seems relevant to the system at hand.

Class A and class B are associated if

- an object of class A sends a message to an object of class B
- an object of class A creates an object of class B
- an object of class A has an attribute whose values are objects of class B or collections of objects of class B
- an object of class A receives a message with an object of class B as an argument

– in short, if some object of class A has to know about some object of class B. Each link, that is, each instance of the association, relates an object of class A and an object of class B. For example, the association called borrows/returns between LibraryMember and Copy might have the following links:

- Jo Bloggs borrows/returns copy 17 of *The Dilbert Principle*
- Marcus Smith borrows/returns copy 1 of *The Dilbert Principle*
- Jo Bloggs borrows/returns copy 4 of *Software Reuse*

Discussion Question 33

As an alternative to calling this association borrows/returns, we (the authors) could have chosen to have two separate associations, one called borrows and the other called returns. Indeed if, instead of considering who borrows and returns a copy, we had been considering who is the author of a copy and who owns it, we would have chosen to have two separate associations. What's different about the two situations? Do you agree with our choice?

Discussion Question 34

Think about how the cases of association listed above overlap, and consider whether any of them should be removed. It is arguable, for example, that if an object of class A receives a message with an object of class B as argument, but does *not* later send that object a message or store it in an attribute, then this should not count as an association. In fact such a situation is often, though not always, bad design anyway. Construct some examples and consider whether you think they are sensible. Do you have an opinion on whether this should count as association?

The secret of good object oriented design is to end up with a class model which does not distort the conceptual reality of the domain – so that someone who understands the domain will not get unpleasant surprises – but which also permits a sensible implementation of the required functionality. When you develop the initial class model, before you have identified the messages which pass between objects, you necessarily concentrate on the conceptual aspect of the model. Later, when we use interaction models to check our class model, we will be more concerned with whether the model permits a sensible implementation of the required functionality. However, the process isn't that you first develop the conceptual

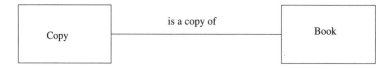

Figure 5.2   Simple association between classes.

model, and then forget about conceptual relationships to develop the implementation class model. Throughout the development, you aim to develop a model which is good in both conceptual and implementational aspects. Success in this is a large part of what leads to a maintainable system, because such a model tends to be comparatively easy to understand, and therefore comparatively easy to modify sensibly.

In Figure 5.2 we can see how UML represents a general association between two classes, by drawing a line between their icons. This is usually annotated in various ways. It should normally at least have a label giving it a name, for readability. We can include an arrow in the label to show which way round it applies. In Chapter 6 we will discuss the use of arrows on the association line to denote *navigability*: does the book know about the copy, or vice versa, or both? You might like to think about these questions now: some experts feel strongly that it is important to answer such questions early, others disagree.

Discussion Question 35
What are the advantages and disadvantages of deciding about navigability at this stage?

In the earliest stages of the development of a model it is often enough to draw a single line, indicating but not tying down the existence of some coupling. As the design matures, this line may be replaced with several, indicating different sorts of association. Some sorts of association are so common that UML has a predefined way of showing them; others can be defined by the designer as needed. We will look at different forms in Chapter 6.

TECHNICAL UML NOTE

The definition of association that we use in this book is a *dynamic* one: if at runtime objects may exchange a message, there must be a navigable association between their classes. Sometimes it is convenient to take a more restrictive *static* view, in which class A only has a navigable association to class B if an attribute of A contains an object (or collection of objects) of class B. UML does not specify which definition to use: it sometimes refers to static associations as 'real' or 'actual' associations, but dynamic associations are also mentioned in UML.

One annotation which is often used early on is the *multiplicity* of an association. Although it may not always be clear initially and may change with subsequent refinement of the design, this is so fundamental that we will spend some time thinking about it here.

5.2.1 Multiplicities

In the example in Chapter 3, we showed a 1 at the Book end of the association is a copy of, because every copy (that is, every object of class Copy) is associated by is a copy of with just one book (object of class Book). On the other hand, there may be any number of copies of a given book in our system. So the multiplicity on the Copy end is 1..*.

As you see, we can specify:

- **an exact number** simply by writing it
- **a range of numbers** using two dots between a pair of numbers
- **an arbitrary, unspecified number** using *

Loosely, you can think of UML's * as an infinity sign, so the multiplicity 1..* expresses that the number of copies can be anything between 1 and infinity. Of course, at any time there will in fact be only a finite number of objects in our whole system, so what this actually says is that there can be any number of copies of a book, provided there's at least one.

We can also specify a choice of multiplicities by giving a comma separated list of multiplicities: for example 3, 12..15, 901..* is an unlikely multiplicity saying that there can be exactly 3, or else between 12 and 15 (inclusive) or else at least 901, of whatever it is.

Q: Express in UML that a Student takes up to six Modules, where at most 25 Students can be enrolled on each Module.

Q: Consider the various ways in which such an association can be implemented in your programming language.

> **Discussion Question 36**
> Express in UML the relationship between a person and his/her shirts. What about the person's shoes? Do you think you have exposed a weakness in UML? Why, or why not?

> **Discussion Question 37**
> The number zero can never be a meaningful multiplicity, or can it?

> **Discussion Question 38**
> The existence of a multiplicity greater than one is sometimes assumed to mean that objects of that class must exist as a collection of some sort. Is that a safe assumption?

5.3 Attributes and operations

The system that we build will consist of a collection of objects, which interact to fulfill the requirements on the system. We have begun to identify classes and their relationships, but this cannot proceed far without considering the state and behavior of objects of these classes. We need to identify the operations and attributes that each class should have. Some will be obvious; others will emerge as we consider the responsibilities of objects and the interactions between them.

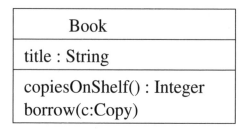

Figure 5.3 A simple class model, with attribute and operation.

5.3.1 Operations

Most important are the operations of a class, which define the ways in which objects may interact. As we said in Chapter 2, when one object sends a message to another, it is asking the receiver to perform an operation. The receiver will invoke a method to perform the operation; the sender does not know which method will be invoked, since there may be many methods implementing the same operation at different levels of the inheritance hierarchy. The *signature* of an operation gives the selector, the names and types of any formal parameters (arguments) to the operation, and the type of the return value. Here, as usual, a type may be either a basic type or a class. Operations are listed in the bottom, third, compartment of a class icon.

Q: Revisit the example in Chapter 3 and derive operations for all the classes there.

5.3.2 Attributes

The attributes of a class – which, as discussed in Chapter 2, describe the data contained in an object of the class – are listed in the second, middle, compartment of a class icon. Figure 5.3 is a version of the Book class icon which shows that each object of class Book has a title, which is a string, and understands a message with selector copiesOnShelf, which takes no argument and returns an integer, as well as borrow, which takes as argument an object of class Copy and returns no result.

Notice that we do not include attributes that simply implement the associations shown in the class diagram. For example, we do *not* show that Book has an attribute copies in which to store the collection of references to the Copy objects associated with the Book. The final implementation probably will have such an attribute, but to show it would add extra notation to the diagram without adding useful information. (It would also imply a decision about the navigability of the association, which would arguably be premature. Navigability is discussed further in Chapter 6.)

Q: Look for any obvious attributes that might exist for the other classes in the example from Chapter 3.

Views of operations and attributes   Just as with associations, we have a conceptual approach and a pragmatic approach, which we attempt to make consistent.

The conceptual approach involves identifying what data is conceptually associated with an object of this class, and what messages it seems reasonable to expect the object to understand. The latter view can lead you into an anthropomorphic view of objects as having an intelligence of their own – 'If a book could talk, what questions would you expect it to be able to answer?' – which some people find disconcerting, but which can nevertheless be worthwhile!

Pragmatically, we have to check that we have included enough data and behavior for the requirements at hand. To do this, we have to start to consider how the objects of our classes will work together to satisfy the requirements. One very useful technique for doing this is CRC cards, which we describe later in this chapter.

5.4 Generalization

Another important relationship which may exist between classes is *generalization*. For example, `LibraryMember` is a generalization of `MemberOfStaff` because, conceptually, every `MemberOfStaff` is a `LibraryMember`. Everything that every `LibraryMember` can do can certainly be done by every `MemberOfStaff`. So if some part of our system (e.g. the facility to reserve a book) works on an arbitrary `LibraryMember`, it ought to work on an arbitrary `MemberOfStaff` too, since every `MemberOfStaff` *is* a `LibraryMember`. On the other hand, there may be things that don't make sense for every `LibraryMember`, but only for a `MemberOfStaff` (e.g. borrow journal). `MemberOfStaff` is more specialized than `LibraryMember`; or `LibraryMember` is a generalization of `MemberOfStaff`.

In other words, an object of class `MemberOfStaff` should *conform* to the interface given by `LibraryMember`. That is, if some message is acceptable to any `LibraryMember`, it must also be acceptable to any `MemberOfStaff`. `MemberOfStaff`, on the other hand, may understand other, specialized messages which an arbitrary `LibraryMember` might not be able to accept – that is, a `MemberOfStaff`'s interface may be strictly broader than `LibraryMember`'s.

From this we can see that to say that a generalization relationship exists between classes is to make a strong, though informal, statement about the way the objects of the two classes behave.

> An object of a specialized class can be substituted for an object of a more general class in any context which expects a member of the more general class, but not the other way round.

This takes us to a further rule about the design of classes where one is a specialization of the other.

> There must be no conceptual gulf between what objects of the two classes do on receipt of the same message.

Stating this more precisely is surprisingly difficult: see Panel 5.1.

PANEL 5.1   Design by Contract 2: substitutivity

In this panel we continue the discussion of the contract that an object must fulfill, by considering how this concept is related to inheritance. An object of a subclass is supposed to be usable anywhere that an object of the superclass was usable. In other words, the subclass is supposed to fulfill the contract entered into by the superclass. Let us examine what that means in practice.

The easier aspect is what it means for the attributes of the class and the class invariant. (Recall from Chapter 3 that a class invariant is a statement about the values of attributes of a class that must hold for all objects of the class.)

Q: In Chapter 2 we said that a subclass could have extra attributes and operations as well as those of its superclass, but that it could not drop any of the superclass's attributes or operations. Why? What about operations that are not in the object's public interface?

Q: If a superclass has a class invariant, does the subclass need a class invariant? What should the relationship be between the two invariants? Give examples of correct (substitutive) and incorrect inheritance in this case.

Substitutivity needs checking if the subclass overrides any of the superclass's methods: that is, defines its own methods to implement the operations. We said that the new methods must do conceptually the same job; now we will be more precise. The overall slogan for the subclass, seen as a subcontractor, is

---

Demand no more: promise no less.

'Demand no more' describes the circumstances under which the subclass must accept the message (without complaining). It must be prepared to accept any arguments that the superclass would have accepted. Therefore its precondition must be *no stronger* than the precondition of the superclass's implementation. It may be that the subclass's implementation is an improvement on the superclass's implementation in the sense that it works in more situations: that's fine.

'Promise no less' describes what the client can assume about the state of the world after the operation has been carried out. Any assumption which was valid when the superclass's implementation was being used should still be valid when the subclass's implementation is used. Therefore the subclass's postcondition must be *at least as strong* as the superclass's version.

Behavioral subtyping, often known as Liskov substitutivity after Barbara Liskov who popularized it, is a strong and precise version of this slogan. Suppose some program expects to interact with an object of class c, and that instead it is given an object s of class s, a subclass of c. If Liskov substitutivity holds, there is some object c of class c which could be used instead of s without altering anything about the behavior of the program.

Discussion Question 39
Construct a few examples to see what this means in practice. Are there circumstances under which this requirement might be too strong? Too weak?

Q: In your programming language, if a subclass overrides an attribute or operation from a superclass, is it allowed to change their types? In what way?

Consider the list of cases in which two classes were associated (Section 5.2). We should perhaps add 'knowingly' to some of the cases: class A and class B are associated if an object of class A *knowingly* sends a message to an object of class B, and so on. Suppose the code of class A mentions an object which the writer of class A expected to belong to class B. The point is that the object could actually belong to any subclass of class B, and – if substitutivity holds – class A will still work as expected. It is not useful to add an association between class A and every subclass of class B: this would clutter the diagram without adding any new information.

In other words, if there is an operation such as borrow(c:Copy) defined for any object of the class LibraryMember, the way that operation is carried out should be clearly comparable to the way it is carried out for a MemberOfStaff. Their behavior doesn't have to be identical, but it must be similar enough that other operations which rely on what the operation borrow(c:Copy) does when requested from an object of a more general class (LibraryMember) will also work with an object of a specialized class (MemberOfStaff).

Figure 5.4 shows how generalization is shown in UML.

5.4.1 Using English to check whether a generalization exists

Class Bar is probably a generalization of class Foo if it is true that *every* Foo *is a* Bar. Often we just talk about 'is a' relationships – *a* Foo *is a* Bar.

However, if we rely too naïvely on this check, it is very possible to come unstuck, because of the ambiguous nature of English. For example (from Fowler and Scott's book, *UML Distilled*, page 91 [20]), you might casually say 'a Border Collie is a Breed' and conclude that Breed is a generalization of Border Collie, which is rubbish. Try out 'every Border Collie is a Breed' which is more obviously rubbish.

The problem is actually that the statement in English 'a Border Collie is a Breed' is wrong to start with, since it relates a single instance of Border Collie to a collective noun, Breed. It should have been 'Border Collie is a Breed'. Putting in 'every', replacing the initial 'a', helps to show that the original claim was nonsense.

5.4.2 Implementing generalization: inheritance

One way (not the only way) to implement a generalization is by *inheritance*. Whereas generalization is a conceptual relationship between classes, inheritance is an implementation

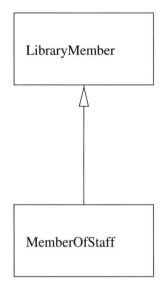

Figure 5.4   A simple generalization.

relationship.[3]

Instead of duplicating the definition of LibraryMember, and possibly adding to it, to define MemberOfStaff – which would be possible, and there would still be a generalization between LibraryMember and MemberOfStaff – we often choose to use inheritance, which is provided in object oriented programming languages, to define MemberOfStaff in terms of LibraryMember. We discussed inheritance as a technical concept in Chapter 2; here we need to consider the pragmatic issues of how inheritance is used.

Inheritance is not the silver bullet it may appear to be. The main problem is that a subclass is dependent on its superclasses, so using inheritance tends to increase the coupling in a system. If a superclass is later changed, even in ways which do not affect its behavior, this may force the recompilation of subclasses, or even make changes to their code necessary. This is sometimes called the *fragile base class problem*. Another effect of the tight coupling between subclass and superclass is that, even if you are confident that a superclass is correct, it is not usually possible to make use of this confidence to reduce the amount of testing that has to be done on the subclass. We will return to this when we consider testing in Chapter 19.

Because of these problems we recommend that you use inheritance between classes only when it models a conceptual generalization relationship. It is tempting to use it for convenience in other cases, but it is not usually worthwhile; an implementation using composition is often more robust. Suppose, for example, that we have a class List available and that we wish to implement a class AddressBook in which the addresses are stored in a List. A classic mistake is to make AddressBook inherit from List. A better

---

[3] When the two notions are distinguished at all – as we remarked in Chapter 2, they are sometimes loosely used as synonyms.

solution is to make an `AddressBook` own a `List`, for example by having an attribute
`addresses : List`.

Discussion Question 40

Why is the composition solution better than the inheritance solution? Compare the effort
involved in initial development of the `AddressBook`. Then compare the changes required
if the `List` implementation or interface changes, and those required if it is decided to use
a different class instead of the `List` (`Dictionary`, say).

Q: Are `Book` and `Journal` related by generalization?

5.5   The class model during the development

As we have mentioned, the class model will be developed gradually over several iterations
of the system's design. We start by recording conceptual relationships and capabilities,
independently of any implementation as far as possible.

Later we add more detail, introducing new operations and more specific associations.
Attributes are added in this refinement process, which is repeated until we are satisfied that
our design is complete and consistent. Some experts, notably Fowler and Scott in [20], like
to formalize this process as that of moving from a model drawn from one *perspective* to one
drawn from another, e.g. from the conceptual perspective to the specification perspective.

Models vs diagrams   Remember that in Chapter 4 we explained the distinction in UML
between a *model* of a system, which is a collection of model elements representing a view
of the design at some level of abstraction, and a *diagram* of that model, which is a way of
representing the model graphically: we also warned that although the distinction is sometimes important, in practice the terms model and diagram are often used interchangeably.
Here is a case where it is important to distinguish between them.

There is a single class model – the UML notation guide more accurately calls it the static
structural model, since as we shall see it can represent more than just classes – for a given
system, and each class of the system appears in it just once. The class model describes the
overall static structure of the system. It can, however, be described by several different class
diagrams for legibility. Similarly, although each class occurs just once in the class model, it
is possible to represent a class more than once on a class diagram. You might want to do this
if the layout of the diagram is such that it is more readable that way. However, since in the
underlying model there is only one model element representing the class, it is vital that two
iconic representations of the class in a diagram do not give conflicting information about
the class. A CASE tool can help to ensure this consistency. Without one, we recommend
that you do not represent the same class more than once on a class diagram.

5.6   CRC cards

One common way of checking for a good design and guiding its refinement is to use CRC
cards. CRC stands for Class, Responsibilities, Collaborations. CRC cards were introduced

(and described in a paper [2] at the major OO conference OOPSLA'89) by Kent Beck and Ward Cunningham, as a technique to help programmers with experience in non-OO languages to 'think objects'.

Although CRC cards are not part of UML, they add some very useful insights throughout a development, including in the very early stages when you are identifying classes and their associations. We will therefore make a short detour to look at how to create and use them.

5.6.1 · Creating CRC cards

On a small card, we record:

- **the name** of a class, at the top;
- **the responsibilities** of the class, on the left-hand side
- **the collaborators** of the class, which help to carry out each responsibility, on the right-hand side of the card.

The responsibilities of the class describe at a high level the purpose of the class's existence: they are connected with the operations the class provides, but are more general than that might imply. For example, 'maintain data about the book' is acceptable as a description of a responsibility, though there might be many associated operations necessary for getting or resetting the various bits of data concerned.

A class should not normally have more than three or four responsibilities, and many classes will have only one or two. If a class does end up having more responsibilities, consider whether you can describe them more concisely, and, if not, consider whether it would be better to split the responsibilities and have two or more classes. You will probably identify one or two responsibilities of the class immediately – if a class had no responsibilities, you would not have invented it – but the responsibilities will be revised as you use the CRC cards.

Too many responsibilities corresponds to low cohesion in your model; too many collaborators corresponds to high coupling. Using CRC cards can help to identify and fix both of these faults in your model.

At the beginning, you may not know which other classes a class has to collaborate with in order to fulfill a responsibility; this becomes clear as you use the cards. If an object of one class collaborates with an object of another, it does so by sending it a message; so a class has an association with each of its collaborators. Using CRC cards is the best way we know to work out in which direction associations should be navigable, and it can also help to identify the associations, especially between classes that do not represent real-world objects.

5.6.2 Using CRC cards in developing a design

You can use CRC cards to walk through use cases, working out how the class model provides the functionality required by the use cases, and where the missing bits are. (You can see this as discovering the collaborations and interactions which realize your use cases. We will discuss how to record this information permanently in UML notation in Chapter 9.)

A possibly useful technique is role playing. If you are working in a team, each person can take on one or more CRC cards' responsibilities, where the complete set of cards represents the classes responsible for one major aspect of the system's responsibilities. You can test the completeness of your design by working through the various scenarios of the relevant use cases.

First pick a typical scenario from a use case. For example, in the `Borrow copy of book` use case, start with the scenario of a borrower successfully borrowing a book. As the design becomes more solid, anyone who suspects that there may be a problem with the design can suggest a scenario that may illustrate the problem (e.g. what happens if there is no copy available). The initial request is given to the person whose CRC card represents a class whose responsibilities include realizing the scenario; this represents an object of that class receiving a message from the initiator of the scenario. If the object needs assistance from one of its collaborators, it will, in the eventual implementation, send it a message requesting it to perform an operation. Each operation which an object may be asked to perform should form part of one of the responsibilities of the object's class; the responsibilities of a class can be seen as a summary of the operations it can perform. When you first use CRC cards, you will probably just consider whether it is broadly reasonable to expect a particular collaborator to be able to help perform a particular part of a responsibility; later, you can examine the interactions in more detail to design the actual collection of operations for each class.

If there is a missing link – something has to be done, but no class has the responsibility of doing it – this means the design is faulty or incomplete. You might need to create a new class, change the collaborations and responsibilities of an existing class or both. It's important to remember that the changes you make must preserve the overall sensibleness of the models: avoid jumping at the obvious fix for the particular problem case that has turned up, without thinking about the other implications of the change. It's often useful to write a new card for a class if you've substantially altered its original card.

Notice that the system actually works by means of *objects*, rather than classes, communicating: you will need to bear in mind whether a CRC card for a class is always representing the same object of that class, or whether several different objects of the class are involved.

A useful side-effect of working through examples in this way is that it builds a team spirit and gives everyone a feeling that they own a stake in the design. Naturally some teams will find the technique more useful than others!

As an alternative, especially where you are working alone, you can arrange the cards to represent relationships between them – you can consider this as drafting a class model. For example, some people like to pile cards related by generalization together, with the most abstract at the top, so that you use the specialized class only when the particular specialization is relevant.

5.6.3 CRC card example

Figure 5.5 is an example drawn from the case study in Chapter 3. We start by drawing some CRC cards for the classes `LibraryMember`, `Book` and `Copy`. Our decisions are based on our intuition about how instances of these classes will collaborate. We can then check how a particular use case might be carried out.

Although the amount written on each card is quite brief, this is not a toy example: its scale is about right. Crowded CRC cards mean either badly expressed responsibilities or non-cohesive classes.

LibraryMember	
Responsibilities	**Collaborators**
Maintain data about copies currently borrowed	
Meet requests to borrow and return copies	Copy

Copy	
Responsibilities	**Collaborators**
Maintain data about a particular copy of a book	
Inform corresponding Book when borrowed and returned	Book

Book	
Responsibilities	**Collaborators**
Maintain data about one book	
Know whether there are borrowable copies	

Figure 5.5 Example of CRC cards for the library.

If we follow through the processing of a request by a BookBorrower to Borrow copy of book, we can check if any other classes would need to be involved. We can also check the messages that might need to be sent. If a responsibility cannot be met by an object, it needs to either add to its own definition or define a collaboration with another class which can meet it.

We can also explore the generalization relationship between LibraryMember and MemberOfStaff by seeing how far they share responsibilities and collaborators. We find that all the responsibilities of a LibraryMember are shared by a MemberOfStaff, but not the other way round. This confirms our earlier impression that a MemberOfStaff is a specialization of a LibraryMember. More generally, we can watch for opportunities to *refactor* the class model into a better one.

5.6.4 Refactoring

Refactoring is the process of altering the class model of an object oriented design without altering its visible behavior. For example, if at any stage you become aware that an operation doesn't fit properly in the class where it is – the responsibilities are not allocated to classes in the best possible way – a refactoring step would be to make the necessary changes to put the operation where it should be, updating whatever code and design documentation needs to be modified.

The WRITE ONCE rule is a good source of refactoring steps. For example, if you find you have two classes with overlapping responsibilities and behavior, you can often usefully factor out the common behavior into a new superclass from which both inherit. In fact, this process can help with one of the hardest aspects of object oriented analysis and design, namely finding the right abstractions which will make the design clean and robust. Such classes often do not show up at all in the requirements document – because they are not domain classes themselves, although they express what several domain classes have in common – so noun identification will not find them. See Kent Beck's book [3] for many refactoring ideas.

Q: Work through the example of borrowing in the library, using the CRC cards shown and modifying them if necessary.

Q: Try a similar analysis for returning a book and for borrowing and returning a journal.

SUMMARY

This chapter introduced class diagrams, which represent the static structure of the system to be built. We discussed how classes and their associations can be identified, and the concept of multiplicity of an association. We showed how a class's attributes and operations are shown. Next we covered generalization, which can be implemented for example by inheritance. Finally we discussed the role of the class model through the development, and illustrated the use of CRC cards for validating a class model.

DISCUSSION QUESTIONS

1. Why should classes have names in the singular? Do you think there are any exceptions?
2. What are the advantages and disadvantages of formally deciding from what perspective you're drawing a particular class model?
3. Under what circumstances could you have classes in your model that don't correspond to domain objects? Can you think of any examples where this seems necessary in the library example?
4. How are the associations set up in the implementation? How, if at all, should your class model describe this? Does it depend on the stage of development? How?
5. Consider the dynamic and static notions of association mentioned in the Technical UML Note in Section 5.2. Construct a small example of classes which are dynamically but not statically associated, and consider the two versions of the UML class diagram you get by adopting either notion. What do you think are the advantages and disadvantages of each convention? What does the *absence* of an association between classes mean, in each case?

CHAPTER 6

More on class models

In this chapter we consider other features of UML class diagrams. They are less central than the ones described in Chapter 5, and you may choose to skip this chapter on a first reading. However, one of UML's strengths is its expressiveness, and here we give a taste of that, covering most (but not quite all) features of class diagrams.

Along the way we'll discuss a few aspects of UML which are not specific to class models, but which we use here for the first time. These are *constraints*, UML's main extensibility mechanisms (*stereotypes*, *properties* and *tagged values*), *interfaces*, *dependencies* and *packages*.

We begin by considering extra information that may be recorded along with an association between two classes.

6.1 More about associations

6.1.1 Aggregation and composition

Aggregation and composition are kinds of association: instead of just showing that two classes are associated we may choose to show more about what kind of association this is. Aggregation and composition are both ways of recording that an object of one class *is part of* an object of another class.

For example, Figure 6.1, drawn from the case study in Chapter 15, shows that a `Module` is part of an `HonoursCourse`. This notation, with the open diamond, denotes aggregation, which is the more general way of denoting a part–whole relationship in UML. Notice that the diamond goes at the end of the whole, not the part. We can still use all the other notation

Figure 6.1 An aggregation.

that goes with associations. For example, we can show multiplicities just as with a normal association. Notice that an object is allowed to be simultaneously part of several other objects: in our case, a single Module could be part of several different HonoursCourses. (For example, Software Engineering with Objects and Components 2 is part of both the Software Engineering and the Computer Science honours courses.)

We normally don't bother to name an aggregation association, since the name of the association would normally be 'is a part of' and this is reflected in the aggregation notation already, so there's no need to put it in words too. However, if it helps to name the association (for example, if we want to describe the function of the part in the whole) that's perfectly legal.

From this lack of any new restrictions we see that aggregation is essentially a conceptual notion: seeing an aggregation in a class model should help you to understand the relationships between the classes at an informal level, but it doesn't give you any more formal information about how they must be implemented or what you can do with them. (Although see Discussion Question 47 later in this chapter: it is arguable that an aggregation should imply some things, even though in UML it currently doesn't.)

Composition is a special kind of aggregation which does impose some further restrictions. In a composition association, the whole *strongly owns* its parts: if the whole object is copied or deleted, its parts are copied or deleted with it. (In order for this to be implementable the association must be navigable from the whole to the part, although UML does not explicitly specify this.) The multiplicity at the whole end of a composition association must be 1 or 0..1 – a part cannot be part of more than one whole by composition. The example with Module and HonoursCourse does not fit these restrictions, so a composition would not be appropriate in that case. On the other hand, consider a Noughts and Crosses (Tic-Tac-Toe) application of the game framework considered in Chapter 16, which might sensibly be implemented in terms of classes Square and Board. Each Square is part of exactly one Board, and it wouldn't be sensible to copy or delete a Board object without copying or deleting the Square objects that make up the Board. So in this case composition is appropriate, and we show it in Figure 6.2. Composition is shown just as aggregation is, except that the diamond is filled in.

Figure 6.2 A composition.

WARNING

In our experience people new to object oriented modeling use aggregation and composition far too often. Remember that both are kinds of association, so whenever an aggregation or composition is correct, so is a plain association. If in doubt, use a plain association.

Discussion Question 41
Think about some cases where aggregation or composition might be appropriate. For example, what about the relationship between an Employee and a Team? Between Wheel and Car? Account and Customer? Can you describe different contexts, in which classes with these names might arise, where because of differences in the context different relationships would be appropriate?

Discussion Question 42
If you know C++ or another object oriented language which can refer to objects either *by value* or *by reference*: people sometimes distinguish between aggregation and composition by saying that you have aggregation if the whole contains a reference or pointer to the part, and composition if the whole contains the part by value. Consider why this is, and whether it's appropriate.

Mnemonic The stronger symbol, the solid diamond, represents the stronger relationship, composition. When you rub out a solid diamond, you have to delete the inside of the diamond symbol, as well as the border, just as when you delete a composite object you have to delete the parts as well as the whole.[1]

6.1.2 Roles

We have shown how to name an association. Often you can naturally read an association name in both directions ('is taking', 'is taken by'). Sometimes, however, it's more readable to have separate names for the roles that the objects play in the association, either as well as or instead of naming the association. For example, Figure 6.3 makes clear that the role of the Student in this association is that of directee, which might possibly be useful, for example, if directee was a commonly used term in an accompanying document. You can show both an association name and the role names if you like, though this is likely to be overkill in most situations.

Discussion Question 43
Would it be helpful to give role names to the association between Student and Module? Why?

---

[1] Thanks to Ben Kleinman for suggesting this.

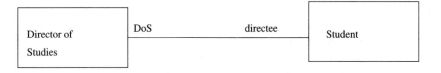

Figure 6.3 An association shown with role names.

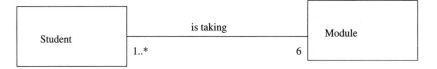

Figure 6.4 Association with no navigability shown.

6.1.3 Navigability

Consider a situation in which we have an association between two classes, for example between `Module` and `Student`, as shown in Figure 6.4. The diagram records that:

- for each object of class `Student` there are six objects of class `Module` which are associated with the `Student`;
- for each object of class `Module` there are some `Student` objects (the number of students is unspecified) associated with the `Module`.

It does *not* yet record, though, whether it should be possible to get hold of these objects in both directions or just one. Should a `Student` object be able to send messages to its associated `Module` objects? Should a `Module` object be able to send messages to the `Student` objects representing students on the course? Both?

We can put an arrow on one or both ends of the association line to represent that it is possible for messages to be sent in the direction of the arrow. For example, Figure 6.5 indicates that a `Module` object can send messages to the objects representing the students on the module, but not vice versa.

We say that `Module` *knows about* `Student`, but not vice versa. Such an association might be implemented, for example, by letting `Module` have an attribute (`students: StudentCollection` say) which was a collection of objects corresponding to students taking the course. This has both good and bad consequences. The application may need this information to be readily available: in our case, for example, we have to produce lists of students for each course, since the lecturers need them, and the easiest

Figure 6.5 Association with one-way navigability shown.

way to do this is to let a `Module` object retrieve a collection of student names by sending a message to each object in such a student collection. However, if class A knows about class B, then it is impossible to reuse class A without class B; so we should not introduce navigability unless it is required for the current application, or there is good reason to think it will be required in future. Sometimes it is essential to allow two-way navigability along an association, but such decisions should be individually justified, rather than being the default.

Discussion Question 44

(After considering Chapter 15.) Should this association be navigable also in the other direction – that is, should `Student` know about `Module`? Why?

Now we have a way of showing that it *is* possible to navigate an association in a certain direction, but we don't have any way to show that it *is not* possible to navigate it. The obvious thing to do is to say that the absence of an arrow means non-navigability: but the problem with this is that when you build your initial, conceptual class model you may (quite rightly) not yet have decided what the navigability should be. UML suggests different conventions; for example, the absence of an arrow may mean non-navigability, or may mean that navigability is unspecified. In this book, if a class diagram shows any navigability arrow you can assume that all such arrows are shown; if it does not, we are not specifying navigability.

Discussion Question 45

When, if ever, might an association be navigable in neither direction?

Discussion Question 46

When should navigability be decided?

Discussion Question 47

According to UML, the navigability of an association is independent of whether the association is an aggregation, a composition or neither. What navigability do you expect an aggregation association to have? What about a composition? Can you say anything definite about what kind of navigability either kind of association must *always* have, to make sense?

6.1.4 Qualified associations

Occasionally it is helpful to give finer detail about an association than we have so far. Consider again the Noughts and Crosses application of the game framework described in Chapter 16, which is implemented using classes `Square` and `Board`, and suppose that a `Square` is identified relative to the `Board` it's on by attributes `row` and `column`, each taking a value between 1 and 3. Forgetting about the fact that the association is a composition for the moment (remember that an association is always correct when an aggregation or composition is correct), the association can be shown as in Figure 6.6.

Figure 6.6   Plain association between `Square` and `Board`.

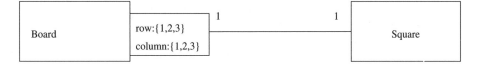

Figure 6.7   Qualified association.

However, this doesn't capture the idea that the nine squares are found by giving the nine possible pairs of values to the attributes `row` and `column`. To do this we use a *qualified association* as shown in Figure 6.7.

The `1` on the right-hand end, attached to `Square`, specifies that if we take a `Board` object, call it *b*, *and* specific values for both the attributes `row` and `column`, then there is exactly one `Square` object which is associated with the `Board` object *b*. The `1` on the `Board` end means the same as usual: each object of class `Square` is on exactly one `Board`.

Essentially for each `Board` we have a look-up table in which we look up a `Square` by its row and column. The conditions we described simply ensure that each `Square` occurs in just one look-up table, just once. Notice that in general there could be more than one object for a given value of the look-up key: the elements in the look-up table could be sets, not just single elements.

In fact we can combine the qualified association notation with the other adornments on associations; for example, we can add back the information that this particular association is a composition, as shown in Figure 6.8.

You may have noticed that we have cunningly not told you what class the attributes `row` and `column` are in! They could be attributes of `Square`; but formally they are attributes of the association. Each link between a `Board` and a `Square` (recall that a link is an instance of an association) has values for `row` and `column`, which identify where the `Square` is on the `Board`.

Q: (Derived from an example in the UML notation guide.) Draw a qualified association between `Person` and `Bank` to record the fact that a `Person` can be associated with many `Banks`, but that given a `Bank` and an account number, there is at most one `Person` with that account number at that bank.

6.1.5   Derived associations

When developing class diagrams you will frequently wonder whether you need to show an association or whether it's enough to deduce its existence from something else on the diagram. For example, if `Student` is associated with `Module` by *is taking* and `Module`

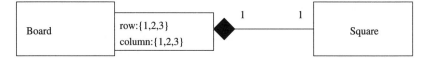

Figure 6.8 Qualified composition.

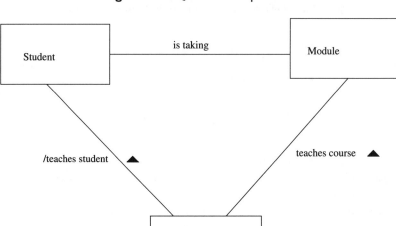

Figure 6.9 A derived association.

is associated with Lecturer by *teaches course*, do we need also to show an association *teaches student* between Lecturer and Student, which might relate a lecturer to all the students taking courses which that lecturer teaches?

Discussion Question 48
What are the advantages and disadvantages of doing so?

We can do so or not, or we can use the third option which UML gives us, which is to show that association as a *derived association*. In other words, it exists automatically once we have implemented the main associations: there is no need for a designer to consider separately how to implement this association. A derived association is shown using a slash in front of its name, as in Figure 6.9. (The black triangles, by the way, can be used on any association name, and simply indicate which direction of the association the name describes.)

TECHNICAL UML NOTE

In UML there can be *derived elements* other than derived associations. In general, a derived element is distinguished from the usual form of the element by adding a slash in front of its name. For example, you can show that an attribute of a class is derived – that is, that you can work out what its value is in a given object if you know the values of all the object's normal attributes, and have access to the other objects which this object knows about – by putting a slash in front of the attribute's name in the class icon. (You may find it clearer, though, to define an operation of the class, which takes no arguments and whose return value is the derived value, instead. It's a matter of taste.)

In the example we gave, there's only one sensible choice of what the derived association must actually be. A Lecturer *l* is associated by *teaches student* to a Student *s* if, and only if, there is some Module *m* such that both *s* is associated with *m* by *is taking* and *l* is associated with *m* by *teaches course*. If we want to record this explicitly on the diagram, we can either write it in words in a note, or write it more formally.

6.1.6 Constraints

A constraint is a condition that has to be satisfied by any correct implementation of a design. For example, a system with associations *teaches course*, *is taking* and *teaches student* has a bug if the condition we added in the previous section is not always satisfied. Constraints can be more general than that, however. They can constrain single model elements, or collections of model elements. One of the most common – and safest – uses is to express a *class invariant*. For example:

```
{self.noOfStudents > 50 implies (not (self.room = 3317))~
```

as an invariant of class Module says that it's always the case for every object of class Module that if the number of students enrolled on the course is greater than 50 then the course does not take place in room 3317 (presumably, because room 3317 seats only 50 people).

This formal constraint is written in OCL, the Object Constraint Language which UML has adopted for this purpose. See Panel 6.1 for more information on OCL.

Another common situation in which constraints may be useful is when there's an 'exclusive or' between two association relations: an object takes part in (a link which is an instance of) exactly one of the associations. For example, in the library example of Chapter 3, we assumed that although there could be several copies of a book, there was only ever one copy of a journal. Now let's suppose we want to model a system in which each Copy object represents either a copy of a Book or a copy of a Journal. We might start off with the diagram shown in Figure 6.10. But this doesn't rule out the nonsensical possibility that a Copy could be associated with both a Book and a Journal, or with neither. To do that, we can use an xor constraint, as shown in Figure 6.11.

The xor constraint is not written in OCL; it's a special predefined constraint which is part of UML.

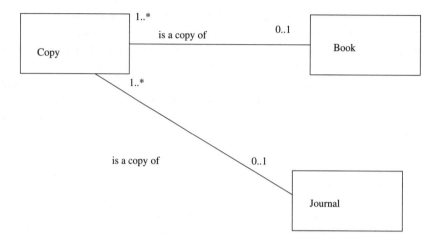

Figure 6.10 An under-constrained diagram.

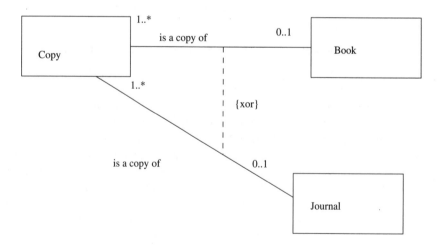

Figure 6.11 Using an xor-constraint.

Discussion Question 49

Can you see a way to solve this problem without introducing a constraint? Hint: consider introducing an extra class.

The fact that UML allows you to add constraints in such a general way increases its power tremendously. However, as always it's important not to be carried away by powerful features! Someone has to read any diagram you write, and this is harder the more complex the diagram is – you should use constraints sparingly, considering in each case whether it's sensible to put in a piece of information. There are also technical reasons for avoiding designs which need to be expressed using constraints which constrain several model elements not contained within one class; as Ian Graham points out, such constraints signal dependencies between the constrained model elements, which may hamper both maintenance and reuse.

Discussion Question 50

In fact constraints can express some of the information which is normally expressed in UML using more convenient specialized notation. How could you specify the multiplicity of an association using constraints instead of the normal multiplicity notation?

PANEL 6.1 OCL, the Object Constraint Language

The Object Constraint Language is intended to be

- formal, so that constraints written in it are unambiguous
- easy to use, so that every developer can write constraints in it

OCL originated in the Syntropy method developed by Steve Cook and John Daniels, and has been developed by IBM as a business modeling language. It is used within the semantics document of UML to place constraints on which UML models are well formed, as well as being available to users of UML to place constraints on their own models.

The UML specification (see this book's home page) includes full details of OCL, and a book [52] is also available.

Combining the two goals of OCL is very hard, and we are not really convinced that OCL completely achieves either goal yet. It does not have a formal semantics, so it can't yet be said to be a formal language. On the other hand it's not clear that a formal language with the kind of power required could ever be really easy to learn. Whilst we encourage you to consider learning more about OCL, we'd also like to give a warning:

WARNING

Whilst using formal notations can be useful provided that the people involved really know how to read and write them, a constraint in clear English is much more useful than a constraint in a formal language that is buggy, or which the intended readers can't understand. So if you and your colleagues are not confident that you know how to write something in OCL, write it in English.

6.1.7 Association classes

Sometimes the way in which two objects are associated is just as important as the objects themselves. Consider, for example, the association between Student and Module. Where should our system record the student's marks on this course? The marks are really connected with a pair consisting of both a student and a module. We might want to implement an object for each such pair: the object would record this student's marks on that course, avoiding confusing them conceptually with any other student's marks on this course, or with this student's marks on any other course. This amounts to treating the association between the classes Student and Module as a class; of course an instance of the association connects a student with a module, and we're now saying that we want there to be data attached to that link. We probably want operations too, if only to set and get the marks. The result is a thing which is both an association and a class, which is unsurprisingly called an *association class*. The notation is shown in Figure 6.12.

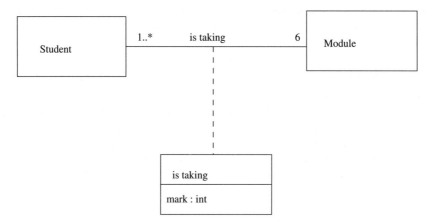

Figure 6.12   An association class.

The class icon and the association line must have the same name, because they are the same thing! This poses a slight problem, since associations normally have verb phrases as

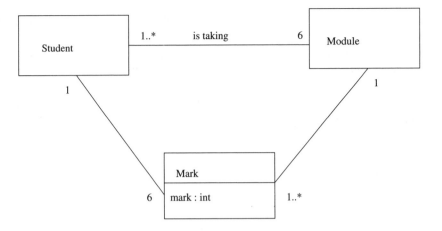

Figure 6.13 Avoiding an association class.

names and classes normally have noun phrases as names. (Also if you use the common capitalization convention that association names are lower case and class names are capitalized, you have to have a special case for association classes, since you can't obey both conventions at once!) You may be able to think of a better name than *is taking* to cover both.

There are other ways to record the same relationship between Student and Module, of course: we could invent a new class, say Mark, and associate it with both classes in the standard way, as shown in Figure 6.13.

Discussion Question 51
What are the advantages and disadvantages of the two approaches? Consider: what happens if the same student takes the same module twice for some reason; whether we need a constraint in either case; whether there would actually be any difference in the implementations which either notation would permit.

6.2   More about classes

In Chapter 2 we emphasized that a class actually serves two purposes: it defines the interface that objects present to the rest of the system, and it defines an implementation of that interface. Sometimes it's important for a design to separate the two concepts, particularly in order to distinguish between different levels of *dependency* between model elements.

There are in fact three variants on the idea of a class – three different ways of classifying objects – which we will consider together. They vary in how much information they contain about attributes, operations, and their implementations. In brief, they are:

1. Interface. An interface specifies a list of operations which anything matching the interface must provide. There are no implementations associated with any of the operations. An interface does not specify anything about the state of an object that matches it; so it

has no attributes, and no association can be navigable from an interface. We'll discuss interfaces in more depth in the next subsection.

2. ≪type≫. A class which has the stereotype ≪type≫ is like an interface except that it can have state, e.g. specify attributes as well as operations. It does not define any implementation.

3. ≪implementation class≫. A class which has the stereotype ≪implementation class≫ defines the physical implementation of its operations and attributes. It can realize a type.

Any object has exactly one implementation class, though it can have several types and match several interfaces. Usually we work with unstereotyped classes, but sometimes the extra precision given by the stereotypes is useful.

PANEL 6.2 Stereotypes

A *stereotype* is UML's way of attaching extra classifications to model items; it's one of the ways that UML is made extensible. It describes a model element, and is placed close to the element on a diagram. For example, Figure 6.14 shows the stereotype ≪interface≫ on a class symbol,[2] and the stereotype ≪use≫ on a dependency arrow. This gives us extra information about the class[3] and about the dependency.

Some stereotypes are predefined in UML; they are automatically available and you can't redefine them. ≪interface≫, ≪type≫ and ≪implementation class≫ are examples. More interestingly, you can define your own stereotype to express whatever extra classification is useful. For example, if you were implementing an application which had persistent classes you might well choose to define a stereotype ≪persistent≫ to show which classes are persistent. UML even permits you to define a new graphic icon to represent a ≪persistent≫ class. The project team needs, of course, to agree on some standard place where invented stereotypes are documented.

In this book we try to comment on the fact, whenever we use a stereotype which is not a predefined part of UML.

6.2.1 Interfaces

An *interface* specifies some operations of some model element, such as a class, which are visible outside the element. It need not specify *all* the operations that the element supports, so the same element could match several different interfaces.

An interface is defined on a class diagram using a rectangle like a class icon, with the operations listed in a compartment of the rectangle just as for a class. The icon is marked with ≪interface≫, and never has an attribute compartment, because an interface cannot

---

[2] An interface is actually not a kind of class; instead, interfaces and classes are both classifiers. There are various reasons for this difference in treatment; for example, it makes it easy for the UML semantics to specify that classes can have attributes but interfaces cannot.

[3] strictly, classifier: see the Technical UML note on p. 88.

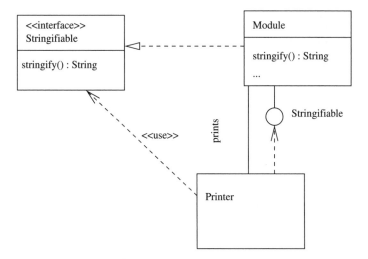

Figure 6.14   An interface and its use.

have attributes. For example, Figure 6.14 defines an interface which is satisfied by anything which understands the message `stringify` and returns a string. The diagram also shows how interfaces are used in UML.

The class `Module` *matches* (or *realizes*, or *supports*) the interface; that is, `Module` has a method `stringify` of the right type. This is shown in two ways, by both:

1. the small circle labeled `Stringifiable` attached to `Module`'s icon;
2. the arrow from `Module` to `Stringifiable`. Notice the *realization* arrow used: it's like a generalization arrow except for the dashed shaft. As the notation suggests, matching an interface can be seen as a weak form of inheritance. `Module` provides at least the operations specified in `Stringifiable`, and may provide more, just as with inheritance between classes. However, `Module` *has* to provide its own implementations, since the interface `Stringifiable` doesn't have any implementations: only the specifications of the operations are inherited.

It's unnecessary to show the same information twice, of course. It may be convenient to omit the realization arrow, especially when a diagram contains many classes that realize the same interface. The class icon of the interface still has to be there, to define what the interface means.

Class `Printer` *depends on* the interface `Stringifiable` only, shown with a dependency arrow to the circle representing the `Stringifiable` interface. That is, `Printer` doesn't care about any other feature of a class; provided it provides the method `stringify` the `Printer` can use it. This is extra information about the association `prints`; it's useful because it means that changes to the `Module` class which don't affect the `stringify` function can be made without fear of affecting `Printer`.

The diagram also shows the dependency arrow with stereotype «use» showing that `Printer` depends on the interface `Stringifiable`. Again, this can be omitted from the diagram without losing information.

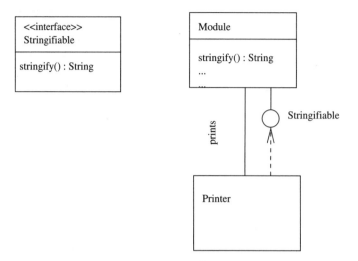

Figure 6.15 More parsimonious notation for interface dependency.

Figure 6.15 and Figure 6.14 carry the same information; which is clearer depends mainly on the aesthetics of your class diagram.

Q: How can an interface be implemented in your language? Write skeleton code that corresponds to Figure 6.14.

As we shall see in Chapters 13 and 14, subsystems and components, not just classes, can match interfaces.

TECHNICAL UML NOTE

In fact, in UML any *classifier* can match an interface. Classifiers include actors and use cases, for example, as well as the classes, subsystems and components we mentioned. The notation is the same as we've described; for example, you could attach a lollipop to a use case symbol. The interface definition itself is always shown as a rectangle.

6.2.2 Abstract classes

A related notion is that of *abstract class*. An abstract class, which we will show using the *property* {abstract} on the class icon, may have implementations defined for some of its operations. However, to say that it is abstract means that for at least one of its operations no implementation is defined. Therefore you cannot instantiate an abstract class. An abstract class in which *none* of the operations have an implementation, and in which there are no attributes, is effectively the same thing as an interface. C++ programmers often use abstract classes to achieve the same effects for which Java programmers use Java interfaces. An abstract class might well be used to implement a UML interface in a C++ application. In this case a class which implements an interface inherits from the abstract class.

Discussion Question 52

In Chapter 2 we said that classes often have a role as object factories. In what sense is an abstract class an object factory?[a]

---

[a] Thanks to Bernd Kahlbrandt for pointing this question out.

PANEL 6.3 Properties and tagged values

We've just seen an example of a *property* being added to an element in a diagram to give more information about it. This is a powerful mechanism in UML, and is the other main way, apart from stereotyping, in which UML is made extensible.

Just as objects have values for their attributes, model elements, such as classes, have values for their properties. Properties are essentially to do with the *model* rather than the implemented *system*. For example, in a UML model every class has a Boolean property isAbstract, which is intended to have value true if the class is abstract and false otherwise. There's no suggestion that there should be an actual attribute isAbstract anywhere in the system: the property just provides a systematic way for a designer to record the design decision that this is an abstract class.

Different kinds of UML model elements have different properties available for recording appropriate decisions. Another particularly useful one is the isQuery property of operations. If a developer specifies that an operation has its isQuery property set to true, this records the design decision that invoking the operation should not affect the state of the system in any way. Such operations can be used whenever it's convenient in the model and as many times as you like, without fear of causing unwanted side-effects. For example, they can be used in conditions or constraints without causing confusion.

Any property can be written on a diagram by adding a label {propertyName = value} near the name of the element to which the property applies. Because so many properties are Boolean-valued with names isSomething, UML provides a short form for those. We could write in full {isAbstract = true}, but we can instead write just {abstract}. Notice the similarity to how we write constraints: in both cases, the expression is written in curly brackets near the element name. You could think of a property as a kind of constraint.

The predefined properties of each kind of model element are described in the UML Semantics document [50]. You can also define your own *tagged values*. That is, for any element of your model you can define a name (a tag) which should be filled in with a value. For example, if you wanted to record who was to write the code for a class and who was to review it, you might define two tags author and reviewer to apply to each class. Your class diagram could record the information; for example, by inserting {author = ''Perdita Stevens'', reviewer = ''Stuart Anderson''} near the name of the class. Of course, this will only be really useful if you have both an agreed set of tags among the development team, and some tool support for managing and displaying the tags.

What is the difference between defining a new tagged value, and defining a new stereotype? Stereotyping is a more powerful, heavyweight option, which is especially useful when you want to make several specialisations to a kind of model element. Defining a tagged value is a more lightweight mechanism, for when you just want to associate a little more data with an element.

6.3 Parameterized classes

A parameterized class is not actually a kind of class! It can be seen as a kind of function: instead of taking some values and returning a value, though, a parameterized class takes some classes and returns a class. It is sometimes called a *template*: the idea is that it has some slots into which you put classes, to get a new class. The classic example is List⟨T⟩, which, given a class C to substitute for the formal parameter T, describes the class of lists of C objects. For example, an object of class List⟨Student⟩ represents a list of students, whereas an object of class List⟨Game⟩ represents a list of games. We could, of course, implement new classes StudentList and GameList without needing any special facilities. However, lists of students and lists of games will have a lot in common: they will both provide operations for adding and deleting elements of the list, for example, and the code for both is likely to be identical, regardless of whether the elements of the lists are Students or Games. A parameterized class allows us to take advantage of this fact by reusing the same parameterized class in both cases. By defining a parameterized class once, and then using it twice, we may save both development and maintenance effort. In UML we show a parameterized class using a variant on the class symbol which has a small dashed rectangle in the top right corner, in which the formal parameters of the parameterized class are listed. The types of the members of the class can (and almost always do) mention the formal parameter. There are two ways of showing that a class is the result of applying a parameterized class to an argument. We show them both in Figure 6.16.

Notice that in Figure 6.16 we show one dependency but not others. Both instantiations depend on the parameterized class, as well as on their respective parameters. We omitted, for example, the dependency of List⟨Game⟩ on List⟨T⟩ because that dependency is clear from the name of the class.

Q: Why couldn't we build class StudentList from class List using inheritance?

Not all languages support this way of constructing classes directly (sometimes known as *genericity*); C++ does, but Java, for example, does not. Even if the language to be used in a project does not support parameterized classes, the design may sometimes be made more readable using the notation.

> **Discussion Question 53**
> Another way to get the reuse benefits in the List example might be to define a single, non-parameterized class List in terms of a very general class such as Object, of which every class is a subclass, and then rely on substitutivity to let you put any object of any class into a List. This is often done in languages which don't support parameterized classes directly. What advantages and disadvantages does this approach have, compared with a parameterized class List? How else might you achieve some of the same reuse benefits?

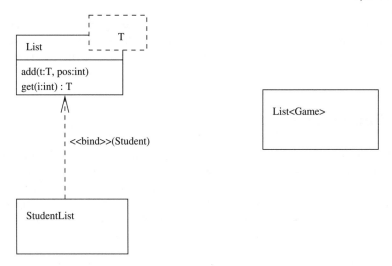

Figure 6.16 A parameterized class and its uses.

6.4 Dependency

We have now seen several examples of a dependency between two classes (and in one case between a class and a parameterized class – remember a parameterized class is not really a class!). Recall from Chapter 1 that A depends on B if a change to B may force a change to A. We can show a dependency between any two UML model elements (and just about anything in any UML diagram is a model element). In each case, the dependency of A on B is shown by a dashed *dependency arrow* from A to B, like the one in Figure 6.16.

Notice the difference between a dependency between two classes and an association between the classes. An association between two classes represents the fact that *objects* of those classes are associated. A dependency is between the classes themselves, not between the objects of those classes.

In fact when there is a dependency between classes it is usually possible, and preferable, to be more specific about the nature of the dependency. For example, a class always depends on a class from which it inherits, so there is no need to show a dependency explicitly in such a case.

6.5 Components and packages

Dependencies are most commonly used in UML between *packages*. A package is a collection of model elements, and defines a namespace for the elements. For example, a package might be a collection of related classes and the relationships between them, or a collection of objects and relationships between them. It is often convenient to be able to package things like this, either because they form a component or simply to divide work into team-sized chunks. A package can be shown on a class diagram (or indeed any other kind of diagram) as a rectangle with a 'tab' in the top left-hand corner. If a diagram shows a dependency or association linking a package to something, this means that there is some element in the package which has the dependency or association. We do not need to specify which. We will talk about components, packages and subsystems in more detail in Chapters 13 and 14.

6.6　Visibility, protection

Classes often have attributes or operations which are not available to every client of the class. UML allows the use of symbols +, # and – to distinguish between public, protected and private members of a class. Public members can be accessed by any client of the class. The exact meaning of protected and private is language dependent. Private members can normally only be accessed by members of the same class. Protected members normally have wider access than private members, but not so wide as public members.

SUMMARY

This chapter considered some advanced features of UML class diagrams, and UML's main extensibility mechanisms: stereotypes, constraints and tagged values. We described some ways of giving extra information about the association between classes, considering aggregation and composition, roles, navigability, qualified associations, derived associations and association classes. We also covered constraints, which are a general feature of UML that can be used for a wide variety of purposes; here we discussed their use for giving class invariants and for recording the relationships between various associations. Next we considered interfaces, which, again, can be applied more generally. We mentioned abstract classes, and so-called parameterized classes, which are not really classes at all, but rather are functions which take one or more classes as arguments and return classes as the result. Finally we considered dependency and visibility.

CHAPTER 7

Essentials of use case models

Use cases document the behavior of the system *from the users' points of view*. By 'user' in this case we mean anything external to the system being developed which interacts with the system. A user might be a person, another information system, a hardware device, etc. Use case modeling helps with three of the most difficult aspects of development:

- capturing requirements
- planning iterations of development
- validating systems.

Use cases were first introduced by Ivar Jacobson in the early 1990s, as a development from the earlier idea of *scenarios*. Scenarios still exist in UML, and we'll discuss them later in this chapter.

A *use case diagram* is comparatively easy to understand intuitively, even without knowing the notation. This is an important strength, since the use case model can sensibly be discussed with a customer who need not be familiar with UML. To see this, look at Figure 7.1, which shows the use case diagram from the introductory case study in Chapter 3, before we look at the elements of a use case model in detail.

The diagram shows, not a single use case, but all use cases for the given system. An individual *use case*, shown as a named oval, represents a kind of task which has to be done with support from the system under development. (The UML standard calls this a 'coherent unit of functionality': we prefer the term 'task'.) Of course the use case diagram shows only a small part of the information we need. Each use case is also described in detail, usually in text. The use case diagram can be seen as a concise summary of the information contained in all the descriptions of the use cases.

An *actor*, usually shown as a stick person, represents a kind of user of the system (where, remember, by *user* we mean anything external to the system that interacts with it – do not be misled by the human appearance of the icon into thinking the actor must be human).

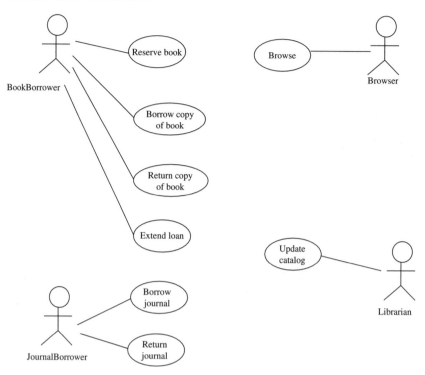

Figure 7.1 Use case diagram for the library.

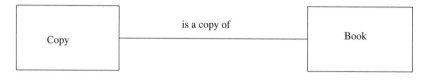

Figure 7.2 Simple association between classes.

There is a line connecting an actor to a use case if the actor (more correctly, someone or something playing the role represented by the actor) may interact with the system to play some part in the task.

A use case diagram is rather like a class diagram in the sense that the icons represent *sets* of things and *possible* interactions, rather than individual things and definite interactions. In Chapter 5 we discussed the simple association is a copy of between classes Copy and Book, shown in Figure 7.2, which represents a *relation* between the set of objects of class Copy and the set of objects of class Book. That is, an individual object myCopy of class Copy and an individual object thatBook of class Book might or might not be related. In the same way, the very simple communication relation shown in Figure 7.3 shows that there's a relation between the set of BookBorrowers, and the set of *scenarios* in which a BookBorrower reserves a book from the library. A particular BookBorrower might or

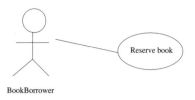

Figure 7.3 Simple communication between an actor and a use case.

might not be involved in a particular book–reservation scenario. A scenario is an instance of a use case, just as an object is an instance of a class. We'll return to this point later. For now, notice two things:

- An actor in a use case diagram represents a *role* that someone might play, rather than representing a particular individual. For example, a librarian may also be a book borrower: someone who sometimes plays the role of a librarian may at other times play the role of a book borrower.

- A communicates relation between an actor and a use case doesn't mean that someone in that role is *necessarily* involved in carrying out a task; it just means that they may be, depending on the circumstances.

Now let us consider actors and use cases in more detail.

7.1 Actors in detail

Beneficiaries   Each use case has to represent a task, or coherent unit of functionality, which the system is required to support. Normally this means that the use case has value for at least one of the actors. We call an actor for whom a use case has value a *beneficiary* of the use case. It's important to identify the beneficiaries of each use case, since if a use case has value for a particular actor, that actor will stay connected with the use case throughout the development. (Perhaps the name of the actor may change, and perhaps we may even end up with several actors because we reclassify the roles, but the humans or external systems represented by the actor will always be represented somehow.) However, if an actor is not the beneficiary of a use case, then the connection between the actor and the use case is less certain. There may be other ways of providing the same value, that is, satisfying the same requirements. For this reason developers need to be aware of who *needs* a use case and who is involved in it without getting benefit from it.

Q: Consider the use case `Borrow copy of book` in the library system. We did not show the librarian as an actor connected with this use case. What would have been the advantages and disadvantages of doing so?

> **Discussion Question 54**
> It is sometimes argued that only actors who are beneficiaries should be shown on a use case diagram, because which other actors are involved in realizing a use case is a design decision, not part of requirements analysis. What do you think, and why?

There are circumstances in which nobody who interacts with a system to carry out a task actually gets benefit from it: the beneficiary's interaction with the system in that task is indirect. See Section 7.4.1.

Identifying actors   Potential human users of a system tend to be comparatively easy to identify.[1] In order to develop a use case model you need to identify the different roles that these humans may play, remembering that one person may play different roles at different times. Identifying roles is rather like regarding users from the system's point of view. If Mary Smith and Joe Bloggs might both be involved in some part of the system's behavior (e.g. reserving a book), and it 'makes no important difference to the system's behavior' whether it is interacting with Mary Smith or Joe Bloggs, this is likely to mean that Mary Smith and Joe Bloggs are both capable of playing the role represented by a particular actor in connection with the use case representing that task.

> **Discussion Question 55**
> What differences in a system's behavior do you think might be *important* in this context? Can you make this precise?

There are some subtleties which we'll return to later in this chapter and in the next, but normally any human who interacts with the system will be represented by at least one actor in the use case model. Of course a user who plays several different roles is represented by several actors, one for each role.

Non-human actors   The situation with non-human actors tends to be less clear, mostly because it's less clear what should count as an external system or device. For example, a keyboard doesn't count as a device which interacts with the system, because there is a human operating the keyboard. Showing the keyboard would not be useful; instead, we will naturally abstract away from the fact that the human operator hits a keyboard whose key presses are sent to the system, and show an actor representing the human interacting directly with the system. What if we consider a system which gets input from a barcode reader? From a clock? From the Internet? From a different computer system within the same company? What if the system sends output to such an external system or device? Where are the boundaries between systems? For example, suppose that our library system allows users to request books on inter-library loan from another library, and that when such a request is placed the system contacts the other library via the Internet. What actor should be shown on our use case diagram? The Internet? The other library system? Neither?

The decision is a pragmatic one: you do whatever seems likely to be most useful, and different people have different views. Even if it is clear what an external system or device is, there is a question about which such things should be shown on a use case diagram. Fowler and Scott [20] discuss the possible views, which we can summarize as saying that you may show interactions with external systems:

1. always
2. when it is the other system or device that initiates the contact

---

[1]   If they aren't, be very suspicious: you may possibly be being pushed into embarking on the surprisingly common task of building a system which somebody wants built but which nobody really wants to use!

3. when it is the other system or device that gets value from the contact.

Other people again think that actors should always represent humans: for example, that we might consider showing the other library's librarian as an actor, but not the other library's system. The danger with this view is that it means you may have to understand irrelevant things about how an external system works, in order to know what human roles are involved.

TECHNICAL UML NOTE

In fact in UML role tends to be used to denote what an object or an actor does in one specific collaboration: so technically an actor plays a different role in each use case and is a *coherent set of roles*. You may prefer to think of an actor as a person 'wearing a particular hat'.

7.2   Use cases in detail

We said that a scenario is an instance of a use case, as an object is an instance of a class. As with objects and classes, it's easier to describe what a scenario is than what a use case is, since a use case describes a set of related scenarios.

A scenario is a possible interaction between the system and some people or systems/devices (in their various roles). The interaction can be described as a sequence of messages. For example, here are two scenarios:

- Book borrower Mary Smith borrows the library's third copy of *War and Peace*, when she has no other book out on loan. The system is updated accordingly.
- Book borrower Joe Smith tries to borrow the library's first copy of *Anna Karenina*, but is refused because he already has six books out on loan, which is his maximum allowance.

Discussion Question 56
What are the messages, in each case? Should 'message' mean the same in this context as it did in Chapter 2?

Both of these scenarios are possible instances of the use case Borrow copy of book. Notice that not only the interactors, but even the outcome, differed between the two cases. This is common. Just as not all objects in the same class send the same messages during their lifetime, scenarios in the same use case can involve different behavior. The scenarios in a use case should have in common that they are all attempts to carry out essentially the same task, even though the use case includes unusual or alternative courses.

So a use case embodies a, possibly complex, set of requirements on the system, which will start to emerge during initial requirements capture and will be refined as the system is developed. We need some way to record the detailed information we have about what a use case involves: what are the possible scenarios, and what determines which of them applies in any given set of circumstances? This is usually done by associating a textual description with the use case. A tool may allow the tool user to click on the oval icon representing a use case in order to see the text that gives the detailed description of what that use case is.

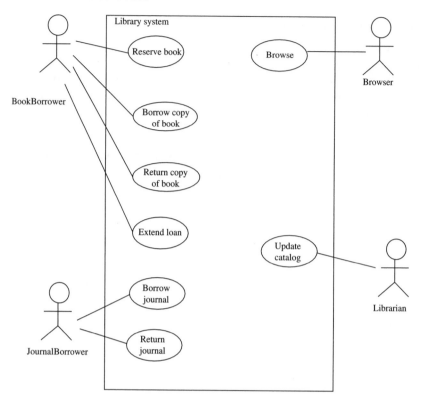

Figure 7.4 Use case diagram for the library.

A UML *activity diagram*, or a description in some formal language, may also be used, and similarly associated with the use case it describes.

Later we need to be able to show how the designed collection of classes and components enables the system to realize the use case. A use case may be associated with *interaction* diagrams which show how it, or some subset of the scenarios it includes, is realized in a particular system design.

7.3 System boundary

Optionally, there can be a box around the use cases in a use case diagram, labeled with the name of the system. The box represents the system boundary. An example is shown in Figure 7.4.

This can be useful when modeling a complex system which is split into different subsystems: you could have one use case diagram for each subsystem, in which case the system boundary may help to make it immediately clear which subsystem is being modeled. When drawing a use case diagram to represent a simple system, though, it is common to omit the box, and we shall do so in the rest of this book.

7.4 Using use cases

7.4.1 Use cases for requirements capture

Use cases can help with requirements capture by providing a structured way to go about it:

1. Identify the actors.
2. For each actor, find out

    • what they need from the system: that is, what use cases there are which have value for them;
    • any other interactions they expect to have with the system, that is, which use cases they might take part in for someone else's benefit.

For purposes of prioritizing the work and planning iterations of the development, you also need to know *how much* someone needs a given use case to be realized.

It may be helpful to list which actual people or systems can carry out the role of each actor, but that is not usually recorded in the UML diagram. In discussing the system with potential users, it is necessary to find out which actors they might be in the use case diagram and to find out if there are any functions they believe they would participate in which are not currently included.

As we remarked when considering beneficiaries of the system as actors, there may be aspects of system behavior that don't easily show up as use cases for actors. We connect an actor with a use case only when the actor participates in a use case, not, more generally, when an actor is in any way concerned about the existence of a use case. So there may very well be cases when a task is essential, but not particularly valuable to any of the actors which participate in it. The classic example (mentioned in [20], for example) is when a utility company sends quarterly bills to each of its customers. The company as a whole gets benefit from it; but the only obvious actor in the use case is the customer, and possibly the company's mailing office, which doesn't itself particularly benefit from sending out the bill. You should show such tasks as use cases when you discover them, even though they are not of direct benefit to any of the actors involved. (Be careful, though, to ensure that the use case does represent a real requirement.)

7.4.2 Use cases through the development

Planning   Before we can carry out a sensible estimation and planning process for the whole project, we need to have a list of all the use cases for our system, together with:

• a good idea of what each means
• an understanding of who wants each and how much
• knowledge of which use cases carry most risk
• a plan for how long it should take to implement each use case.

A point which sounds elementary is that you should not plan to deliver a system in less time (total effort, from all the developers involved) than the sum of the times for the use cases you plan to deliver![2] Performing this arithmetic can be a useful antidote to over-optimism.

---

[2] taking into account any reuse you can predict.

When (and it is when, rather than if) you find that the system absolutely has to be delivered sooner than that, you must undertake negotiation with the customer about which use cases should not be provided in the first release. (Kent Beck calls this the *planning game*, which captures the fact that it has rules, for example about how time works, which can't be broken even to oblige the customer.) This is one of the places where it makes a difference at what level of granularity use cases are described. The identification of functionality which is common to several use cases and can therefore be reused is also important: we'll discuss this in the next chapter.

Once you know which use cases you are contracted to provide, you have to decide in which order to implement them, and which use cases belong in which iteration of the system. (Remember that an iteration may be low level, internal to the project, or may be high level or external, that is, may result in a system delivered to the customer. The customer is involved in the decision about which use cases should be provided in external iterations, but not in decisions about the internal iterations.)

Political aspects   Remember the 25% of systems that were never delivered? It wasn't because the developers decided to go on holiday instead: it was because the project got canceled. That is, someone somewhere decided it wasn't worth going ahead with. How do we stop that happening to our project?

If we've captured requirements in terms of use cases and actors, we are likely to have a very good idea of which use cases – i.e. which aspects of the system's behavior – are most important to which people. So, other things being equal, we want to be able to demonstrate the system doing something valuable to the most influential people *first*. As soon as possible, we want to make sure that everyone who has the power to scupper the system (and remember this may include people who don't have formal power in the organization!) has some good reason not to do so. This means that they must see that if the system is completed and delivered, they will get something they want, which they will lose if they get the project canceled.

Comparing use cases which are important to a given person, of course other things being equal we should implement the highest priority ones first.

Of course, it may be decided not to *start* a project if the use case analysis does not demonstrate that it will provide enough benefit. This is another way to reduce the probability that a given project gets canceled!

Technical aspects   Another criterion, which may conflict with the ones above, is that we should deliver the use cases associated with highest risk first, so as to tackle the greatest risks when we still have contingency to tackle them, and so that we don't get tied into a design which will not allow us to deal with the hardest (highest risk) use cases.

Discussion Question 57
In other circumstances, we may tackle the *easiest* parts of a problem first. When is this the right approach?

Notice that the way in which the use case is described will vary through the development process. To begin with it's important that we identify *what* the system should achieve in each use case, not *how* it should achieve it. Later we'll choose an implementation. This may well involve changing the actors; probably not the one who wants the use case, but the ones who take part in a 'helping' capacity.

System validation Each use case describes a requirement on the system, so a correct design allows each use case to be carried out; that is, it *realizes* each use case. An obvious, and very useful, technique for validating a system design is to take each use case in turn and check that the design allows the use case to be carried out. This is sometimes called walking the use case.

The same technique can be used to derive system tests: there should be tests of each use case, and where a use case includes significantly different families of scenarios, an example of each family should be included. For example, the library system must be tested to see both that it does allow a user to borrow a book, and that it does not allow any user to borrow too many books at once. The need for these tests is immediate from the use case model.

7.5   Possible problems with use cases

As we've seen, use cases can help with some of the most difficult aspects of system development, namely requirements capture, planning, iteration management and test planning. However, some experts, notably Meyer [36], feel strongly against them. We too have some reservations, but these apply more strongly to the features of use case modeling described in the next chapter than to the simple form discussed here. Use case modeling should be used with caution, however, since:

1. There is a danger of building a system which is not object oriented. Focusing on use cases may encourage developers to lose sight of the architecture of the system and of the static object structure, in the rush somehow to deliver the use cases which are required in the current iteration. Later, if the functionality of one use case has already been developed, it may be hard to justify the time to modify the design to maintain its integrity with respect to subsequent use cases. We may end up back where we started, developing a top-down, function-oriented, unmaintainable, inflexible system. This danger can be lessened by careful management of the beginning of each iteration. If the previous iteration left the system in a state which is unsatisfactory, it should be *refactored* before any new functionality is added, and the plan for the iteration should allow for this.

2. There is a danger of mistaking design for requirements. We've already seen one example of how this can happen: the assumption that an actor is involved in a use case from which it does not get value is normally a design decision, not a constraint. More generally, requirements by use cases may encourage developers to think too operationally: users are likely to describe the use case as a very concrete sequence of interactions with the system which is one way, not the only way, of achieving their real goal. For example, users naturally think of the things that have to be done happening in some order, perhaps the order in which they are done at present, even though another order might be just as appropriate. It's important that developers distinguish between requirements and candidate designs.

3. There is a danger of missing requirements if too much reliance is put on the suggested process of finding the actors and then finding the use cases that each actor needs. As mentioned, not all requirements emerge naturally in this way. This danger can be lessened by doing use case analysis and conceptual class modeling in parallel.

Discussion Question 58

One tactic might be to develop a use case model in which only the actors who need a given use case communicate with it; the 'helper' actors would not be shown. What would be the advantages and disadvantages of this approach?

PANEL 7.1 Use case driven development?

'Use case driven' is a buzz phrase often associated with UML, introduced in [29] and picked up by much of the UML community. What does it mean, and are we advocating it?

In essence, the idea is that use cases are the most important aspect of the design process. They are not developed to do requirements capture and then abandoned once design starts: they should be used throughout the project, to track changes and define iterations, for example. This approach helps keep the focus where it should be, on the users' requirements. There is an overlap here with *user centered design* which we will briefly consider in Chapter 19.

More controversially, [29] advocates examination of the use cases as a principal method of finding objects and classes, for example, as well as a principal method of finding components and ways of using them. However, we have described some of the dangers of over-reliance on use cases. In particular, we do not believe that examination of the use cases is *on its own* a good way to find objects and classes. We think instead that the development of the conceptual class model should proceed in parallel with the development of the use case model, and that each will feed into the other. Some classes will be discovered by examining the use cases. Some use cases will be discovered by examining the classes. We don't consider it useful to classify ourselves as advocating 'use case driven' or 'data driven' or 'responsibility driven' development. A good OO development will always include aspects of all three approaches.

SUMMARY

This chapter introduced simple use case models and showed how they are used to specify the behavior of a system in a design-independent way. We discussed how to identify actors, use cases and the communication relationships between them, and how to use the use case model in the context of a development project. In the next chapter, we will consider further features and uses of use case diagrams. In Chapters 9 and 10 we will show how interaction diagrams are used to demonstrate how a system design realizes a use case.

DISCUSSION QUESTIONS

1. Consider the actors in the library example, and consider the sets of people who may be represented by each actor. Consider the intersections between the sets: for example, the set of people (if any) who sometimes play the role of book borrower and sometimes

the role of librarian. Is any set contained in another? Do you think it would be helpful for the diagram to show the relationships between these sets of people as relationships between the actors? Why, or why not? If so, how?

2. Are there any interesting relationships between any of the use cases? If so, what are they? Again, would it be useful to represent them on the diagram, and if so, why and how?

3. We said that a use case should normally have value for at least one of the actors. Give some examples, from systems you know, of use cases which have value for more than one of the actors involved.

Chapter 8 shows how to represent some relationships between actors and between use cases in UML: you may find it interesting to compare what UML provides with what you thought you might want.

CHAPTER 8

More on use case models

In this chapter we consider further aspects of use case models and their use in development. We will discuss

- how and why we may show relationships between use cases
- how and why we may show relationships between actors.

The reader should be warned that each of these features makes a use case model more complex (though possibly smaller). At the beginning of the previous chapter we claimed that an important strength of use case diagrams is their simplicity. There is an obvious conflict here. Moreover, there is considerable scope for disagreement on exactly how the features we describe here should be used, and the UML community does not yet seem to have reached consensus. The relationships between use cases, in particular, have changed since UML1.1 (and the first printing of this book) and may change again. We recommend a KISS approach: if in doubt, don't use these features.

Finally we shall discuss the circumstances in which an actor in the use case model should be modeled by a class in the system, since this often causes confusion.

8.1 Relationships between use cases

There are two main kinds of situations in which we may want to document a relationship between two use cases. On the use case diagram, this is shown as an open-headed dashed arrow between two use case ellipses (it's the same arrow that is used to show other kinds of dependencies). The two cases are distinguished by being given different *stereotypes*: the first is given the stereotype ≪include≫, the second is given the stereotype ≪extend≫. (Stereotypes are explained in Panel 6.2.)

8.1.1 Use cases for reuse: ≪include≫

The most vital case is when we are able to factor out common behavior from two or more of our original use cases, or (better still) when we discover that we can implement part of one of our use cases by using a component.

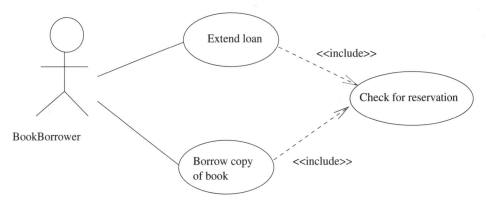

Figure 8.1 Use case reuse: ≪include≫.

For example, notice that the descriptions of the use cases Borrow copy of book and Extend loan both mention the need to check whether there is an existing reservation on the book. If there is, then the loan cannot be extended nor can the book be borrowed. We might choose to show this common feature of the two use cases on the use case diagram, as shown in Figure 8.1. Note that the arrow goes from the 'user' use case to the 'used' use case, and is labeled (with the stereotype) ≪include≫, to represent that *the source use case includes the target use case*. More precisely, scenarios which are instances of the source use case contain subscenarios which are instances of the target use case. If the target use case changes to contain different scenarios, the source use case will be affected because its longer scenarios will change too; but the target use case does not depend on the source use case.

There is of course a corresponding decomposition of the detailed use case descriptions. The new descriptions might read:

- **Borrow copy of book** A BookBorrower presents a book. The system checks that the potential borrower is a member of the library, and that s/he does not already have the maximum permitted number of books on loan. This maximum is six unless the member is a staff member, in which case it is 12. If both checks succeed, the system checks whether there is a reservation on the book (use case Check for reservation); otherwise the system refuses to lend the book. If the book is reserved, the system refuses to lend it. Otherwise it records that this library member has this copy of the book on loan and prompts for the book to be stamped with the return date.

- **Extend loan** A BookBorrower asks (either in person or by telephone) to extend the loan of a book. The system checks whether there is a reservation on the book (use case Check for reservation). If so, the system refuses to extend the loan. Otherwise it records that this library member's loan of this book has been extended, updating the records of both. It prompts for the book to be marked with the new return date. This is done by restamping it, if the borrower is present in person; alternatively if the extension is being done by telephone, the borrower is asked to alter the return date.

- **Check for reservation** Given a copy of a book, the system searches the list of outstanding reservations for reservations on this book. If it finds any, it compares the number of them, n, with the number of copies of the book known to be on the reserved book shelf, m. If $n > m$ then the system returns that this copy is reserved, otherwise that it is not.

Discussion Question 59

Is this the best factoring of functionality? How do you go about comparing this factorization with others? Can you do it based on a use case model alone?

Documenting shared or reused functionality like this on a use case diagram has several advantages:

- It is a convenient way to record the decision that a component is to be used, or to avoid recording the same information in more than one detailed use case description.
- Factoring out parts of the use case description can make the use case descriptions shorter and easier to understand, provided that the included use cases are themselves coherent units of functionality.
- Identifying common functionality between use cases at an early stage can be a way of discovering possible reuse of a component that can implement the shared functionality. As we discussed in Chapter 7, the use case diagram is an important input into the planning process. Therefore it is useful to know where functionality is shared between use cases; this lets you avoid budgeting the time for the functionality twice, which you might do if you did not discover the shared functionality until later. Notice, however, that you would not develop a detailed plan on the basis of the use case model alone, so ≪include≫ is not the only way to achieve accurate plans.

However, there are also certain pitfalls associated with identifying and documenting reuse in this way, especially if the included use cases represent small pieces of functionality:

- There is a serious danger that by looking for reuse in the functionality-oriented use case model, we effectively revert to a top-down functional decomposition style of design: exactly the inflexible style that object orientation is supposed to help avoid.
- A use case model incorporating ≪include≫ is harder for someone not skilled in UML to read, so it begins to lose its attractiveness as a customer-visible document. Moreover the more complex the use case diagram the harder it is to keep up to date, especially if it is allowed to incorporate information about design as well as about the requirements.

To tackle the first point, it is advisable to develop the conceptual level class model in parallel with the use case model, and to use techniques like CRC cards to ensure that any reuse shown on the use case diagram makes conceptual sense at the object level too. Conversely, of course, CRC card use and similar techniques can help to identify shared functionality, which might then be shown in the use case model.

How much functionality needs to be shared, before it is worthwhile to document the shared section as a separate use case? As a rough guideline, you should probably separate out shared functionality only if the time taken to develop it is significant in planning terms, which would normally mean that the time that has to be set aside to do it is greater than the minimum unit of time in which the plan is formulated, perhaps an 'ideal engineering day'. In the case we illustrated, that is unlikely to be true, so you probably would *not* in practice want to separate out this use case.

8.1.2 Components and use cases

Components and use cases interact in (at least) two related ways. We first consider the impact of *using* a component on the use case model, and then consider how a use case model can help to specify a component.

If we are to be serious about doing component-based design, it's essential to think about using components as early as possible, in fact from the very beginning of the project. There are several reasons for this.

Firstly, we will certainly need to adapt the way we describe the use cases to match the available components; we may well need to negotiate changes in the requirements themselves to make good use of available components. This may sound radical: but consider the parallel case in, say, architecture. You are unlikely to be asked exactly what size and shape you want your doors. More likely, you will be asked to choose from a range of available shapes and sizes, each with its own cost; if it's possible at all to specify that you want a round, green door with a brass knob, you can expect to pay a much higher price for it, and to wait longer, than if you want something standard. It seems reasonable to say that if the software industry is to make the shift to component-based engineering, our approach to flexibility of requirements will similarly have to change.

> **Discussion Question 60**
> Do you agree? Or do you think, for example, that the inherent flexibility of software will be enough to mitigate this?

Secondly, if we will be able to implement some requirement using a component, we want to know before we expend time and effort working out how to build it ourselves.

We meet here for the first time a question which will recur: when we use a component which we don't have to develop, do we show it on our design diagrams? Or do we treat it as though it were part of the programming language, and just use it? Either is possible; which is best depends on what the component is (and to some extent on taste). For example, suppose we use an `OrderedCollection` class from a library of collection classes, to order the items on an overdue book list. There's probably no value in showing `Order things` as a ≪include≫d use case; this piece of functionality is too small. However, if we use a more complex component we probably do want to show it.

Naturally if we are planning to develop a reusable component that will include some, but not all, of the functionality of a given use case, it will also make sense to describe the proposed component clearly by its own use case(s). The main difference between a use case for a component and a use case for a whole system is that the actors that interact with a component might be objects external to the component, rather than humans or external systems or devices. An object external to the component looks like an external system or device from the point of view of the component; we've just shifted perspective. For example, if `Check for reservation` is a component which should be documented separately, its documentation might include the detailed description given above and the very simple use case diagram shown in Figure 8.2.

As we mentioned before, this small example is probably too simple to be worth treating in this way.

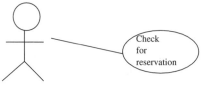

ReservationChecker

Figure 8.2 A use case diagram describing a component.

Summary: using ≪include≫

Consider using a ≪include≫ relationship between use cases

- to show how the system can use a pre-existing component
- to show common functionality between use cases
- to document the fact that the project has developed a new reusable component.

A project will probably begin by developing a simple use case diagram that does not make use of the features described in this chapter; a diagram that makes use of ≪include≫ is probably best viewed as a refinement of such a diagram, in which some design decisions have been made.

8.1.3 Separating variant behavior: ≪extend≫

If a use case incorporates two or more significantly different scenarios – that is, several different things may happen depending on circumstances – we may decide that it would be clearer to show these as a main case and one or more subsidiary cases. When to do this is a matter of judgment, since we can always show variant cases in one use case. For example, we could separate `Borrow copy of book` into the normal case in which the user is allowed to borrow the book, and the unusual case in which the user is not allowed to borrow the book because s/he has already borrowed the maximum number of items.

We use the ≪extend≫ arrow from the less central case to the central case, as shown in Figure 8.3. Beware: the arrow goes from the exceptional case to the normal case, which most people think of as being 'the other way round' from the ≪include≫ arrow!

Again there is a corresponding decomposition of the use case description. In the new version of the description of the normal case we must show:

- the condition under which the exceptional case applies;
- the point at which the condition is tested and the behavior may diverge: this is the *extension point*.

UML permits (but does not require) the condition to be shown by the extension arrow, and the extension point to be recorded in the ellipse for the central use case, as shown in Figure 8.4. This is probably most useful if you are using a formal or semi-formal description language to describe the use cases.

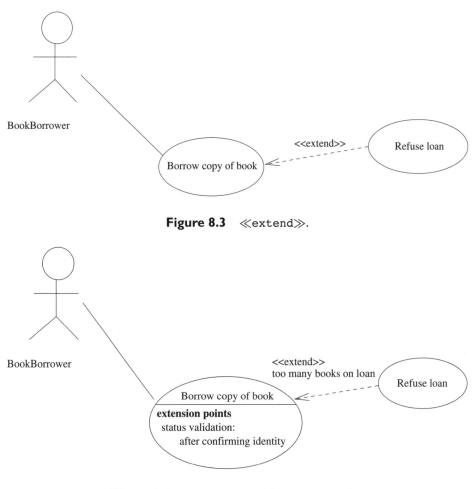

Figure 8.3 ≪extend≫.

Figure 8.4 ≪extend≫ with extension point.

8.2 Generalizations

Two actors, or two use cases, can be related by generalization, just as two classes can be.[1]
For example, in the library example, every human `JournalBorrower` *is a* `BookBorrower`,
because the people entitled to borrow journals are also allowed to borrow books. We may
choose to record a generalization relationship between the corresponding actors using the
same notation that is used for classes, as shown in Figure 8.5.

When use cases are related by generalization the idea is to show a task and a specialized
version of it. Again, we use the standard generalization arrow, which goes from the specialized use case to the more general use case. For example, if we have a use case `Reserve`
`book`, we might have a specialization of it called `Reserve book by telephone`. This

---

[1] Classes, actors and use cases are all classifiers in UML and any classifier can be generalized.

BookBorrower

JournalBorrower

Figure 8.5 Generalization between actors.

might be useful if the library system needed to behave differently for a telephone reservation; for example, if it means that the user's library card number has to be entered manually since the card cannot be scanned. This is very similar to ≪extend≫ and it is arguable that UML should not have both. A rule of thumb is that if you want to describe extra behavior which should sometimes be added depending on "run-time" conditions, you probably want ≪extend≫, whereas if you want a label for a specialized version of a whole task, you probably want generalization.

8.3 Actors and classes

It is very common for a system to interact with an actor (instance) and also to have an internal system object representing the actor instance. There are two main kinds of situation in which this can happen:

1. The system may need to store data about an actor, typically a human in a certain role. For example, the library system needs to know which people are entitled to borrow books, and how many books each of them currently has on loan, in order to carry out the Borrow copy of book use case. In an object oriented system, this is likely to mean that there is a set of real people who can take the role described by a given system actor, and also a set of system objects, one for each person, which store information about the people in that role.

Figure 8.6 These two symbols mean the same.

2. A subtly different situation is when the system *wraps* an external system in order to provide a manageable way for parts of the system to access the external system and vice versa. For example, an external transaction processing monitor might be accessed by sending messages to an internal TPMonitor object, which in turn invokes the real functionality of the external system. Or a separate user interface program might be represented inside the system by a UI object which in fact mediates between the external UI program and the main system, passing messages both ways.

The features of these two cases can be combined: for example, one of the easiest ways to provide a simple user interface to a system, which can handle the system needing to respond to different users in different ways, is to make the use cases which can be initiated by Jane Bloggs available as methods of a system object representing Jane Bloggs. An example of this is the way we implemented the `Borrow copy of book` use case in Chapter 3.

It is, however, easy to get confused and important to remember where the system boundary is. The main difference is that you can program system objects to do what you want, but not system actors!

> **Discussion Question 61**
> What are the advantages and disadvantages of representing actor instances as system objects?

8.3.1 Notation: actors as classes

Just to make things even more confusing, you will see people say that actors are classes, with the stereotype ≪actor≫. This is true at the notational level: an actor can be represented by a class icon with the stereotype ≪actor≫ instead of by a stick figure, as in Figure 8.6. (However, as we remarked earlier, in fact actors and classes are both classifiers, rather than either being a kind of the other.)

SUMMARY

In this chapter, we showed how the ≪include≫ relation can record what functionality is common to several use cases, and how the ≪extend≫ relation can record what happens in unusual cases. We discussed generalization between actors and between use cases, and the relationship between actors and classes. In the next two chapters we will demonstrate how interaction diagrams can record how objects interact to realize use cases.

DISCUSSION QUESTIONS

1. We've suggested that the version of a use case diagram using the features described here should be used in conjunction with a simpler form as described in the previous chapter. How do you think a CASE tool could sensibly support this?

CHAPTER 9

Essentials of interaction diagrams

We've now seen the two most important UML models:

- the use case model, which describes the tasks which the system must help to perform
- the class model, which describes the classes which are intended to achieve this and the relationships between them.

In Chapter 5's discussion of CRC cards, we began to address, informally, the issue of how to ensure that the class model is capable of realizing the use cases. UML's *interaction diagrams* allow us to record in detail how objects interact to perform a task.

The main use for such diagrams is to show how the system realizes a use case, or a particular scenario in a use case. We'll consider other uses at the end of the chapter.

We may use CRC cards to explore which objects interact and how, and we may use interaction diagrams to record precisely what happens. This is useful for exploring several possible options in difficult cases. Interaction diagrams can also be an aid to communication between developers, if several different people or groups develop bits of a single interaction. You would not normally expect to develop interaction diagrams for every use case or for every operation: as always, you do it when the benefit is likely to outweigh the cost. If you have a CASE tool which can use the interaction diagrams to help with code generation, this makes it more likely to be worthwhile to develop interaction diagrams.

UML provides two sorts of interaction diagram, *sequence* and *collaboration* diagrams. They show almost the same information; given an underlying class model, some CASE tools can generate one from the other. Which is better depends on what aspect of the interaction you need to concentrate on: we'll come back to the question after showing simple forms of both.

In this chapter we will describe the *instance* forms of both kinds of interaction diagram, and we will consider only straightforward procedural interactions. In Chapter 10 we will consider more advanced features, such as the *generic* forms of the diagrams and the features that are useful for describing concurrent systems.

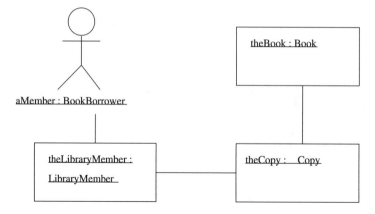

Figure 9.1 A simple collaboration, showing no interaction.

TECHNICAL UML NOTE

UML isn't always completely clear about whether a feature can be used on sequence diagrams, collaboration diagrams, or both. Wherever two interpretations are sensible, we assume that features are intended to apply to *both* sorts of interaction diagrams.

9.1 Collaborations

Collectively, the objects which interact to perform some task, together with the links between them, are known as a *collaboration*. For example, Figure 9.1 shows a collaboration which is appropriate for realizing the use case `Borrow copy of book` which we briefly considered in Chapter 3.

A collaboration, without any interaction shown, is rather like an *instance* of *part* of the class model. It shows objects, links and actors.

Objects   Each object is shown as a rectangle, which is labeled `objectName: className`. Here `className` must be the name of a class in the class model. There need not be an object of every class, because some classes will be irrelevant to the particular collaboration we're considering. There may be two or more different objects of the same class.

It may have occurred to you that object names like `theLibraryMember` are not very informative. If, as here, such a name doesn't make the diagram more readable, it can be omitted; the object rectangle could be labeled just `: LibraryMember`.

Links   Links between objects are shown like associations in the class model. Since a link is an instance of an association, there should be an association in the class model between the classes of any two linked objects. Again, the collaboration doesn't have to include links for all associations, just the relevant ones.

You can show extra information about the nature of the link here, as in the class model. For example, arrows on the lines can be used to show navigability or the association names can be shown, if you judge that it makes the diagram clearer.

Actors   Actors can be shown as on a use case diagram. If the collaboration is describing the realization of a use case, the actors in the collaboration will correspond to the actors which are connected to the use case in the use case diagram. There may be several actors, but there will always be one which initiates the use case: we will call this the initiator.

TECHNICAL UML NOTE

We are choosing to avoid one of the more complex aspects of UML. When we draw a diagram involving an object `theLibraryMember`, we don't really have any particular object in mind: for example, we don't care what the library member's name is. We could equally well be representing Kent Beck borrowing *Formal Methods for Fun*, or Amir Pnueli borrowing *Prototyping for Managers*. That is, many different actual objects could play the *role* of `theLibraryMember`. It is possible to make this idea precise by explicitly describing the different roles that objects of a given class can play. UML allows interaction diagrams to involve objects, roles, or both. However, for most purposes it is clearer and simpler to use objects which are informally representative, so this is what we will continue to do. Technically, our diagrams are at the instance level, not the specification level, and we do not use explicit roles.

9.2   Interactions on collaboration diagrams

Next we consider how to show an interaction on a collaboration diagram: that is, how to show the sequence of messages that pass between the linked objects.

Use CRC cards or some other technique to decide what the sequence of messages should be. Here we are considering only one particular interaction: for example, we decide to show the case of `Borrow copy of book` in which the user is permitted to borrow the book, rather than any of the possible variants in which the user has too many books on loan or the book is reserved. (By the way, if it's completely obvious what messages must pass you should consider whether or not it's worthwhile to draw the interaction diagram at all. It may be, for example if the diagram will help people communicate.)

Record the messages next to the links on the collaboration diagram. For example, Figure 9.2 shows the normal case of `Borrow copy of book`. Each labeled arrow represents a message sent from the object at the tail of the arrow to the object at the point of the arrow. So there must be a link between those two objects, and it must be navigable in the direction of the message. Furthermore, the target object must understand the message. That is, the class of the object at the point of the arrow must provide the appropriate operation. Developing interaction diagrams can help to identify associations between classes, and operations needed on classes.

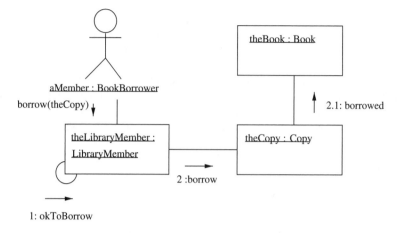

Figure 9.2   Interaction shown on a collaboration diagram.

It is normal to revise the class model as you develop interaction diagrams. However, it's essential to make sure the class model stays sane!

The most obvious solution to the immediate problem may not be the best overall: you may have to revisit previous decisions to get a solution that works well in all cases. It's essential to keep the models consistent: a CASE tool and/or a configuration management tool can help.

Activations: flow of control   In *procedural* interactions (as opposed to those involving concurrency, which we consider in Chapter 10), exactly one object is computing at any one time. An object starts to compute when it receives a message; at this point it is said to have a live *activation*. Eventually it should return a response to the sender of the message. In between it may just compute, or it may send messages to other objects to get them to compute. If it sends a message, it still has a live activation, but it can't do any more computing until it sends a response to the message. That is, the message is *synchronous*, and sending a message passes control to the receiver of the message. At any time, there is a stack of live activations, each associated with an object which has received a message to which it has not yet replied. The object associated with the top activation has control and is computing; objects whose activations only appear lower down the stack are waiting for replies to messages they have sent. The top object can send a message, in which case the receiver of the message gets a live activation which becomes the new top of the stack. Alternatively the top activation may finish its computation, reply to the message which caused this activation, and be removed from the stack. The activation below it becomes the new top activation, and its associated object – which sent the message which has just been replied to – regains control.

In ordinary procedural systems, which are all we've considered so far, only an actor can initiate activity, that is, send a message 'out of the blue'. A system object sends messages only after it has received a message (and before it has replied to it).

You can think of control as a token that gets passed as a message along the links in a collaboration diagram, and then passed back when the message is dealt with. We don't explicitly show these returns. To keep track of what the stack of objects with live activations is, the messages are uniquely numbered with a nested numbering scheme. The first message from one object to another (i.e. not counting the message from the actor to an object that kicks the interaction off – that message is unnumbered) is numbered 1. Whenever an object O receives a message, the number of that message will be used as a prefix of *all* the messages that are sent until O sends a response to the message. For example, if the message that activates O is number 7.3, all messages sent from then until the response to that message are number 7.3.something. If O sends a message to another object P, that message is numbered 7.3.1. If after getting a reply to message 7.3.1, O sends another message, it will be numbered 7.3.2, and so on.

Q: If after receiving message 7.3.1 from O, object P sent a message, what would its number be?

> **Discussion Question 62**
> You might think it would be more obvious just to number all the messages 1, 2, . . ., rather than using this nested scheme. What difference would it make? Can you construct a situation in which it would be ambiguous?

Q: If messages 2.4.1, 2.4, and 2.4.1.7 have been sent but not replied to, what can you say about the objects which sent and received each message? Which are active? How many, and which, are computing?

Q: Is it possible for messages 4.5 and 4.6 both to have been sent and not replied to? Why? Can you generalize?

9.3   Sequence diagrams

A sequence diagram shows the objects and actors which take part in a collaboration at the top of dashed lines. The line represents time as seen by the object: it is the object's *lifeline*. Time is assumed to pass as we move from top to bottom of the diagram. You show a message as an arrow from the lifeline of the sender to the lifeline of the receiver. Later messages are further down the page. Figure 9.3 (also used in Chapter 3) shows the sequence diagram version of the simple collaboration diagram we used above.

The order in which you show the objects doesn't matter, though it will make for a more readable diagram if you put the objects which take part earliest furthest to the left, so that most messages flow left to right.

When an object has a live activation, we show a narrow rectangle covering its lifeline. Optionally you can shade the parts of the activation in which the object is actually computing. Again optionally, we can show when the responses to messages happen: though as we discussed above, an object ceases to have a live activation exactly when it responds to the message that caused the activation, so you can tell when the responses happen by looking at the activations.

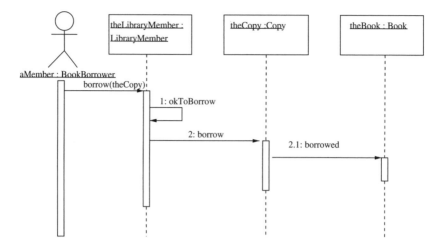

Figure 9.3 Interaction shown on a sequence diagram.

Q: Why do message arrows always point at the top of activation rectangles, never part of the way down? Why are messages from an object to itself an exception to this rule? (See below for more on this.)

Notice that even though the links between objects are not explicitly shown on a sequence diagram, there still is an underlying collaboration, just as there is in a collaboration diagram. If two objects exchange a message, there should be an association between their classes.

PANEL 9.1 Where should messages go? Law of Demeter

As we have said, underlying every interaction there is a collaboration: a set of objects with links between them. We have said that objects should exchange messages only when there is an association between their classes (or they're in the same class). But this is not a design guideline, since if objects *can* exchange a message then by definition there is an association between their classes: if in the class model it looks as though there isn't, this is just a bug in the model.

Consider the class diagram fragment in Figure 9.4.[1] In this case we only show the explicit navigabilities: for example, the arrow from Job to EverythingController illustrates that each Job object can send a message directly to the associated EverythingController. (This might be because each Job had a reference to an EverythingController; in fact in the real-life case there was a single global EverythingController.) We don't show an arrow from Job to JobController. The reason is that if a Job object wants to send a message to its JobController (which it frequently did, in the real-life case) it must first send the message getJC to the EverythingController, with itself as parameter ('give me my JobController'). The EverythingController looks up which JobController

---

[1] Real commercial example: class names have been changed, but were similar in meaning.

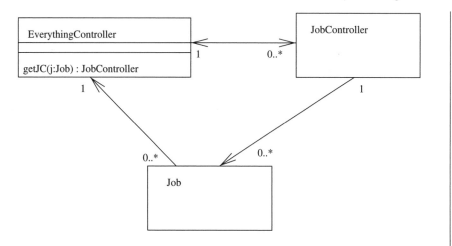

Figure 9.4   Bad design, breaking the Law of Demeter.

controls this job, and returns a reference to that `JobController`. The `Job` can now use that reference to send a message to the `JobController`.

Discussion Question 63

What alternative ways are there for providing `Job` with access to the behavior `JobController` provides? Why do you suppose this way was chosen?

Discussion Question 64

What else is suspicious about this design?

The main problem with this kind of design is that it is hard to maintain. If `JobController` changed, or if it was decided to alter the relationship between `EverythingController` and `JobController`, clients of `EverythingController` would have to be examined to see whether they had to change too. In a sense `EverythingController` exposes not only what should be its own interface, but also the structure of the class diagram to which it's attached. Its interface is much bigger than it looks.

Following the Law of Demeter allows designers to avoid 'this kind of design'. It says that in response to a message *m*, an object *O* should send messages *only* to the following objects:

1. *O* itself
2. objects which are sent as arguments to the message *m*
3. objects which *O* creates as part of its reaction to *m*
4. objects which are *directly* accessible from *O*, that is, using values of attributes of *O*.

Q: How does the design above disobey the Law of Demeter?

> **Q:** Consider again the case of an `AddressBook` which is implemented using a `List`. We have already (in Chapter 5) ruled out as bad design the idea of allowing `AddressBook` to inherit from `List`, and have said that instead `AddressBook` should own a `List` by aggregation. Why should `AddressBook` not have a method returning the `List` to objects which want to add or remove addresses from the book? What should it do instead?
>
> The Law of Demeter is described in [34]. It is a small part of what Karl Lieberherr, its inventor, calls *adaptive programming*. We do not have space to describe this here, but there are some links from this book's home page.

9.4 More advanced features

9.4.1 Messages from an object to itself

An object may, and frequently does, send a message to itself. On a collaboration diagram you show a link from the object to itself, and messages pass along that link in the usual way. On a sequence diagram, you show a message arrow from the object's lifeline back to itself. There is a problem, though. We said above that when an object receives a message it gets control, and a new live activation of that object gets added to the top of the stack of live activations. In this case the object already had a live activation when it sent the message; now it has a new, different activation because it's also the receiver of the message! That is, this object is associated with two different activations on the stack. We can show this using a nested activation; the narrow rectangle representing the new activation is shown slightly offset from the rectangle representing the old activation, so that it is visible.

Figure 9.5 shows a version of the sequence diagram with all these optional features shown.

In pure object oriented programming, every function invocation is the result of a message, and objects may send messages to themselves so often that an interaction diagram becomes cluttered. You might choose to omit messages from an object to itself, counting such things as internal computation within the object.

> **Discussion Question 65**
> Does doing so create any problems or ambiguities? If so, how should they be resolved? Consider a case where an object sends a message to itself, and part of its reaction to this message is to send a message to a different object.

9.4.2 Suppressing detailed behavior

It is often sensible to describe interaction at a higher level, rather than showing every message between every pair of objects. To do this we define a (full) *sub-collaboration* of a collaboration. Given a collaboration, that is, a collection of objects and links between them, a sub-collaboration is a subset of the objects, together with the links connecting those

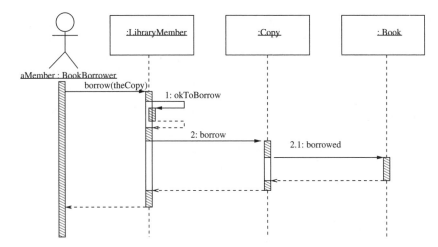

Figure 9.5 Interaction shown on a sequence diagram, with optional features.

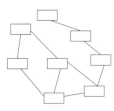

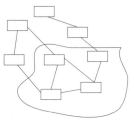

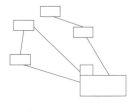

Complex collaboration

Identifying a sub-collaboration

Replacing with a package

Figure 9.6 Using a package to simplify a collaboration.

objects. We can collapse the objects in the sub-collaboration together, and regard them as one *package*. Figure 9.6 shows how this might be done. We should give the package a name, and treat it as though it were one object.

TECHNICAL UML NOTE

In UML *package* is a very general term for a grouping of model elements. Sending a message to a package just means that some object in the package is sent the message: a package isn't a real thing with an interface of its own. See Chapter 14 for more about packages.

The UML documentation says that a collaboration can be shown at different levels of granularity, but does not specify in detail exactly what these different levels of granularity are, or how they should be shown. We suggest using packages for this because it seems useful, but this is intelligent guesswork, not something explicitly described in UML.

Any link between an object outside the package and one inside becomes a link between the object outside and the package. Links between two objects inside the package disappear, and messages between such objects need not be shown; this is what makes the packaged diagram simpler. We can use a package symbol to represent the whole package, and the whole package will have just one lifeline in a sequence diagram.

Discussion Question 66

An object has a class which specifies, among other things, what messages can be sent to the object. What messages should we be able to send to a package? After reading subsection 6.2.2 on Interfaces in Chapter 6, consider how you might show this. Consider this again after reading Chapter 14!

Discussion Question 67

What makes a group of objects a good or a poor candidate for packaging together like this?

Discussion Question 68

We've described the process of packaging *existing* objects together to form *new* packages. What about defining the packages and their interactions first, and then defining what objects are in the packages?

Discussion Question 69

(After reading Chapter 6.) Should there be any connection between the objects packaged together in an interaction diagram and the classes packaged together in a class diagram? Consider this again after reading Chapter 14.

9.4.3 Returned values

Sometimes it is useful to name the value which is the response to a message; for example, often the value returned from one message is an argument to a later message. Values being returned are shown on the original message arrow, by showing an assignment to a new variable name. The assignment statement binds the variable, which can then be used in messages which are sent after the response from the message has been received. Figures 9.7 and 9.8 (which also shows creation and deletion of objects, to be described in the next subsection) show an example, in both sequence and collaboration diagram form.

Discussion Question 70

Would it ever be useful to name the return value from a message even if it wasn't mentioned in a later message?

9.4.4 Creation and deletion of objects

The set of objects involved in an interaction is not always static; objects may be created and deleted during an interaction.

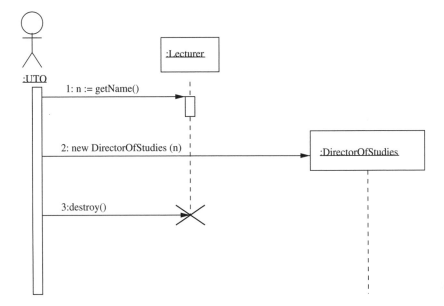

Figure 9.7 Sequence diagram: creation and deletion of objects, and use of return value.

Collaboration diagrams These show which objects are created and destroyed during an interaction by adding the constraints {new} and {destroyed} respectively after the label in the object box. Notice that this is a feature of the interaction, not of the collaboration. If an object is both created and destroyed in the same interaction, it can be labeled {transient}, which is short for {new and destroyed}.

Sequence diagrams These show an object being created by putting its object box part-way down the page, at the point where it is created. Destruction of an object is shown by its activation ending with a large X. If the object is destroyed by another object (rather than destroying itself) there is a message from the deleting object into the X.

Figures 9.7 and 9.8 show an object being created, in both sequence and collaboration diagram versions, and another being deleted. The example is an extension of the case study in Chapter 15: it describes a scenario of a possible use case Promote lecturer, which is not described in Chapter 15. A lecturer, described by an object of class Lecturer in the system, is promoted to being a director of studies (that is, a lecturer with special responsibilities for particular students). A new object of class DirectorOfStudies must be created, and the old Lecturer object must be deleted. (In some programming languages this could have been done by changing the class of an existing object.)[2]

Message names for creation and deletion The mechanisms for creating and destroying objects are language dependent. It is usually possible to initialize an object with some values

---

[2] We assume that promotions happen between academic years, so that there are no Module or Student objects associated with the Lecturer object that have to be reassociated with the new DirectorOfStudies.

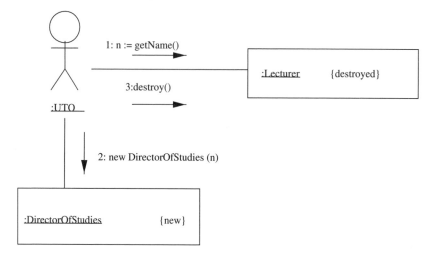

Figure 9.8 Collaboration diagram: creation and deletion of objects, and use of return value.

at the same time as creating it; it can be convenient to show this on an interaction diagram using a message called something suitable like new or create, with the initializing values as arguments. Of course this isn't a normal message to an object, since the object doesn't exist until after the message has arrived!

Many languages (for example Java and Smalltalk) are *garbage collected*: that is, objects are automatically destroyed at some time when there are no references to them in the system (roughly speaking). In this case the programmer does not need to delete objects explicitly. (This eliminates a large class of programming errors: in fact it is so useful that Bertrand Meyer made the presence of such automatic memory management one of his Seven Steps to Object Oriented Happiness [36].) Such languages normally have conventions about how one object makes it clear to the garbage collector (and any reader of the code) that it no longer needs another. For example, it may change a reference that previously pointed to the object to point somewhere else. When no part of the system is using an object it will be garbage collected. In languages where the programmer must manage memory explicitly, it is crucial that an object destroys only the objects for which it is responsible, such as its solely owned parts: see the discussion of composition in Chapter 6. It is also important that some object *does* destroy an object which is no longer needed: failure to do so leads to 'memory leaks'. In order to avoid both kinds of problems, the design must specify where the responsibility for destroying each object lies.

Discussion Question 71

If the system is to be implemented in a garbage-collected language, is it ever sensible for an interaction diagram to show an object being destroyed? If so, when and why?

Q: How are objects created and destroyed in the languages you know? Develop a simple sequence diagram in which:

1. an object O receives message m from an actor;
2. O creates a new object P;
3. P sends a message to Q;
4. After receiving the response from Q, P returns;
5. O destroys or forgets P, following the conventions of your language.

Then write code to implement this scenario.

Q: If, on receiving a message, an object does some computation and then destroys itself, what can the return value from the message be? If your language supports explicit destruction of objects, write a method in which the receiver of the message destroys itself.

9.4.5 Timing

The major advantage of sequence diagrams over collaboration diagrams is their ability to represent the passage of time graphically. So far we have let the diagram indicate only the relative ordering of messages. Sometimes, however, the actual times are important. A system in which actual times are important is called a *real-time system*; if there are definite constraints on the times when things happen that the system must satisfy without fail, it is called a *hard real-time system*.

UML allows times and timing constraints to be represented on sequence diagrams in two ways. First, and most intuitively, you can let distances on the lifelines represent intervals of real time, either exactly or loosely, so that the vertical distance between two messages indicates the elapsed time between the messages. This tends to be inconvenient in practice as a way of getting more than an intuitive understanding of the relative timings of events, though you could experiment with drawing the diagrams on graph paper! More usefully, you can write timing constraints in terms of names for the arrows on your diagram.[3] You can use the message selector as the name if there is one and it's unambiguous: for example, in Figure 9.9 `borrowed` is used as the name of message 2.1. Alternatively you can give the arrow its own name, and show this by a "timing label" on the same level in the diagram. In Figure 9.9 we give the names A and C to the initial message and the return from it. Then in the simplest case, you just use the name to represent the time when whatever the arrow represents happens. For example, if the time between two consecutive messages being sent must be no more than 5 microseconds, we could add the labels A and B in the margin of the diagram level with the message arrows. Then we could record in the margin the *constraint* $\{B - A < 5 \text{ microsec}\}$.

A further refinement is to consider the time taken for messages to pass between objects. So far we have drawn message arrows horizontally, which intuitively suggests that the message takes (virtually) no time to arrive. If the time taken for a message to arrive is significant as a fraction of the time for the whole interaction, it may be clearer to show the message arrow slanting downwards. If an arrow is named A and you write A as a time in a timing constraint, then strictly speaking you are referring to the time at the tail of the arrow (for example, the time when the message is sent: indeed, you can write `A.sendTime()` if

---

[3] UML's treatment of timing has recently changed, and is slightly inconsistent in version 1.3: we give one sensible interpretation.

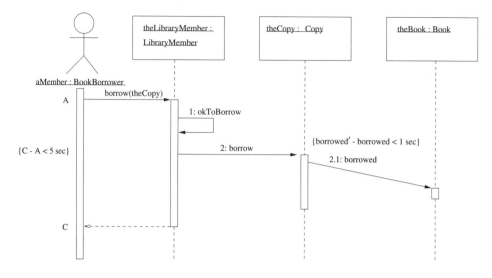

Figure 9.9 Showing timing constraints on a sequence diagram.

you prefer). You can write the time at the head of the arrow, for example the time when the message is received, as A' (or $A.\texttt{receiveTime()}$). Figure 9.9 illustrates the notation, showing that the book borrower is not supposed to have to wait more than 5 seconds for confirmation that s/he can borrow a book (and the unrealistic suggestion that message 2.1 might take a significant time to arrive, but with the constraint that it should not take more than 1 second).

Discussion Question 72
Can you show the more general constraint that no message in a diagram should take longer than 3 milliseconds to arrive? What kinds of constraints might be useful?

9.5 Interaction diagrams for other purposes

So far we've been using interaction diagrams to show how a complete system realizes a use case. They can also be useful for describing other behaviors. Here are some examples.

9.5.1 Show how a class provides an operation

When an object receives and acts upon a message, it will initiate an interaction with various other objects in the system. An interaction diagram can be used to show which objects are involved and what messages pass. Whatever it was that sent the original message is external to this collaboration, so it is represented as an actor (perhaps $\texttt{Initiator}$).

9.5.2 Describe how a design pattern works

We will discuss design patterns in Chapter 18. In UML the structure of a design pattern is treated as a parameterized collaboration, into which classes are plugged to get an actual collaboration. The interaction between the objects of these classes can be described using interaction diagrams.

9.5.3 Describe how a component can be used

The simplest kind of component, one which is self-contained and provides just an interface describing what it can do, can be treated throughout as a black box. However, components sometimes have more complicated interfaces to the rest of the system than this; they can have several points of connection to the rest of the system, each requiring the presence of an object which provides a certain interface. In such a case it can be important to understand how the component expects to interact with these objects which are external to it. An interaction diagram which is part of the documentation of the component can represent each such object as an actor. The user of the component then has to ensure that the objects that play these roles interact as expected with the component.

SUMMARY

We discussed how to use interaction diagrams – collaboration and sequence diagrams – to describe how objects interact to achieve some piece of behavior. Collaboration diagrams are better at showing the links between the objects; sequence diagrams are better for seeing the sequence of messages that passes. Interaction diagrams can be used to describe how a system realizes a use case, or for various other purposes including showing how a class realizes an operation or how a complex component is to be used.

CHAPTER 10

More on interaction diagrams

In this chapter we consider two classes of more advanced features of interaction diagrams. We will consider:

- generic interaction diagrams, with conditional and iterated message passing
- concurrent systems.

10.1   Generic interaction diagrams

In Chapter 9 we considered the *instance* form of interaction diagrams, in which there was a single possible sequence of messages. Because a use case can include substantially different scenarios, it is sometimes useful to show conditional behavior or a variable number of iterations in an interaction diagram, to cover a variety of situations.

As with any situation in which advanced features of UML can be used to increase expressiveness, there is a serious danger of defeating the object,[1] by developing a diagram which is too complicated to read.

TECHNICAL UML NOTE

The UML documentation says that a generic interaction diagram shows *all* possible sequences of messages that can occur, e.g. all scenarios in a use case, in contrast to an instance interaction diagram which shows just one sequence or scenario. We think you could legitimately use the generic form to show more than one sequence while still not showing all possible sequences, so we won't stress this point. However, if you find yourself wanting to take such a half-way position, it might be worth considering whether it's a sign that the use case in question is too complex, and should be split.

---

[1]   pun intended.

10.1.1   Conditional behavior

A message may be *guarded* by a condition. We can see this in several of the examples in the case studies. The message is sent only if the guard evaluates to true at the time the system reaches that point in the interaction.

To show a guard we write the condition in square brackets in front of the message. This represents a simple `if` condition. A condition represents a boolean expression, i.e. it evaluates to `true` or `false`. UML does not lay down what conditions can be: you could express them in English, OCL, your target programming language or another notation. Of course the project must agree what to use and be consistent.

Several messages can leave the same point on the sender's lifeline, guarded with different conditions. In this case at most one of the messages will be sent, in a sequential system. That is, you must make sure that the different conditions are mutually exclusive (at any one time, at most one of the conditions can evaluate to true) – otherwise you are accidentally describing a concurrent system, in which two messages are sent at once! Such a sequence diagram might be implemented using an `if-else` or `case` or `switch` construct. Figure 10.1 illustrates the notation.

Q: What is the difference between the two sequence diagram fragments shown in Figure 10.1? Write a code fragment to implement each. Could they ever behave differently in a way that mattered? What are your assumptions?

Q: Why does the second message arrow in the first example start sloped and then become horizontal again? Would it matter if it were sloped all the way?

Showing conditional behavior raises a problem which will be familiar to students of quantum physics and readers of science fiction! If the sequence diagram has a point where there are two (or more) possible futures – a conditional message send – then what happens to all the objects after a sequence passes the branch point may depend on which branch the sequence took. In the left-hand fragment of Figure 10.1 there are actually three possible 'worlds': one in which *i* was 0, so just the top message was sent; one in which *i* was 1, so just the bottom message was sent; and one in which *i* was neither, so neither message was sent. What happens, for example, if both messages were being sent to the same other object? In any given situation, only one of the messages will be sent to the object, so the sequence diagram shouldn't make it look as though it's possible for both to be sent in the same sequence of messages. But we have to show both of them somehow, because the point of the diagram is to show all the things that could happen!

UML solves this problem by letting the lifeline of any object which could be affected by such a conditional message split into branches. An example is shown in Figure 10.2.

> **Discussion Question 73**
> When should the branches of the lifeline be allowed to join up again?

> **Discussion Question 74**
> Do you think the numbering of the messages in Figure 10.2 is reasonable, or should the branching be reflected in the numbering scheme somehow? If so, how?

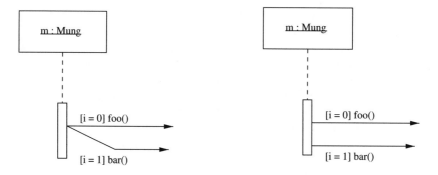

Figure 10.1 Two sequence diagram fragments.

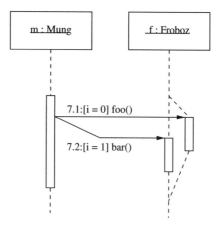

Figure 10.2 Fragment of sequence diagram with branching lifeline.

Conditional behavior on collaboration diagrams Conditional messages can be used in collaboration diagrams, but there is no equivalent of the branching lifeline, so for all but the simplest conditionals a sequence diagram is probably a better choice.

10.1.2 Iteration

Consider a scenario in which one object sends a message to another some number of times. If the number of times is fixed – it's the same for all scenarios in the use case – it would be possible to show the message that number of times on the interaction diagram. It would, however, be extremely inconvenient to have to do this, especially if sending the message caused a further chain of messages every time. Worse, if the number of times the message was sent varied between scenarios in the same use case, it would not in general be possible to show this. Just as in programming languages, we need a loop, or *iteration*, construct.

UML allows a message to be marked with an asterisk to show that it is sent repeatedly. In the simplest case, we need not specify how many times it is sent; but more often we combine the asterisk with an iteration clause, which is an expression in square brackets like (but not to be confused with) the condition on a conditional message. The iteration clause somehow describes how many times the message will be sent. Again, the expression can be anything the project agrees to use. Examples might include:

- [i := 1..10] (the message will be sent 10 times)
- [x < 10] (the message will be sent repeatedly, until x becomes less than 10)
- [item not found] (the message will be sent repeatedly, until the item is found).

Q: What program fragments would you expect to implement each of the examples?

Q: What is the difference between a message marked with * and one marked with *[true]?

If sending a message *m* which has an iteration clause results in some other messages being sent, then of course they will be repeated every time *m* is sent. Because this is the only way to make the diagram make sense, we do not need to repeat the iteration clause on the later messages. Indeed we must not, because that would describe nested iterations. Figure 10.3 represents the message a being sent twice, and each time it is sent it results in message b being sent. So the overall sequence of messages will be abab which is commonly what we want. Figure 10.4 is the same except that each time message a is sent it results in message b being sent *twice*: the overall sequence of messages is abbabb.

10.2 Concurrency

The interaction diagrams we've considered so far show how to describe the unfolding of a use case or operation in terms of messages and responses which are passed one at a time among actors and objects. We have assumed that with each message, the sender waits for a response before continuing with its own actions. At most one of our objects is computing (performing useful work) at any one time. Of course this is the usual case, since many applications are designed to run on single computers which have only one processor.

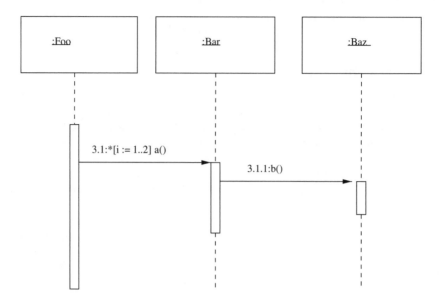

Figure 10.3 Sequence diagram fragment: iteration showing messages abab.

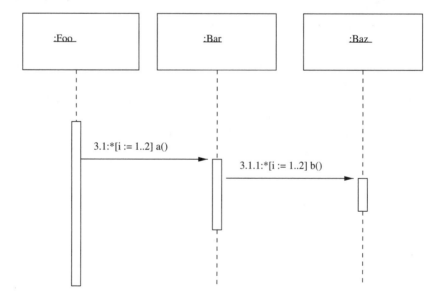

Figure 10.4 Sequence diagram fragment: iteration showing messages abbabb.

Systems like this are sometimes called procedural or single-threaded, because there is a step-by-step procedure with a single thread of execution. On an instance form sequence diagram, you can even envision this as a single thread, laid out along the message arrows, down the activations and back along the returns. One piece of thread will suffice to cover all the arrows! (Beware, though: the word procedural is also used in several other senses.)

However, many systems today are not single-threaded; they are *concurrent* in some way. Some examples of kinds of concurrent systems are:

- distributed systems, in which computation proceeds simultaneously on different processors (each requiring at least one thread of execution)
- multi-threaded applications, in which several threads of execution proceed in parallel, possibly by being scheduled onto one processor or possibly using several
- many reactive systems, which get input (data or events) from the environment in a variety of ways and have to react, often satisfying real-time constraints.

These categories overlap, and are not exhaustive. The common feature is that several things may be going on at once in the system we are building; several objects may be computing at the same time, several messages may be sent at the same time.

In fact developers often have to consider concurrency even when each application they design is single-threaded. If several applications are running at the same time on different processors (perhaps on different networked machines), we have multiple flows of control. External systems that are represented as actors often have their own flows of control (and of course human actors always do!). The concurrency just becomes more obvious when the system being designed consists of several interacting applications.

Concurrent systems are often confused with real-time systems, because real-time systems are often concurrent and vice versa. However, the concepts are quite different and do not always occur together: a single-threaded system can be a real-time system, and a concurrent system need not be.

Q: Give examples of a single-threaded non-real-time system; a concurrent non-real-time system; a single-threaded real-time system; a concurrent real-time system. (You may need to use a broad definition of system.)

Q: (Particularly relevant if you're using Java.) Do you have facilities available to write multi-threaded code? Investigate how this can be done, and write small sample programs.

> **Discussion Question 75**
> In what ways can several single-threaded applications interact?

It is beyond the scope of this book to consider concurrent application design in depth. In the rest of this chapter we will try to give just a flavor of the considerations that arise.

10.2.1   Modeling several threads of control

There are (at least) three ways a new thread of execution can start up:

1. A single existing thread can be split into several threads. That is, an object which is computing (e.g. because it just received a message) can send two messages concurrently. This can be shown on a sequence diagram as two message arrows leaving the same point – like the alternatives of conditional message sending described above, but without the restriction that the conditions have to be mutually exclusive.

   On a collaboration diagram we use the messages' sequence numbers to show which messages are concurrent. Recall from Chapter 9 that numbers are used to represent sequential messages in the same activation, and if there are several nested activations – caused by messages that have been sent but not yet replied to – there will be several numbers separated by dots, with the first activation on the left and the most recent activation on the right. For example, message 2.13.4 is sent from the activation that was caused by message 2.13, after message 2.13.3. (In fact in a procedural system, message 2.13.4 can't be sent until after the *reply* to message 2.13.3 has been received – if there are messages 2.13.3.1, etc., they all have to have completed too before we can go on to message 2.13.4.) The change when we consider concurrent systems is that we can use names (strings of letters) instead of numbers, to show messages which are sent concurrently. For example, messages 2.13.A and 2.13.B are both sent concurrently within the activation caused by message 2.13.

   Q: Draw a sequence diagram in which messages with the following sequence numbers appear (they won't be in this order, and you will need some other messages too): 2.B.2, 1, 2.A.

   Discussion Question 76
   Is this numbering sequence enough? Can you illustrate a sensible sequence of messages that can't be numbered using this scheme?

2. An actor, or an *active object*, can send a message 'on its own initiative' without necessarily having received a message itself first, while there is already computation going on somewhere else. This is in fact almost the definition of an active object: an active object is one that owns its own thread of control. Indeed, the canonical examples of active objects are objects that represent processes or threads. An active object is shown in UML just like any other object except that it has a heavy border.

   Q: Does your programming language support active objects? What classes can active objects have?

   The decision of how to assign concurrent processes to different processors is recorded in UML *deployment diagrams*, which are described in Chapter 13. The decision is likely to be made at an early stage of a project, as part of deciding its architecture.

3. An object can send an *asynchronous* message to another object – that is, it can cause another object to start computing without having to stop computing itself. This is harder to describe using the thread metaphor – the sender splits its single thread into two, cuts one off and hands it over to the receiver of its message!

Interaction type	Symbol	Meaning
Synchronous or call	$\rightarrow\!\!\blacktriangleright$	The 'normal' procedural situation. The sender loses control until the receiver finishes handling the message, then gets control back, which can optionally be shown as a return arrow.
Return	$\leftarrow\!-$	Not a message, but a return from an earlier message. Unblocks a synchronous send.
Flat	$\rightarrow$	The message doesn't expect a reply; control passes from the sender to the receiver, so the next message (in this thread) will be sent by the receiver of this message.
Asynchronous	$\rightharpoonup$	The message doesn't expect a reply, but unlike the flat case, the sender stays active and may send further messages.

Figure 10.5 Variants of message sending in sequence diagrams.

In the latter two cases, the nested form of numbering may not be useful, because the execution is not nested: the objects are concurrent. You can use the straightforward numbering sequence 1, 2, ... instead.

UML has defined a small number of variants of simple message passing, to allow concurrent systems to be described. As with all aspects of UML, further variants may be added, by using stereotypes to extend the core language. In the rest of this chapter we look at the predefined variants and consider examples where they might have an effect. We list the variants in Figure 10.5.

WARNING

In Figure 10.5 we show what UML describes, but in fact conventions differ so you may see variants.

Not all the messages in an application have to be of the same type. Some objects may be interacting synchronously, i.e. as non-concurrent parts of a single component, while messages between other objects may be asynchronous. This might happen, for example, when some messages are being sent to a separate, independently executing component.

For our example we consider again the student registration system developed in Chapter 15. Suppose that the use case `Register for modules` (slightly more sophisticated than anything discussed in the chapter) is as follows. This use case assumes that each `CS4DirectorOfStudies` (each director of studies of a CS4 student, as actor: we write DoS for short) has pre-approved certain module combinations, possibly on a per-student basis. For example, the most standard combinations might be pre-approved for all students, and a particular non-standard combination might be approved for a particular student, after the student has discussed the choice with the DoS. You might model this by a use case `Approve combinations` with the DoS as actor.

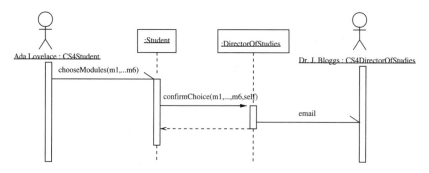

Figure 10.6 Asynchronous message-passing.

Register for modules The student visits a Web page and chooses a selection of modules. On confirmation, the system records these choices. Not necessarily immediately, the system does one of three possible things:

1. If the combination is pre-approved for this student, sends a confirmatory email to the student and records that student on the modules named.
2. If the choices are not pre-approved for this student, but are legal according to university regulations, sends email to the student's director of studies. The system's responsibilities end here: the DoS will contact the student, and may approve the choice using use case `Approve combinations`.
3. If the choices are illegal according to university regulations, sends email explaining the problem to the student.

Q: If you are familiar with Web programming, consider how such a system might be implemented, and write a more detailed (use case?) description making clear your high level decisions, for example which parts of the system are in what language and run where. What are the advantages and disadvantages of your description, compared with the one above? Do you think it appropriate for a use case description to include the extra information? Why?

Figure 10.6 shows one possible realization of the scenario of this use case described as 2. We use asynchronous messages between system objects and actors to represent both the student submitting course choices and the email message sent by the system.

Q: Could we have used flat messages instead of asynchronous ones?

Q: Develop realizations of the other scenarios in this use case. (You will need to read Chapter 15 first.)

Discussion Question 77
Would it ever be useful to use these features of interaction diagrams even if the final system was to be single threaded?

SUMMARY

This chapter covered two more advanced aspects of UML interaction diagrams. First we discussed generic interaction diagrams, which allow us to show more than one scenario on a diagram, by permitting the expression of conditional and iterated message passing. Then we very briefly introduced some features suitable for modeling concurrent systems.

CHAPTER 11

Essentials of state and activity diagrams

So far we have described:

- how to describe the requirements of a system using use cases
- how to model the static structure of a system – including what classes there are and what messages objects of those classes accept – using a class model
- how to model how objects interact to satisfy the requirements – by describing the messages that pass between them – using interaction diagrams.

We haven't discussed, though, how to model an object's 'decision' about what to do when it receives a message. Two interaction diagrams may show objects of the same class receiving the same message, but responding differently. This is often reasonable, because an object's behavior may be affected by the values of its attributes. In order to implement, maintain or test the class, we need to understand what the dependencies are between the *state* of an object and its reactions to messages, or other events. As we shall see in this chapter, UML's *state diagrams* (or statecharts, or statechart diagrams) record these dependencies in a convenient way. In this chapter we will consider the commonest use of state diagrams, namely to show how an object reacts to receiving a message by sending messages.

With a little lateral thinking, we shall be able to use much of the same notation to describe complex activities. The idea is that moving on from one (sub)activity to the next when the first activity is completed is rather like an object moving from one state to a significantly different one when it receives a message. We shall see that *activity diagrams*, which are a variant on state diagrams adapted to show the connections and dependencies between activities, can be an aid to understanding complex activities. Sometimes there is a choice between using an activity diagram and using an interaction diagram; we will discuss the choice.

11.1   State diagrams

Let us start with a very simple example in which an object receives a message and what it does depends on the values of its attributes and links.[1] In our library system an object of class `Copy` may have a boolean attribute `onShelf`, which is intended to record whether the object describes a copy of a book which is currently in the library, or one which is currently on loan. The interface of class `Copy` specifies that the object should be willing to accept the message `borrow()`. This is intended to inform the `Copy` object that the real-world copy has just been borrowed from the library. This message *should* only arrive when the object's `onShelf` attribute is `true` – if the real-world copy is being borrowed, it must have been in the library! The `Copy` object's reaction should be to set its `onShelf` attribute to `false` (keeping itself in step with the aspect of the real world it is supposed to describe), and to send a message to its associated `Book` object to inform it, in turn, that this copy has just been borrowed.

What should happen if the `borrow()` message arrives when the `onShelf` attribute is `false`? This means that something has gone seriously wrong – the state of the system does not correctly describe the state of the real world – so it would not be appropriate for the `Copy` object's reaction to ignore the problem. Instead it should somehow signal an error, perhaps by writing an error message to a log.

The value of the copy's attribute `onShelf` is important for understanding the behavior of the object, at the level of what messages it sends after receiving a message itself. We can name the two significantly different *states* of a `Copy` object `on the shelf` and `on loan` and record the messages that cause it to move between the states as the *events* that cause *transitions* between states, as shown in Figure 11.1. (We haven't shown what the object should do if it receives an unexpected message; this is discussed in subsection 11.1.1.)

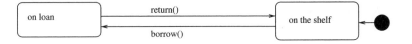

Figure 11.1   State diagram of class `Copy`.

The black blob with an arrow into the `on the shelf` state is a *start marker*. It means that when a new object of class `Copy` is created, it starts off in state `on the shelf`. Start markers are optional. It's useful to show them when objects of the class are always started in one state. For example, this is the case if objects of a class are always created with the same default values of their attributes. However, often objects are created with values of their attributes given as part of the create instruction (arguments to a constructor, for example). In that case, the initial state of the object varies depending on how it is created, so no start marker should be shown.

Q: (Why) is it reasonable to suppose that a `Copy` object is always created in the `on the shelf` state, that is, with `onShelf` true?

---

[1] By 'what it does' we mean what messages it sends, not just what arguments or return values it chooses: we may say its behavior depends *qualitatively* on the values of its attributes and links.

Q: How are the initial values of the attributes of an object set in your programming language? For example, can the class definition specify default values? If so, can you still choose to override the defaults when you create an object?

Discussion Question 78

Consider the alternative of having just a single message, say `borrowOrReturn`, in response to which a `Copy` object toggles the value of `onShelf`. What are the consequences of such a design change?

11.1.1 Unexpected messages

In Figure 11.1 we have not shown arrows to represent the receipt of message `borrow()` in state on loan or the message `return()` in state on the shelf. Under normal circumstances, such messages should not arrive: if they do, it's a bug. However, the class defines the interface that an object of class `Copy` must satisfy, and this interface contracts a `Copy` object to accept messages `borrow()` and `return()`. So the code of class `Copy` will have to do something if these 'wrong' messages do arrive, like report an error in a certain way. The decision about what should happen in unexpected circumstances like these is an *architectural decision* which should be made and documented once, so that we do not have to record separately what happens on any such event. A common solution is to have a single, globally accessible object of a class `Error`, whose sole responsibility is to report errors. Any object which receives a message it was not expecting sends a message to the error object describing what happened. We are using the convention that if a state diagram does not show how a message is handled in a particular state, it means that the message should never arrive when the object is in that state. We show error handling messages only if something special is required in this particular case.

TECHNICAL UML NOTE

In fact our convention is a departure from UML, which specifies that an event, such as the arrival of a message, that does not trigger a transition is simply ignored. This will be important when we consider other kinds of events in Chapter 12. Our convention is commonly used in practice, because it is very convenient, but it applies only to the arrival of messages that are in an object's interface.

Discussion Question 79

How else might unexpected messages be dealt with? What are the advantages and disadvantages of the approaches you consider?

11.1.2 Level of abstraction

The state diagram for `Copy` showed only two states, although there are presumably many different possible settings of the attributes of a `Copy` object. (We have not defined the attributes of class `Copy` completely, but probably it has some kind of library number, some record of which book it's a copy of, and possibly more.) This is because most of the different settings of the attributes are equivalent as far as our current concerns go: the behavior of a Copy object does not significantly depend on which Book it's a copy of, for example. What is significant may depend on what aspect of the system you're interested in. However, in the final implementation, the values of an object's attributes determine which state of the state diagram it is in. In fact, the state of the object also depends, in principle, on the objects it is linked to and *their* attributes and so on ... However, systems in which two objects with the same attribute values could be in different states of a state diagram tend to be hard to understand and maintain. Given the values of all the object's attributes, you should be able to identify exactly one state on the state diagram which the object must be in. It is sometimes helpful to record the range of attribute values that a state covers in the state diagram. For example, we could add the *constraint* {onShelf = true} to the on the shelf state of the state diagram, and {onShelf = false} to the on loan state. Exactly one of these constraints should always be true. This is overkill in our simple example, but is useful when a more complex combination of attributes determines the state in a state diagram.

Q: What is the smallest number of states that there could be in a correct state diagram for class Copy? Can you say anything about the largest number of states? Consider drawing state diagrams with (a) the smallest possible number of states, (b) some number of states larger than two. Are you convinced that the diagram with two states is more useful?

> **Discussion Question 80**
> (After reading Chapter 6.) What difference does it make if the class has a class invariant?

11.1.3   States, transitions, events

Figure 11.1 demonstrates the most important elements of a state diagram, namely:

- **states** shown as boxes with rounded corners
- **transitions** between states, shown as arrows
- **events** that cause transitions between states. So far we've only considered the most common kind of event, namely the receipt of a message. This is shown just by writing the message (including the names of its arguments, if any) on the transition arrow
- **start marker** shown as a black blob with an (unlabeled) arrow into the initial state of the diagram.

It will not surprise you to know that a state diagram can also show a *stop marker*. This is a black blob with a ring round it, and means that the object has reached the end of its life, and will be destroyed. There can be several stop markers in one diagram, or none.

Q: What's the difference in meaning between a state with no outgoing transitions at all, and one with an arrow into a stop marker?

Figure 11.2 State diagram of class Copy, with actions.

11.1.4 Actions

We said that state diagrams were useful for understanding how an object's reaction to a message depends on its state; for example, we want to show what messages it sends. An object sending a message in response to being sent one itself is an example of an *action* being an object's reaction to an *event*.

> An event is something done to the object, such as it being sent a message. An action is something that the object does, such as it sending a message.

We can show the action after the event on the transition, separating the two by a slash. Figure 11.2 shows the Copy object sending messages borrowed(self) and returned(self) to its associated Book object, as part of its reaction to receiving the borrow() and return() messages.

Analyzing the notation: the slash (/) shows that what follows is an action. book followed by a dot identifies the object to which a message is being sent: we are assuming that the Copy class includes an attribute book to implement the association between Copy and Book shown in the class diagram of Figure 3.5. Finally returned(self) is an example of a message including a parameter; in this case, the message returned expects an argument which is an object of class Copy, to say which copy has just been returned, and in this case the Copy object sends itself (more precisely, in most languages, a reference to itself).

> **Discussion Question 81**
> In Chapter 5 we said that it is not useful to show attributes of a class whose sole purpose is to implement the associations shown in the class diagram: this violates the WRITE ONCE rule which states that wherever possible, you should avoid recording information twice if that means you have to keep the versions consistent (see Chapter 2). Yet here we needed some way to refer to the Book object associated with the Copy object. Do you think our decision to invent an attribute book of Copy for the purpose was reasonable? Should we now update our class model to show this attribute? What are the options, and what are their pros and cons?

Writing an action on a transition is a convenient thing to do in this case. However, suppose you have several different ways of entering the same state (which is perfectly legal, indeed quite common) and that the same action should happen when you enter the state, regardless of what transition is happening. You could show the action on each of several transitions, but this is both tedious and error prone – it violates the WRITE ONCE rule, again. Instead, we can show our intention directly, by writing the action inside the state, as a reaction to the special event entry. There is implicitly an entry event every time the object enters a state, though we don't show or consider these events unless we want to associate actions

Figure 11.3   State diagram of class `Copy`, with `entry` actions.

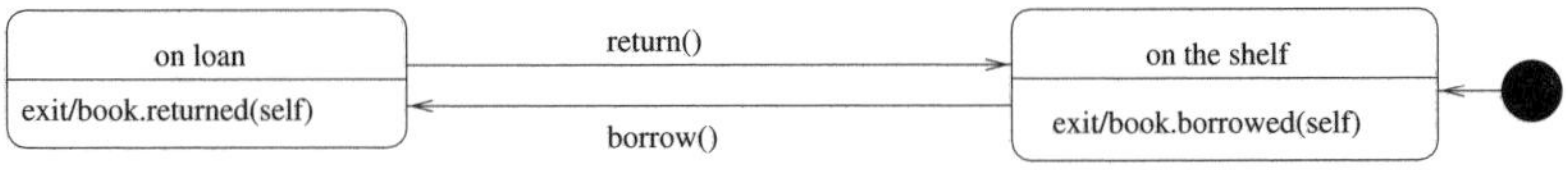

Figure 11.4   State diagram of class `Copy`, with `exit` actions.

with them. Similarly, we can show actions which should happen whenever a given state is left by associating the action with an `exit` event in a state. Figure 11.3 shows the use of an entry event; Figure 11.4 shows the use of an exit event. Both of these diagrams mean exactly the same as Figure 11.2! You can use any combination of these actions.

Q: In what order do you think the actions `foo()`, `bar()` and `baz()` will be executed in Figure 11.5?

Q: Draw some more state diagrams for `Copy` with the same meaning as those above.

> **Discussion Question 82**
> Even though Figures 11.2, 11.3 and 11.4 mean the same, there are various reasons why you might prefer one form. Consider maintenance, for example. What do you think?

In fact this use of entry and exit events shown inside a state is a special case of more general notation, which we shall return to in the next chapter.

11.1.5   Guards

Sometimes the occurrence of the same event in the same state may or may not cause a change of state, depending on the exact values of the object's attributes. (That is, we need to care about more detail than just what state of the state diagram the object is in.) We can show this using the same conditional notation that is used in generic interaction diagrams (Chapter 10).

To illustrate this, let us return to the example of the state diagram of class `Book`, which we first showed in Chapter 3. `Book` objects have a slightly more interesting state than `Copy`

Figure 11.5   Several actions in one diagram.

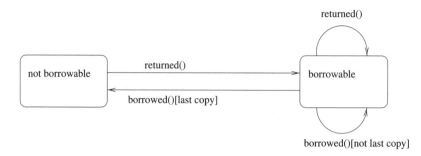

Figure 11.6 State diagram for class Book.

objects, because there can be many copies of each book, and a Book object is borrowable provided that there is *at least one* copy on the shelf. Therefore the borrowed() message causes a state change out of state borrowable only if this is the last copy on the shelf; otherwise, the Book object remains borrowable. Figure 11.6 illustrates this using the two (mutually exclusive) conditions [last copy] and [not last copy]. As in interaction diagrams, a condition can be expressed in careful English, in a programming language, in OCL, or any other convenient notation the project may decide on.

Since the reverse state transition, where a returned() message is received in the not borrowable state, is unguarded, such an event will always cause the Book to change to the borrowable state, as we'd expect.

Figure 11.6 also illustrates that a transition can lead from a state back to the same state. We need to be able to show such transitions if we follow the convention we mentioned earlier, that the absence of a transition showing the arrival of some message indicates that it's an error for that message to arrive. If we omitted the self-transitions in the example, our convention would mean, for example, that it was an error for someone to return a copy of a book when there was already a copy of the same book on the shelf!

Q: Why are there no guards on the returned event?

Discussion Question 83
Why can we not just add an extra state to show a Book with one copy remaining and so avoid using guards? If you cannot see a reason, try drawing the state diagram that would result.

In the next chapter we will see further state diagram notation; for example, UML can show nested state diagrams and diagrams in which several things happen concurrently.

PANEL 11.1 Designing classes with state diagrams

The state diagram of a class should be as simple as possible. The more the behavior of an object depends on its state, the harder it is to understand. Classes with complex state diagrams cause several related problems.

First, it is harder to write the code for such a class correctly; the method implementations end up having many conditional sections.

Secondly, it is harder to test the class. We shall return to this topic in Chapter 19: you might like to think now about how you would test the Book class, and about how the tests required relate to the state diagram. (It's worth remembering that there is often a choice about how much detail to show in a state diagram. Of course, showing less detail for the same class does not really reduce the number of tests required, though it may reduce the number you know you need!)

Thirdly and most importantly, it is much harder for external code to use a class correctly if the behavior of the class depends on its state in a complex way. For example, the client has to make sure that it does not send a message to an object when the object is in a state where that message causes an error. Either the external client has to somehow keep track of what has been done to the object, so that it can work out what state the object will be in, or it has to query the object about its state before it sends the message. In the first case, to be confident about the correctness of the whole system you have to convince yourself that the client is always correct in its assumptions about the state of the object. The second case may be safer, but it also results in extra querying messages being sent, which is more to understand and get right, and also takes time.

Q: What is the relationship between the state of a Book object and the states of the associated Copy objects?

So if you have a class with many states, it is worth considering whether there are better designs. Sometimes a single class with many states can usefully be split into two or more classes with simpler behavior. For example, instead of a single Copy class with two states, we could consider having two classes, say CopyOnShelf and CopyOnLoan. Then instead of state changes we'd have creation and deletion of objects of these new classes. Whether this is an improvement depends on the circumstances, and in particular on whether the smaller classes seem like good classes in their own right or not. If it seems natural to think of the state change as being a case of an object of one of the candidate new classes *changing into* an object of another candidate new class, the splitting is likely to be good design. If this seems unnatural, it is less likely to be helpful.

> **Discussion Question 84**
> Consider in detail the changes that would be necessary if we split the class Copy as described above. Do you think this would be an improvement, or not?

> **Discussion Question 85**
> Another major factor in making this kind of decision is how often the change of state or class is likely to be needed. Why is this important?

Discussion Question 86

Consider the CS4 Administration System described in Chapter 15. Instead of the two classes `Lecturer` and `DirectorOfStudies`, we could have had a single class `Lecturer` with an attribute `isDirectorOfStudies`. Consider what difference this would make, and whether you think it would be an improvement.

Discussion Question 87

Many people (Clemens Szyperski in [45], for example) say that a *component* should not have any persistent state, so in particular its state diagram should have just one state. Why is this?

11.2   Activity diagrams

Activity diagrams describe how activities are co-ordinated. For example, an activity diagram may be used (like an interaction diagram) to show how an operation could be implemented. An activity diagram is particularly useful when you know that an operation has to achieve a number of different things, and you want to model what the essential dependencies between them are, before you decide in what order to do them. Activity diagrams are much better at showing this clearly than interaction diagrams.

Activity diagrams are also useful for describing how individual use cases unfold and may depend on other use cases. Often the use cases that you uncover happen not in arbitrary orders but as part of the overall *workflow* of an area of the customer's activities. For example, sometimes the updating of data as part of one use case must be finished before another use case, which reads that data, can be started. The two may represent separate tasks, so that it is sensible for them to be separate use cases, but not to be independent.

In both cases, activity diagrams record the dependencies between activities, such as which things can happen in parallel and what must be finished before something else can start. As this suggests, the fundamental block in an activity diagram is an *activity*, and a transition out of an activity normally means that the activity has been completed.

TECHNICAL UML NOTE

At the UML semantics level, activity diagrams are state diagrams extended for convenience with some extra notation, though this extra notation means they can look quite different.

We remark that although activity diagrams can be useful for modeling workflow, there is a lot more to business modeling than this. There are some extensions of UML for business modeling; but UML has been criticized for being weak in this area.

Elements of activity diagrams

- **activity** is shown as a named box with flat top and bottom and rounded sides. Technically this is a sort of state which is left, not in response to some event arriving from outside, but when the activity it represents is finished. The activity can involve many steps, including waiting for events, though this detailed activity is not usually shown.

- **transition** is shown as an arrow, as in a state diagram. Transitions in an activity diagram are normally not labeled, because the transitions are caused by the completion of the previous activity (rather than by another kind of event) and it is normally more convenient to include actions in the activities rather than putting them separately on the transitions. However, there can be several outgoing transitions each with a guard, if the next activity depends on the situation.

- **synchronization bar** is a thick horizontal bar describing the co-ordination of activities. Once *all* the activities which have transitions leading into the bar are complete, the bar can be passed. At that point, all the transitions leading out of the bar are fired, so the activities to which those transitions lead are started in parallel. That is, the synchronization bar provides a way to express things like waiting for all subtasks to finish before proceeding (*join*), and starting several subtasks in parallel (*fork*).

- **decision diamond** is used to show decisions, as an alternative to guards on separate transitions leaving the same state.

- **start and stop markers** are used as in state diagrams.

The main differences between activity diagrams and state diagrams, apart from the extra notation just described, are that

- activity diagrams do not normally include events, because the only events of interest are the completions of the subactivities, which don't have to be shown explicitly;

- activity is intended to proceed, following the flow described by the diagram, without getting stuck. So, for example, if there are guards on transitions out of an activity, normally exactly one of them should be satisfied. This isn't a universal rule: sometimes you might want a final step of activity in some circumstances but not others, in which case it might be correct to have non-exhaustive guards, that is, for it sometimes to be the case that no guard is satisfied. However, if you use a decision diamond rather than just guards, then UML says the options must be exhaustive.

   This is different in spirit from state diagrams, where it's often perfectly acceptable for an object never to reach some of its potential states: there's no implied 'correct sequence' of states.

   Figure 11.7 shows the workflow in the library from Chapter 3 as an activity diagram. This does not describe how the library information system works: it describes the human interaction into which the system must fit. Understanding this kind of business context should help you to develop a genuinely useful and usable system; you may sometimes find it helpful to develop diagrams like this one to clarify your understanding. We use the synchronization bar to show the start and end of a concurrent activity, where the librarian submits a borrow request to the system and returns the book to the shelf.[2] We see the

---

[2] Actually this is a loose use of 'concurrent', but one that's common in UML. Probably the librarian cannot do these two activities at the same time: what we mean is that it doesn't matter what order they happen in.

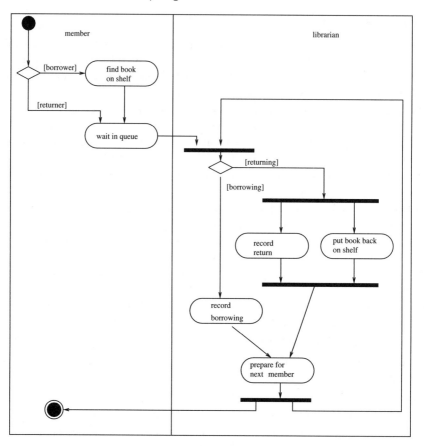

Figure 11.7 Business level activity diagram of the library.

merging of a customer's activities with those of the librarian and the end of this phase when the customer completes and the librarian returns to service the next customer. The diagram also illustrates the use of decisions to show branching of behavior.

Q: Redraw Figure 11.7 to show an activity when the librarian stamps a borrowed book. Should this be concurrent with an existing activity?

Q: Redraw Figure 11.7 to show the detailed activities within the library system itself.

Partitions and swimlanes An activity diagram may contain several groups of related activities. They may be related according to which objects or actors perform them, which use cases they form part of, or any other basis that appears useful. Illustrating this can be achieved by splitting the diagram into partitions, known as *swimlanes*, which group the activities accordingly.

Figure 11.7 has partitioned the library into actions performed solely by customers and those involving the librarian.

Q: Redraw Figure 11.7 to show activities partitioned in correspondence with the use cases in Chapter 3.

Q: Draw an activity diagram to represent the operation `borrow` on a `LibraryMember` object (described as a sequence diagram by Figure 3.6). Show things happening in sequence only when they must.

SUMMARY

We described how to use state diagrams to model the way that significant changes in an object's attributes affect the way it reacts to events, such as messages. We emphasized that, although if an object has such complex behavior it can be useful to show it in a state diagram, it is better to avoid designing classes with complex state-based behavior where possible. We also discussed activity diagrams, which model the dependencies between activities, such as the operations involved in the realization of a use case, or the use cases of a system.

CHAPTER 12

More on state and activity diagrams

This chapter considers some less usual, but sometimes useful, features of UML state and activity diagrams. We will consider

- how to show events and actions, other than message-passing, in state diagrams
- compound states, where a single state of a state diagram has a fine structure which we want to show
- concurrent compound states, where several state machines execute independently; this is useful for modeling concurrent systems.

12.1 Other kinds of events

UML classifies the events that may cause a state transition like this:

- **Call event**: the receipt of a message requesting that an operation be performed. This is the commonest case, which we considered in Chapter 11. As we saw, the event includes the parameters to the message, as well as its selector.
- **Change event**: occurs when a condition changes from false to true. A change event is written as the keyword when followed by an expression describing the condition, written in parentheses, e.g. when(X=10). A change event is useful to describe the situation in which an object changes state because it alters the value of its attributes after receiving a *reply* to a message that it sent, rather than as an immediate result of the object receiving a message. There is an example of this in Chapter 16, where a CurrentPosition object sends a message to a Game object, the reply to which will be used as the new value of the CurrentPosition's toMove attribute, which says which player's turn it is next. Depending on this new value, CurrentPosition may or may not make a state transition. We model this with the event when(toMove = A).
- **Signal event**: the receipt of a *signal*. Like a call event, a signal event may have parameters enclosed in parentheses. A signal must be defined as a special kind of class, with the

keyword ≪signal≫ before its name, no operations and the signals parameters in the attributes compartment. Signals may be related to each other by generalization, but must not be related to normal classes.

- **Time event**: in general an expression denoting a length of time which must elapse after a named event, but most often written, using the keyword after, relative to the time at which the current state was entered, e.g. after(0.5 seconds).

12.2 Other kinds of actions

We have seen that state diagrams can show messages which an object sends in reaction to an event. In fact, UML allows a much more general notion of actions. Figure 12.1 shows a possible state diagram for class Average of the simulation system described in Chapter 17. An Average object waits for update messages from the simulation objects in a model. Such a message sends a new value, which must be added to the current total held in the attribute sum. The number of updates received so far, held in the attribute observations, must also be incremented. There are several points to notice:

1. As usual, UML does not prescribe the syntax of the actions; you will probably find it convenient to write them in English, pseudocode or the target programming language. They must not, of course, refer to anything that the object cannot reasonably be considered to know about. They can sensibly refer to attributes, operations and links of the object, and to any parameters on the message that triggered the transition.

2. An *action sequence* is shown by separating the actions with slashes. The actions are executed from left to right (although in this case that doesn't matter).

3. We have shown update(val: Real) as an *internal event*, by writing it inside the box (as we did with the special events entry and exit, in Chapter 11). The difference between this and a self-transition shown as an arrow from the state to itself is that when we write the event inside the state, the entry and exit events of the state are not triggered. The idea is that showing an arrow from the state to itself corresponds to the object first leaving the state (so the exit event occurs) and then re-entering the same state (so the entry event occurs). Showing the event inside the state avoids causing entry and exit events to happen.

4. Occasionally one-state diagrams like this are a convenient way to show how the object reacts to events. Even the name compartment of a state is optional: since there is only one state we haven't named it here.

Q: Represent the same information on a diagram designed for clarity, rather than to demonstrate as many points about UML as possible!

> **Discussion Question 88**
> Reconsider the Book class in the library example. How could it show more information? Do you think this would be useful?

Q: Draw a state diagram for a Copy in the library where, if it is not returned within three weeks, it becomes overdue. (You will need to make appropriate changes to the class definitions.)

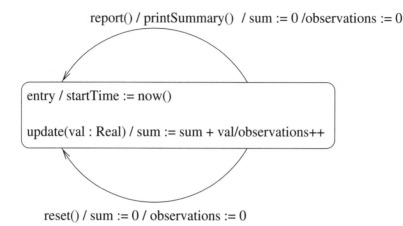

report() / printSummary()   / sum := 0 /observations := 0

entry / startTime := now()

update(val : Real) / sum := sum + val/observations++

reset() / sum := 0 / observations := 0

Figure 12.1   State diagram for class `Average`: not good style!

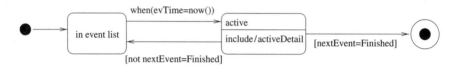

Figure 12.2   State diagram for class `Customer`.

12.3   Looking inside states

So far we have considered states as single entities, without internal structure. Occasionally it is useful to consider a state as containing an internal behavior which can itself be represented as a state diagram. Such states are referred to as *compound* states.

Strictly speaking, we have already considered such compound states, when we looked at the way that internal events are handled. An internal event and its resulting action sequence is implicitly a single transition within an internal (nested) state machine.

Figure 12.2 shows the high level state diagram of a `Customer`, which is being modeled as an `ActiveEntity` in the simulation model of a simple queue for service, using the discrete event simulation package described in Chapter 17. The `Customer` object is either active or in the event list, waiting for its next chance to be active. The line `include/activeDetail` in the `active` state shows that `active` is a compound state: there is a detailed state diagram called `activeDetail` nested in the active state. Figure 12.3 shows this nested state diagram. The start and end markers are compulsory for compound states, although they are optional for simple states. The reason is that we need to know where to start the internal state machine, and to know when it has terminated. When the compound state is reached by an outside transition, its start state is entered. When its internal state diagram reaches its end state, there is an implicit 'completion' event. This doesn't have a name, so transitions out of a state with a nested state machine may be unlabeled, like transitions out of activities in activity diagrams. As in activity diagrams, there can be several transitions

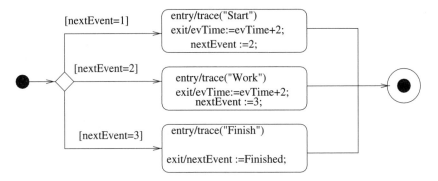

Figure 12.3 Nested state diagram `activeDetail` for class `Customer`'s `active` state.

each with a guard; at most one of the guards should evaluate to true.

Figure 12.3 shows that the `Customer` enters one of three internal states depending on the current value of the attribute `nextEvent`. These substates represent

1. waiting to join the queue,
2. waiting in the queue for service,
3. waiting for service to be completed once it reaches the server.

In all cases this simply means setting a value for `evTime` indicating the duration of the activity, and setting an appropriate value for `nextEvent`.

> **Discussion Question 89**
> In fact Figure 12.3 shows a rather degenerate state diagram. Why? How else could you model this behavior?

12.4 Concurrency within states

In Chapter 11 we saw that activity diagrams can express several activities happening at once, using synchronization bars to express the forking and joining of subtasks. In fact state diagrams can use this notation too, to show forking and merging of concurrent sub-machines. It is also possible to draw a nested state where the internal behavior is made up of independently executing regions. Regions are separated by dashed lines, as in Figure 12.4. Each region has its own start state and end state.

Q: In our example there are no transitions from a state in one concurrent region to a state in another. Do you think such a transition would ever be reasonable? If so, develop an example and decide what it means.

The two state diagrams in this example are equivalent, showing how entry into a state with internal concurrency reaches the start state of all its regions simultaneously and how transitions leaving the state fire only when all regions have reached their end state.

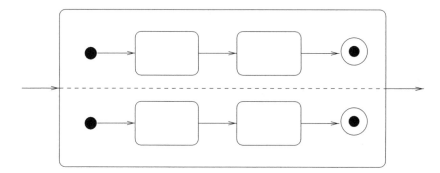

(a) State with internal concurrency

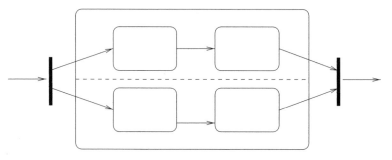

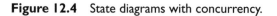

(b) Equivalent state with external synchronization

Figure 12.4 State diagrams with concurrency.

SUMMARY

In this chapter we considered some further features of UML state and activity diagrams. We considered events and actions more general than the message-passing examples in Chapter 11, and went on to consider state diagrams with compound states, with or without concurrency.

CHAPTER 13

Implementation diagrams

Most of the discussion in this book has centered on how to analyze problems and design solutions using object oriented techniques. We have touched on the small scale issues about how the design is turned into code, but we have not considered the overall architecture of the application to be produced, although we said in Part I that such decisions were important. In this chapter we begin to remedy the deficiency.

Q: Are you convinced that we have covered all interesting aspects of the small scale issues?

Given a suitable CASE tool, it is possible to generate code directly from detailed UML models. The tool generates the outline of the code – class definitions, for example, but not usually the implementation of the methods – and you fill in the details.

The implemented system has to run on hardware, meeting its non-functional requirements such as performance and scalability. UML defines two models which describe how your system is implemented. The *component model* shows the dependencies between parts of the code: it is primarily of interest to designers and maintainers of the system, and forms part of the *development view*. The *deployment model* shows the structure of the runtime system: which parts run on which processors and how the hardware is configured to provide necessary resources. It contributes to both the *physical view* and the *process view*.

13.1 Component model

> **WARNING**
>
> As we remarked in Chapter 1, the word 'component' has many meanings. The UML documentation explains what is meant by a component (strictly, component type) in the context of a component diagram: 'a distributable piece of implementation of a system, including software code (source, binary or executable) but also including business documents, etc., in a human system' [49]. In this chapter *only* we will use this definition. Notice that there is no mention in this definition of a component being replaceable or reusable.
>
> Panel 18.1 discusses the various definitions of 'component' but the main point is that you have to know which definition someone is using.

The key word here is *implementation*. So far, all the model elements we have considered have been design constructs, although this is obscured by the fact that we normally use words like 'object' and 'class' throughout the development, whether we are talking about design or about implementation. The design construct that usually corresponds to a component in the sense used in this chapter is a *subsystem*. A subsystem gives a specification (for example, in terms of use cases) and a class structure that realizes the specification. A component can sensibly be thought of as the implementation of a subsystem. We will discuss subsystems in the next chapter. In fact UML does not force components and subsystems to correspond like this, but it is usually good practice for them to do so.

Components are shown as rectangles with two smaller rectangles sticking out, as shown in Figure 13.1. Components may depend on one another; dependencies between components are shown using dashed dependency arrows, which we have already seen used between classes in Chapter 6.

There are various common kinds of components, each with a corresponding common kind of dependency. Classifying them in relation to the compilation process, for example, a component may be:

- source code (e.g. a file containing the code of a class), which depends on any components (not necessarily source code themselves) which have to be available when it is *compiled*
- binary object code (e.g. a class library), which depends on any object code with which it must be *linked* to form an executable program
- an executable application (e.g. the client or server in a client–server application, a bought-in spreadsheet or a database manager) which may depend on other executable programs to interact with it at runtime.

The details are dependent on the programming language being used; you can define stereotypes like ≪compile≫ and ≪link≫ to distinguish between dependency arrows that represent different kinds of dependency. Similarly, you can define any stereotypes that seem useful to distinguish between kinds of components. UML predefines a few: ≪file≫, ≪library≫, ≪executable≫, ≪table≫ (for a database table) and ≪document≫.

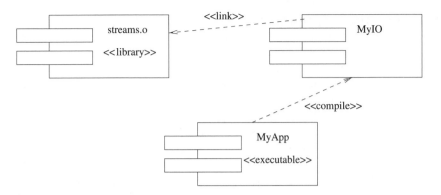

Figure 13.1   A component diagram showing compile time dependencies.

Q: Consider how a makefile expresses dependencies between files: what kinds of dependencies are there? (The answer is programming language dependent.)

Discussion Question 90
There is nothing in UML to prohibit mutual dependency – for example, two components each of which depends on the other. Can this happen in practice for the various kinds of dependency you have considered? What are the implications of it, e.g. for reuse?

Discussion Question 91
How would you classify a shell script? Does it matter?

Discussion Question 92
Under what circumstances, if any, might you want to show a document as a component on a component diagram?

A component, like a class, may realize an interface; that is, it may provide certain operations (see Section 6.2.1). We may show that a component realizes an interface by attaching a small labeled circle to the component symbol. In fact, this is the general UML symbol for interface, and can also be used with subsystems, which we discuss in the next chapter. In all cases, a dependency arrow can point to the interface circle, instead of to the body of the model element, to show that only the operations in the interface are being relied on (as shown in Figure 6.14 of Chapter 6).

Discussion Question 93
Might you want a more general notion of interface than just a collection of operations, for use with components? If so, consider some situations that might call for more general interfaces, and how you might model them in UML.

Component types, component instances Just to add further confusion, the word 'component' is used to mean both a component type and an instance of a component type. Component diagrams show component types, not instances of components. A component type is to a component instance as a class is to an object; however, the distinction can be harder to grasp in this context, because it is common for there to be only one instance of a given component type (at any one time). A component instance is a runtime unit. For example, the executable file containing an application may be represented as a component type, say `MyApplication`. The corresponding component instances are running instances of the application. It would make sense to have several copies running at once, say `a:` `MyApplication`, `b:` `MyApplication`, etc. A component diagram, which is concerned with the structure of the system as artifact, cares only about dependencies between implementation units: what may have to change if I change that bit? A deployment diagram, on the other hand, is not concerned with maintenance, but with particular running programs, their locations and their dependencies at runtime. Therefore a deployment diagram talks about component instances. As always, the name of a model element which is an instance is underlined: Panel 13.1 below for a summary of the classifier/instance distinctions we've seen.

PANEL 13.1 Summary: classifiers and instances

In UML classifiers describe collections of instances. The table defines the classifier/instance pairs we've seen (and will see).

Classifier	Instance
Class	Object
Use case	Scenario
Actor	Actor
Component	Component
Subsystem	Subsystem

Beware the cases where the same word is used for a classifier and for its instances! There is scope for confusion. If in doubt, use the phrases 'X type' and 'X instance' to distinguish.

UML treats all pairs consistently. In each case, the classifier and the instance are shown using the same icon: for example, a rectangle for both a class and an object, a stick person for an actor type and an actor instance. When an icon represents an instance, it is labeled with an underlined string like `instanceName:` `classifierName` (and `instanceName` may optionally be omitted, leaving the colon in place). When an icon represents a classifier, it is labeled just with the name of the classifier, which is not underlined.

The example in Figure 13.1 shows some compile time and link time dependencies for a C++ program which uses a component `MyIO` of specially written input/output functions. This in turn uses the standard language input/output library (here we assume it is the streams package in C++).

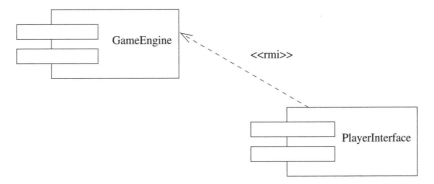

Figure 13.2 A component diagram showing runtime dependencies.

The example in Figure 13.2 illustrates runtime dependencies among components. It uses the example of a simple games package from Chapter 16. Here we assume that the game has been implemented as a client–server application, with the server being the `GameEngine` (including all the classes we talk about in Chapter 16) and the client being the player's interface (the user interface application, which we did not discuss). We have shown a user-defined stereotype on the dependency.

Q: What mechanisms are there in your programming language by which one executable component can use services provided by another?

13.2 Deployment model

The deployment diagram shows:

- the physical communication links between hardware items (machines and other re-sources, such as printers)
- the relationships between physical machines and processes: what runs where.

13.2.1 The physical layer

We start by considering the physical system, which consists of *nodes* with associations between them. A node may be a processor, capable of running software components, or some other device which provide services, such as a printer.[1] As always you can define stereotypes to distinguish between kinds of nodes if it seems useful to do so (see the panel in Chapter 6). Nodes, which represent individual physical things, have node types. For example, Figure 13.3 shows that the node `shillay` has type `Workstation`.

---

[1] UML says that a node usually has at least a memory, but some authors like to use nodes to model much simpler devices.

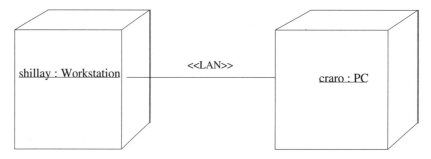

Figure 13.3 A deployment diagram without the software.

Discussion Question 94
Does it matter whether, to describe a kind of node, you use a stereotype or a node type?

Unbroken lines between nodes represent physical connections between machines. (Strictly speaking these are associations, like those in class diagrams, but associations between nodes have to be physical connections.) These may represent cables, local area networks, modems and phone lines or whatever. A link can be given a stereotype, so that it is clear on the diagram what sort of link we have.

Further details may be given as properties within a textual specification of the link or node. This might include a figure for processor power or a bandwidth for a link. Such details are often as important as the topology.

13.2.2 Deploying the software on the hardware

When we add the software components (Figure 13.4), we show how the system is to operate at runtime. Because we are now considering a particular system, the components in a deployment diagram are component *instances*: for example, a particular running instance of an executable application. We show a runtime component inside a node to represent that the component runs on the node. We can also show individual objects, either inside components or separately. As usual, the name of a component instance or an object is underlined, to show that the icon represents an instance, not a type.

Our example allocates two `PlayerInterface` components and a `GameEngine` component to the two machines shown in the previous diagram. The `GameEngine` and one `PlayerInterface` run on the Sun, while the other `PlayerInterface` runs on the PC.

Naturally, if two components are allocated to different nodes but have a runtime dependency between them, there must be a physical link between the nodes!

PANEL 13.2 The deployment model in the project

Although we have left implementation models late in the book, decisions about the structure of the system at this level are normally taken early in the project.

1. Your customer may have existing hardware which the system must use, or you may be developing for a particular market segment. Your system may need to communicate with existing systems, which may restrict what you can consider.

2. The non-functional requirements on the system may determine or influence your decisions about hardware, and low level software such as operating systems. For example, a hard real-time system will normally have to run under a special real-time operating system; a system providing access to mission-critical data might need to run on fault-tolerant hardware with a duplicated database. The performance of the system will be strongly affected by the deployment, and you will need to bear in mind the limitations of the chosen topology during the development. For example, in a client–server application your decisions about how to design the communication between client and server will be affected by the bandwidth available.

3. Decisions about hardware and operating systems are interrelated with decisions about programming languages, component libraries, etc.: you must be able to compile your code for your chosen environment!

4. In a short project, especially one that uses specialized hardware, you may need to order the hardware early in the project, in order not to delay delivery of the system while you wait for it.

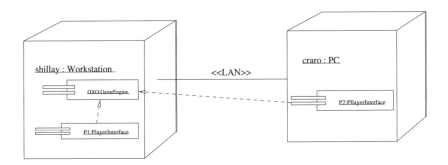

Figure 13.4 A deployment diagram with the software.

SUMMARY

We have considered the two kinds of UML implementation diagrams, component diagrams and deployment diagrams, and how to use them. Component diagrams express the structure of the implemented system, helping to keep track of dependencies to ease maintenance, and to record the reuse of components. Deployment diagrams show how the system is deployed on a particular hardware configuration. In the next chapter we will consider packages and subsystems, which are useful for recording how components are implemented.

CHAPTER 14

Packages, subsystems, models

In the previous chapter we considered the system seen as *components* which can have dependencies between them and can be deployed on hardware. In this chapter we discuss how components may be specified and designed as subsystems. A *subsystem* is a particular kind of *package*, and we will also review the other uses for packages.

UML's treatment of packages has changed between version 1.1 and version 1.3, and we warn that some aspects of UML described in this chapter are still controversial, and may possibly change in later versions of UML.

Remember that a *model element* is UML's general term for more or less anything that can be represented by a diagram element. For example, classes, use cases, actors, associations, generalizations, operations, packages, methods, etc., are all model elements.

14.1 Packages

A *package* is a collection of model elements. There are several reasons for wanting to package some model elements together.

- You may do so purely as a convenience, to hide some irrelevant details on a diagram. We have seen a package used in this way in Chapter 11, where we discussed packaging a subcollaboration, in order to simplify an interaction diagram by hiding irrelevant detail.

- You may do so in order to define the parts of a system to be implemented by each of several teams. A team may choose to represent the part of a system being implemented by another team as a package, which allows them to define the interactions of their bit with the rest of the system, without getting bogged down in detail about how the rest of the system works. As we shall see, the fact that packages provide namespace control is useful.

- You may want to specify and design a *component*, making sure you understand the interactions between the component and the context in which it is used.

(In both of the last two cases you will probably use a particular kind of package called a *subsystem*, which we'll describe below.)

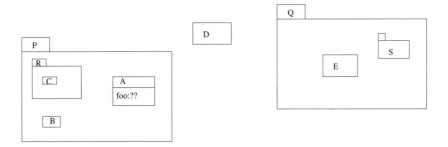

Figure 14.1   Packages and visibility example.

A package is shown on a diagram (any sort of diagram) as a rectangle with a 'tab' on its top edge. The elements contained by a package can be drawn inside the package symbol, but need not be. They usually aren't, since the amount of detail required to show all the contents of a package usually makes this inconvenient: indeed the main purpose of using a package is normally to be able to hide this detail. Instead, the interior of a package is usually drawn in a separate diagram. In a CASE tool this diagram might be hyper-linked to the package icon. It's convenient to write the name of the package on the tab if its contents are shown, and in the body of the package symbol otherwise. Figure 14.1 illustrates all this notation.

You can use package symbols in all kinds of diagrams. You can show dependencies, associations and other relationships between packages when you want to show that *some elements in* the packages take part in the relationship, but prefer to abstract away the information about exactly which elements are involved.

Packages can contain almost any model elements that you wish to group together. As Figure 14.1 shows, a package can even contain another package. The hierarchical view of the system that results can be useful in large systems. As an alternative to showing the hierarchy by including one package symbol in another, you can use a tree structure; see Figure 14.2.

TECHNICAL UML NOTE

However, an ordinary package cannot take part in an interaction, because it is not a Classifier: for example, there is no notion of a plain package having instances or understanding messages. When we showed a package representing a subcollaboration in Chapter 11, we were using the convenient, but purely notational, UML rule that you can draw relationships to a package when what you mean is that some element in the package takes part in the relationship. An alternative would have been to model the subcollaboration as a subsystem, which as we shall see is a special kind of package which is also a Classifier.

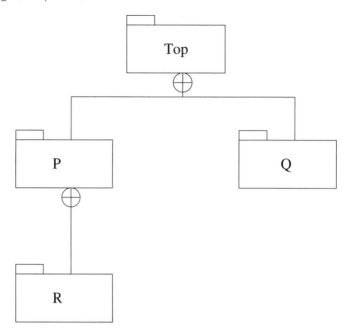

Figure 14.2 A hierarchy of packages.

14.1.1 Namespace control

A package has no real meaning of its own. All its behavior is provided by the model elements inside it, and it doesn't have an interface. The only thing it can do is to define the *namespace* of the elements inside it. The idea of a namespace is simply that within a given namespace, two different things can't have the same name. For example, you can't have two different classes both called Foo in the same namespace; you can't have a use case called Foo and also have a class called Foo, either. In a different namespace, however, another element can be called Foo without causing confusion. We can distinguish between the different things called Foo by specifying which namespace's Foo we mean. For example, a more precise name for the class A shown in Figure 14.1 is P::A, and a more precise name for class C is P::R::C.

The most familiar example of a namespace is a class. You would not expect to be able to have an operation and an attribute both called the same thing, and indeed you can't. There can, however, be operations in different classes both called by the same name, and this does not cause any confusion: if we need to identify which operation we're talking about, we just have to mention the class name to resolve the ambiguity. Package control of namespaces is a generalization of this idea.

This is useful when different teams are developing different parts of a system. It may well happen that two teams happen to use the same name for different purposes. We do not want to find that the UML model resulting from putting their bits together is illegal. If they develop different packages, they work in different namespaces, and such clashes don't invalidate the model. Implicitly, each model element has a 'full name' which is its name within its namespace (e.g. within its package) plus information about what namespace it's in (e.g. the full name of the smallest package that contains it).

Discussion Question 95

If you know a programming language with *overloading*, you might like to worry about a class which defines two methods with the same selector but different parameters. What might be going on?

Importing or accessing a package Every model element is in at most one[1] (most specific) namespace. In general, an element can name (know about) elements which are in its own package, and elements which are in surrounding packages. It can't, however, name elements from packages which don't contain its own. To see what this means, consider what the possible choices are for the class of attribute `foo` of class A in Figure 14.1. It would be legal for the attribute to have class B, because A and B are in the same package. D is also a legal choice, because D is in a package which contains A's package (there is always an implicit top level package, which in this case contains packages P and Q and class D). C is not a legal choice in UML, and neither is E, because these classes are not available in the namespace of A. To sum up:

Things outside a package can't see in.

If some element inside `P` needs to name something in a package (call it `Q`) that doesn't contain `P`, `P` must *import* or *access* `Q`, to make its elements visible inside `P`. For example, if we chose to make attribute `foo` have class `E`, we would have to add a dependency arrow (`---->`) from `P` to `Q` with stereotype ≪import≫ or ≪access≫. The difference between importing and accessing a package is in the way its elements can be referred to. If `P` imports package `Q`, elements of `P` can refer to elements of `Q` just as if they were in package `P`; for example, the class of attribute `foo` could be given just as `E`. If `P` only accesses `Q`, `P`'s elements must specify the package name as well as the element name. For example, the class of `foo` would be given as `Q::E`.

This may seem tedious, but it's a useful way to control dependencies. To name a thing is always to be dependent on it – if the name of a thing changes, everywhere that names it has to change – and if one part of a system is dependent on another we would like that to be explicit, so that changes in one place don't cause unexpected problems elsewhere. Package importing and accessing lets us record the high-level dependencies of parts of a system on one another, without getting overwhelmed by the detail of exactly what in one package depends on exactly what in another. It also allows us to do this without specifying the behavior of a package, if we wish: this is one reason why we sometimes want to use packages instead of subsystems, which we will consider below.

Q: What packaging and namespace mechanisms are there in programming languages you know? How does the namespace control at the programming language level compare with the namespace control in UML? How do you implement an ≪import≫ dependency between packages? What about ≪access≫?

---

[1] usually exactly one, but some model elements, e.g., operations, are not technically in any UML name space (!)

> **Discussion Question 96**
> Consider when you would want to access a package and when you would want to import it. Maintenance of the model will be your main concern.

Visibility So far we have no way to prevent something in a package seeing every detail of everything in a package it must refer to. Returning to the analogy with classes, we expect to have more control than this. A class makes some of its attributes and operations public, so that they can be referred to by anything that can refer to the class at all, while keeping others private. That is, a class can place restrictions on the *visibility* of the elements it owns. Packages can do the same thing. Some elements of a package can be designated public, and others private.

> Things that access or import a package can see public things inside the package, but not private things.

Just as with attributes and operations of classes, you can show whether an element is public or private by putting a + or – in front of its name.

> TECHNICAL UML NOTE
>
> In fact there is a third designation: protected. This behaves as in C++ classes: a protected element is available only within the package and to any specializations of the package. However, UML's concept of specializing packages has been much criticized: we are not going to discuss, or recommend using, generalization between ordinary packages.

14.2 Subsystems

Packages are a useful step toward managing the development of large systems, but they do not allow us to specify what a part of a system should do. To use packages effectively for shared development and for implementing components, we need a way to do this. This is what a *subsystem* provides. A subsystem is a kind of package which has a specification part and a realization part. A subsystem can be shown on a diagram as a package with the stereotype «subsystem», or alternatively with a "fork" symbol near its name; see Figure 14.3.

The specification part, which can include use cases, describes the operations that can be done with the subsystem, without revealing anything about the structure of the system. A subsystem can match interfaces, and this is shown on a diagram just as for classes and components. The realization part can include classes and other subsystems. The way in which the classes provide the functionality promised by the use cases is described by some collaborations, just as we have described at the level of a whole design. All this information can be shown inside the subsystem symbol in a variety of ways: as you can imagine, the diagram gets complicated fast, and you are unlikely to use the notation unless you have

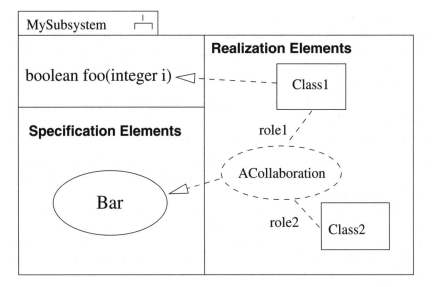

Figure 14.3 A subsystem.

a CASE tool which supports it. Figure 14.3 shows a simple example, in which there are two classes, `Class1` providing the implementation of the subsystem's operation `foo`, and `Class2` which collaborates with `Class1` to provide another, perhaps more complex, piece of subsystem behavior specified in use case `Bar`. The dotted ellipse `ACollaboration` is shorthand notation for a collaboration which is fully described in a collaboration diagram elsewhere; we'll discuss this notation further in Chapter 18.

A subsystem may or may not be *instantiable*. If it is, an instance of the subsystem is a collection of instances of the classes (and, recursively, of any smaller subsystems) which form the realization part of the subsystem. That is, it's a collection of objects, related according to the defined relationships between their classes, which can realize the use cases in the specification part of the subsystem. Subsystems may be related by generalization, although exactly what this should mean is still under discussion.

As mentioned in Chapter 13, there is usually a close correspondence between components and subsystems. A component is an implementation following the design given by the realization part of a subsystem; it satisfies the specification given by the specification part of a subsystem.

14.3 Models

In Chapter 4 we discussed the 4 + 1 view of a system, and we have now seen how the views are described by the various UML models. The UML models don't map exactly onto the 4 + 1 views, but they do cover the necessary aspects. To recapitulate:

- The use case view (the +1) is taken by the use case model.

- The logical view is taken by the class model, and by interaction diagrams and state diagrams to the extent that they are used to specify the logical behavior of the system.
- The process view is taken by interaction diagrams, state and activity diagrams, to the extent that they are used to determine the threads of control of the system, and by deployment diagrams.
- The development view is taken by the component diagrams, and by packages and sub-systems wherever they arise.
- The physical view is taken by deployment diagrams.

In each case, the model includes some model elements but not others. For example, the use case model includes use cases, actors and relationships between them, but not classes and their associations.

Formally, UML defines a *model* to be a package containing the model elements making up a particular view of the system being modeled. A subsystem can have its own models. A model for a system or subsystem must represent the *complete* system or subsystem as seen from the chosen point of view. A model which describes only part of a system belongs in a subsystem package.

> **Discussion Question 97**
> Why do you suppose a model is not allowed to leave out arbitrary parts of the system?

SUMMARY

In this chapter we discussed UML's mechanisms for structuring the development of systems. The most general mechanism is the package, which can contain any sensible collection of model elements. There are two specialized kinds of package. A subsystem has a specification part and a realization part, and can be instantiable; a subsystem typically describes a component. UML's notion of a model formalizes the informal idea of model we've been using all along: a model includes the model elements which make up a particular view of a system at a certain level of abstraction. A model is represented by one or more diagrams.

That completes our study of UML, the language. We have not covered every detail of it; to learn more you could now go on to the official documentation [49] and [50], or to larger books such as those by the Three Amigos. Next, in Part III, we will discuss three case studies.

PART III

Case studies

CHAPTER 15

CS4 administration

15.1	The case study	170
15.2	Discussion	175

In this chapter we will discuss a slightly more complex case study than that in Chapter 3. We will not discuss everything in full detail, and we will not cover the step from detailed design to code, since this is programming language dependent, but Java code for the case study is available from the book's Web page.

15.1   The case study

You are considering tendering for a contract to develop a system to help the computer science department of a university administer its final year ('honours') degree courses. You have been given the following description of the department's current procedures as part of the information on which to base your tender.

Read it carefully, considering what questions you will need to ask, and of whom you might need to ask them, to clarify the requirements.

The current situation

Toward the end of each academic year, the Syllabus Committee in the Department of Computer Science determines which modules will be available to CS4 students in the following year. (A CS4 student is any student who is taking any fourth-year module in the computer science department, whether or not the student is registered for a computer science degree.)

At the end of each academic year, the Head of Department allocates duties to members of teaching staff and others; in particular, one person is assigned to lecture each of the modules which are supposed to be available in the following year. (We'll call these people lecturers for simplicity.)

Each lecturer updates the course handbook entry for his or her module. The CS4 co-ordinator updates other parts of each handbook, and checks the module entries produced by the lecturers. Module entries are written in the LATEX formatting language.

Somebody in the Undergraduate Teaching Office (from now on we'll call any such person 'the UTO') produces the paper version of each course handbook; the CS4 co-ordinator produces the HTML versions by running the conversion application `latex2html` on the LaTeX source.

The CS3 co-ordinator is supposed to give a list of the students entering CS4 from CS3 both to the CS4 co-ordinator, and to the UTO. The CS4 co-ordinator tells the UTO about any students entering CS4 other than from CS3, for example non-graduating students. The UTO keeps the master list of all CS4 students, and updates the mailing list of students taking CS4 modules, which is known by the email address `cs4class`.

Each student is advised by a member of staff acting as a Director of Studies (DoS). A DoS is assigned to a student in their first year of study and remains in that role until they leave.

Students provisionally register for modules by filling in paper forms and handing them in to the Undergraduate Teaching Office. The UTO checks that every student who registers is listed as a CS4 student, and that every CS4 student is registered for a reasonable set of modules. In cases of doubt, the student's DoS is consulted, and may have a discussion with the student.

The UTO then produces lists for lecturers of the students taking their modules. These lists cannot be guaranteed to reach lecturers sooner than week 3. This is, unfortunately, too late to be useful for letting lecturers know how many copies of things to make ....

Questions

Some possible questions are listed below. You may find more: we, the authors, are familiar with the university setup described, and may well be assuming knowledge that you, the readers, don't have. The prevalence of such assumptions is, of course, one of the factors that makes requirements analysis so hard.

1. Which students are we concerned with, and is it always the same set? The text refers sometimes to 'CS4 students' and sometimes to 'students'.
2. What is the CS4 mailing list, and how is it updated?
3. Is there anything else that needs to be updated? Web pages, for example?
4. What are the course handbooks, and how many are there?

Q: Classify your questions according to whether you need to know the answers now, before you can tender, or whether you will simply need to get answers before you can complete the system.

We assume that on further inquiry, we found (among other things) that there is a course handbook for each honours course. 'honours course' and 'degree' are synonyms for the purpose of this application. The honours courses relevant to the system are Computer Science, Computer Science and Artificial Intelligence, Computer Science and Electronic Engineering, etc. The assessment details, and the regulations about what module combinations are acceptable, are different for each of these degrees, so there is a separate handbook for each. However, many modules are acceptable in several different honours courses, and in such a case the description of the module is the same in each handbook. Each student (apart from non-graduating students, who visit the university for just one year, do not get a degree and can do arbitrary module combinations) is registered for one honours course, and receives the appropriate course handbook. The CS4 co-ordinator is responsible for producing all the course handbooks. (In the cases of joint degrees, it is usual for the other department also to produce its own course handbook, so students on joint degrees normally get two handbooks with some duplicated information; but because of the university's structure it is not deemed sensible to try to remove this duplication at present.)

The investigation

The Department has asked you to investigate the possibility of developing a system to automate parts of this process, because they hope it may be possible to:

- decrease the burden of routine work on all staff, especially the CS4 co-ordinator
- allow students to register for modules on-line
- make it easy to obtain (from the UTO) up-to-date, reliable information
- improve the traceability of such information
- make information such as the course handbooks and lists of students taking modules available sooner, by automating their production.

The CS4 administration system should be able to report on any student: for example, whether the student is graduating or non-graduating, what modules the student is taking, what honours course a graduating student is registered for, or which member of staff is the student's DoS.

It also acts as a repository of information on modules: who lectures them, what degree course they're part of, and which students are taking them.

> **Discussion Question 98**
> Do you think the Department's expectations are reasonable? Do you think that an object oriented approach is sensible here?

In this chapter we will not discuss how to implement querying mechanisms; these can be provided sensibly by an off-the-shelf database in conjunction with standard techniques for making objects persistent, which we touched on in the panel on Persistence in Chapter 3.

Q: If you know a database query language such as SQL, draft the queries that we know are required. What assumptions have you made?

With the querying use cases removed, the remaining use cases that we have to provide are:

- `Produce course handbook`
- `Produce CS4 List`
- `Register for modules.`

Figure 15.1 shows the general use case model. Here is a more detailed description of the use case `Produce course handbook`. It takes a conservative view of what work should be done by the system, which is likely to be appropriate in the first iteration of the system (though see the discussion question below).

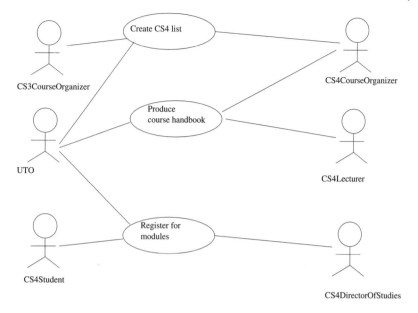

Figure 15.1 Use case model.

Produce course handbook This use case can be used only after the syllabus committee has determined the set of modules which will be available and the head of department has allocated duties to lecturers.

The CS4 course organizer updates the core (module-independent) sections of each course handbook by getting the current text from the system, modifying it and returning the modified version to the system.

The lecturer of each module, similarly, updates the description of the module by getting the text from the system, updating it, and returning it to the system.

These updates can happen in any order. The system keeps track of which updates have been done. Once all updates for the handbook have been done, the system sends the complete text of the handbook by email to the Undergraduate Teaching Office, which prints it and updates the Web pages from it.

Discussion Question 99
Does this provide sufficient value to anybody to be worth proposing as functionality in a first delivered iteration? Or should it be treated as an internal iteration only? If the latter, what functionality would you expect to be required before it was sensible to try it on the users? How would you clarify this?

Q: Develop use case descriptions for the other use cases. When questions arise that in a real project would have to be discussed with the users, record what the issues are and how you have chosen to resolve them in this exercise.

15.1.1 Class model

Q: Draw a conceptual level class model. Include multiplicities, but don't worry about attributes and operations yet.

Figure 15.2 is one possible class model.

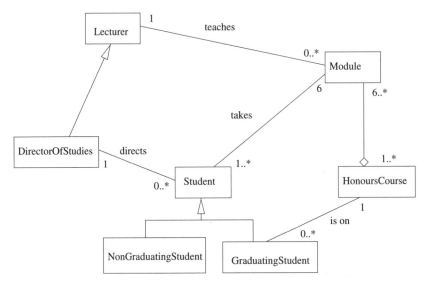

Figure 15.2 Class model.

Discussion Question 100
Figure 15.3 is another. What do you think of it?

Q: In practice not all lecturers will be teaching CS4 modules. In particular, not every DoS will necessarily be a lecturer for CS4. Does the diagram allow for this?

15.1.2 Dynamics

Figure 15.4 shows the CRC cards that we have come up with for the classes involved in the Produce course handbook use case. We can use these to explore how the classes must interact to achieve the use case. We have considered the responsibilities of the classes only with respect to that use case. Even though it would make sense to give each class more responsibilities – and it will probably be essential to do so as we consider more use cases – to add these responsibilities before we have identified a clear need for them would be an instance of inventing requirements, which we forbade in Chapter 3.

Q: Use these CRC cards to help identify the necessary operations of the classes involved in the use case.

Q: Develop the CRC cards for the other use cases and identify the operations associated with these classes.

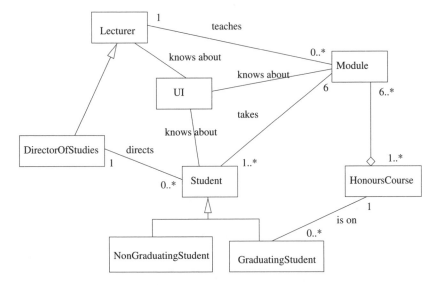

Figure 15.3 Another class model.

15.1.3 State diagrams

There are no classes with interesting state changes.

15.1.4 Activity diagrams

In Chapter 11, we said that activity diagrams can be useful for modeling at the business level, for better understanding how the organization, into which the system must fit, works. Determining what courses there are and who teaches them and then generating the course handbooks is a non-trivial workflow, with synchronizations and task dependencies which the developers will have to understand, particularly if the system is to be further developed to help automate the process. Figure 15.5 is the workflow of the task shown in this way.

15.2 Discussion

Very data-heavy system The major part of the responsibilities of all our classes is to encapsulate data. This shouldn't surprise us, since the main purpose of the system is to maintain data about CS4! But it isn't really typical of OO systems. Classes which do nothing but encapsulate data are often, but not always, a sign that all the behavior is somewhere else, maybe in a single Controller class. This is bad design because it tends to mean that the particular current use of the system (the current set of use cases) is being hard coded. Therefore when your design has such classes you should check that you aren't missing some behavior that goes with the data being encapsulated. In this case, we think what we have is reasonable: our system just doesn't *have* very much in the way of behavior.

Class name: HonoursCourse	
Responsibilities	Collaborators
Keep collection of modules Generate course handbook text	Module

Class name: DirectorOfStudies	
Responsibilities	Collaborators
Provide human DoS's interface to the system	

Class name: Module	
Responsibilities	Collaborators
Keep description of course Keep Lecturer of course	

Figure 15.4 CRC cards needed for `Produce course handbook`.

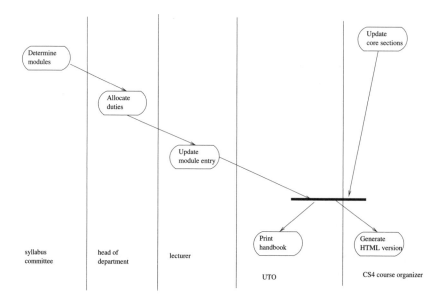

Figure 15.5 An activity diagram for course handbook preparation.

The user interface   We haven't shown the user interface(s), i.e. how the actors get to use these facilities. On reflection, it became clear that a single user interface object was not going to do: different actors need access to different parts of the system's functionality.

Probably, we would end up with something like a Model-View-Controller interface, in which each actor is provided with a different (but consistent) view onto the system. More design work is needed to deal with these aspects, but we leave it there for this example.

Board games

We are asked to deal with the following problem.

> A new company wishes to enter the computer board games market. They intend to produce a range of on-screen versions of well known two-player games, starting with Noughts and Crosses (also known as Tic-Tac-Toe) and Chess.
>
> Two users share a screen and make moves in turn. The program makes sure that only legal moves are allowed and declares the winner.
>
> To make the implementation of new games easy, and to ease the work of maintaining many different games, the company wants to design a game framework, which can be reused as generally as possible.

Discussion Question 101
What questions would you ask your potential client?

One obvious question is 'why do you expect anyone to pay good money for this?'. It isn't obvious that it has any advantages over a physical board game, and it is clear that it has some disadvantages.

Q: List some disadvantages of this product relative to a physical board. Can you in fact think of some advantages?

Discussion Question 102
Suppose you are a provider of software development to this company. Is it your job (that is, your professional responsibility) to question whether the product will be successful? To what extent? Why? Does it depend on who or what kind of company 'you' are?

Discussion Question 103
Suppose that in fact the company hopes that this basic framework can be improved later. What future enhancements can you see?

16.1   Scope and preliminary analysis

Let us suppose that there is some justification for proceeding with the simple framework proposed above.

A major part of the work involved in developing a game will be concerned with the user interface; indeed, this alone might well be a sufficient reason for choosing an object oriented language. It will also influence the choice of language, since you will want a suitable graphical user interface package to be available. For the purposes of this chapter, we will assume that the language is to be Java and that a game is to be implemented as an applet.

This example is more abstract than either of the previous case studies. We are being asked to develop a *framework* for a family of games, not a particular game. What is a framework? In this case, we mean a suitable *architecture* for this class of systems, together with any *common functionality* we can find. (We will discuss general frameworks, briefly, in Chapter 18.) Our aim is to make it easy (quick, cheap) to implement systems for particular games. We will design some abstract base classes, aiming to leave only the details which are specific to a game to be filled in by a later developer, probably by subclassing.

Developing good frameworks (e.g., ones that genuinely do increase the productivity of developers and maintainers) is notoriously difficult, and it's important not to get lost in abstraction. In real life you would not expect to be able to develop a framework for this system without implementing several examples. (James Newkirk and Robert Martin's paper [39] – and there's a link from this book's home page – tells the story of the development of a real framework.) We try here to give the flavor of the process, but undoubtedly the framework presented here could be improved. You should bear this in mind, especially if you use it to develop a game not considered here.

Discussion Question 104
What are the pitfalls in developing frameworks?

There are many Java implementations of these games available on the Web, some with source. You may find it interesting to compare some of them with one another and with what we present here.

16.1.1   Noughts and Crosses (Tic-Tac-Toe)

The game is played on a 3 by 3 square board between two players. The player who starts ('Player X') chooses a square of the board and puts a cross on it. The other player ('Player O') chooses an empty square and puts a nought on it. Thereafter the players continue to alternate, placing their own marks in empty squares. The winner is the first player to complete a straight line (horizontal, vertical or diagonal) of three of their own tokens. If the board is filled without either player achieving this, the game is a draw. Figure 16.1 shows an example of the board after a win by Player X.

16.1.2   Chess

Chess is a much more complicated game and we may pity the developer who has to implement it, however good a framework is provided! The following abbreviated description

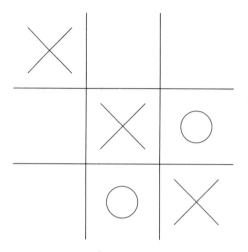

Figure 16.1　Noughts and Crosses (Tic-Tac-Toe).

should be sufficient to bear in mind:

> The game is played on an 8 by 8 square board with pieces of various kinds: pawns, rooks, knights, bishops, queens, kings, each of which comes in two colors, white and black. There are two players, 'Player White' who owns white pieces and 'Player Black' who owns black pieces. The initial configuration is as shown in Figure 16.2. Players alternate moves, normally picking one of their own pieces to move. Which moves are legal depends on what piece is being moved and can also depend on the configuration of other pieces, and on the history of the play. Pieces may be taken. In certain configurations a king is in check. If a player's king is in check the player must move to a configuration in which the king is not in check, if possible. If this is not possible, the king is checkmated and the other player wins. If play returns three times to the same configuration it is a draw.

To develop a framework, we need to consider what these games have in common, and of these things, which are common to all games in the family of board games to be considered. In both cases:

1. The game is played by two players.
2. The game is played on a square, squared board.
3. Players move alternately.
4. To make a move is to alter the state of the board by adding, removing and/or moving some tokens which are things on the board (marks or pieces).
5. Any token on the board is owned by one or other player.
6. All relevant information is available to both players.
7. Which moves are legal depends on the state of the board – which tokens are where – possibly together with other factors like the history of the play.
8. Who wins depends on the same factors.

Figure 16.2   Chess.

Let us suppose that further discussion with your client reveals that features 1, 4, 6, 7 and 8 are expected to hold generally, but that 2, 3 and 5 may fail. We summarize, giving example games that the client cited (but we do not discuss other examples in detail, and it doesn't matter if you don't know the games in question). The board could be any shape (e.g. in the game Hex, whose board is unsurprisingly hexagonal). Its state is determined by the positions of tokens, but tokens need not belong to particular players; a move (as described in item 4) might be legal for either or both players: for example, there could be tokens which either player was allowed to move (e.g. in Kalaha). Players might not always move alternately (e.g. in Draughts or Checkers); whose turn it is might be determined by the history of the play and the state of the board.

Q: Give an example, from a game you know, where the legality of a move depends on the history of the play, not just on the positions of the tokens before and after the move.

Use case analysis does not seem helpful in developing the framework, so we omit the use case diagram.

Q: Draw the use case diagram, and decide whether it was useful to do so.

Let us proceed to identifying classes and relationships. This is much more challenging in this case than in our previous examples, and the noun identification technique alone will not suffice. The technique we adopted, rather difficult to describe, was to begin with a few candidate classes and make a draft class model. Then, considering examples of actual games, we thought through some of the main interactions, beginning to sketch CRC cards as an aid to thought. We went through several iterations of this process before coming up with a class model that seemed to work. Here we try to give a flavor of the procedure, and then mention some of the alternatives we considered.

Our framework classes are:

- `Player`
- `CurrentPosition`
- `Token`
- `Move`
- `Game.`

The names, although as suggestive as we can make them, are not sufficient to explain what is meant. Let us begin to make CRC cards to record the responsibilities of each class, postponing identifying the collaborators that an object of each class will need in order to carry out its responsibilities. We have marked some dubious responsibilities with question marks and notes in square brackets, which is often a useful thing to do with CRC cards when you know that you are unsure about something but want to record it tentatively.

Player	
Responsibilities	**Collaborators**
Maintain any required user data. Identify a player of the game. Provide a visual symbol for the player.	

CurrentPosition	
Responsibilities	**Collaborators**
Maintain data seen by user: position; whose turn it is; eventually who is the winner. Accept a user move and package it for validation.	

Token	
Responsibilities	**Collaborators**
Represent a token of the game. Maintain the position of the token? [Or is this `CurrentPosition`'s job?] Provide a visual symbol for the token.	

Move	
Responsibilities	**Collaborators**
Encapsulate what changes in one player's turn. Know how to confirm itself?	

Game	
Responsibilities	**Collaborators**
Understand the rules of the game: Validate moves. Determine winner. Retain any necessary information about past moves.	

Next let's consider the particular case of Noughts and Crosses (Tic-Tac-Toe). We will need to implement classes which fulfill the responsibilities we identified. For some or all of the framework classes, we will create a specialized subclass that fulfils, for the particular game with which we are concerned, the responsibilities assigned to that framework class. That is, the framework is of the kind sometimes called *architecture-driven*. The intention is that an application developed using the framework gains a sensible architecture from the framework 'for free'. This is a benefit worth having even when, as in the immature example presented here, the amount of code reuse which results from reuse of the framework classes is minimal. A framework matures as it is developed in the light of several applications. Common functionality, which the framework should provide, can be identified when it appears in several applications of the framework. This functionality can then be factored out and made the responsibility of the framework; the existing applications can be *refactored* to take advantage of the new framework. In this way the framework gradually becomes more powerful. Experience of using it in practice is important, though: it is difficult to identify what functionality will be common in the first place.

As a simple naming convention, let us call the specialized class corresponding to `Token`, `OXOToken`, and so on. In some cases we may need to use objects of more than one class to fulfill the responsibilities assigned to an object of a single framework class. The most obvious case is `CurrentPosition`; as we mentioned in Chapter 6, there are obvious domain objects `Board` and `Square` which can collaborate to maintain the position of the game as seen by the user. So we may invent two classes and describe their separate responsibilities thus:

Board	
Responsibilities	**Collaborators**
Maintain data seen by user: position; whose turn it is; eventually who is the winner. Accept a user move and package it for validation.	Square

Square	
Responsibilities	**Collaborators**
Maintain data pertaining to a single square of the board: where it is; whether it contains a token; and if so what kind. Say whether a point falls inside the square.	Token

The (probably abstract) class `CurrentPosition` is realized by a class `Board` which contains nine `Squares`. (That is, `Board` is a subclass of `CurrentPosition`, and it has a non-inherited attribute which is the collection of `Squares`.)

16.2 Interaction

The CRC cards give a starting point for understanding interaction. As an example, we will describe an interaction within the Noughts and Crosses application in terms of the specialized classes.

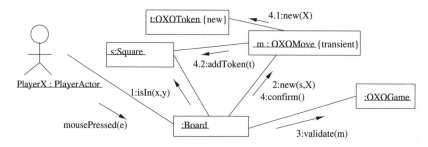

Figure 16.3 Collaboration diagram for an X move in Noughts and Crosses.

The human player interacts with a screen representation of the Noughts and Crosses board, controlled by the Board. The player clicks somewhere on the board, which causes (by standard Java mechanisms) a message to be sent to the Board, with information about where the click happened. The Board, with help from its Squares, works out from the co-ordinates which Square of the Board has been clicked in. The Board knows that it is Player X's turn, so the meaning of the click is that X wishes to place a token on the square. It creates a new OXOMove object which knows which Square and which Player are concerned, and passes the OXOMove to OXOGame for validation. OXOGame checks that there is not yet any OXOToken on the Square. There isn't, so this is a valid move. OXOGame must then check whether this move finishes the game. It does not. OXOGame's reply to the validate message says that the move is OK and that O is now to move. Board asks the OXOMove to update the position it displays to the user – so the OXOMove creates a new X OXOToken on the Square that it refers to, forgets the OXOMove object which is no longer needed (so it will be garbage collected), records that the next move is to be made by O, and waits for the next click, which will represent O's move.

Notice that in the process we have settled, at least in this special case, some of the questions we were dubious about in our initial set of CRC cards. For example, we have decided that it is not an OXOToken's job to know where it is; rather, a Square knows about an OXOToken which is on it, and a Square knows its own position.

Crystallizing this into messages passing, we get Figure 16.3 as the collaboration diagram for a correct Noughts and Crosses move by Player X. We've chosen to show a collaboration diagram rather than a sequence diagram just for a change. You might like to draw the corresponding sequence diagram and see whether you have an opinion on which you consider more readable.

Q: We did not record the detail of the way in which OXOGame carries out its responsibilities. Consider how this can be done. Develop the interaction diagram further.

Q: Consider different scenarios, and consider drawing collaboration diagrams for them. In which cases, if any, would you consider it worth developing a separate diagram? For example:

1. Legal move, not finishing the game, by O.
2. A winning X move.

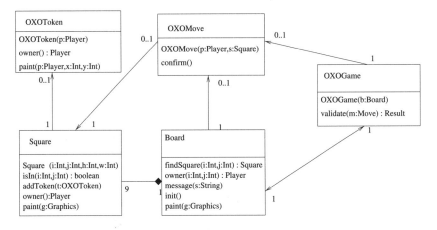

Figure 16.4   Class diagram for Noughts and Crosses.

3. An illegal O move, in which O tries to put an O on top of an X instead of in an empty square.

By exploring the ways in which objects collaborate in this way, we can make decisions about the associations between the classes that implement Noughts and Crosses, their navigability, and the operations that each class must provide. Figure 16.4 shows a possible class model for Noughts and Crosses. We have simplified the diagram (but not the model!) by omitting the base classes of the specialized classes we record, and also by omitting `Player`. The justification for the latter point is two-fold: first, it turns out that there is no need for a specialized subclass of `Player`, and secondly, at this stage a `Player` object is essentially a boolean data item, on which every class (innocuously) depends, so including it would clutter the diagram needlessly. We have also omitted some private operations which occur in the real implementation. If you know Java you will notice some aspects which are peculiar to that language; for example, the fact that `Board` has an `init()` operation instead of a constructor is because we have decided to make a Board an applet.

Q: Go through a similar process based on Chess instead of Noughts and Crosses. How does it differ?

As you will have seen, the details of the interaction that take place when a move happens are different in different instantiations of the framework. However, there is a general collaboration within which such interactions happen. Notice that in the particular case of Noughts and Crosses, the role of `CurrentPosition` was played by `Board` and some `Squares`.

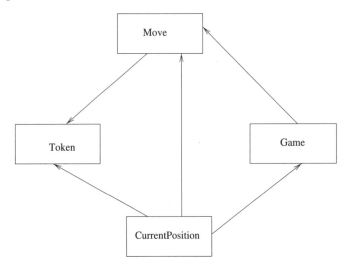

Figure 16.5   Class diagram for games framework.

Q: Draw this general collaboration. Do you need any notation we haven't discussed?

16.3   Back to the framework

Now that we have a reasonable understanding of how one game fits into our initial ideas about how the framework should be, we can make a first attempt at describing the framework itself in more detail. We might want to document how the framework classes work together, in order to help application developers planning to use the framework and/or people developing the framework itself further. It may not be obvious, though, that we have some decisions to make about how it is useful to do so. For example, remembering that most of our implemented classes will be abstract – you can create objects belonging to specialized subclasses, but not objects of the framework classes themselves – what are the associations between framework classes? You could argue that there should be an association between two framework classes when objects of the specialized subclasses *must* be associated, or when they *may* be associated. In a mature framework you might want to make sure that all associations were determined by the framework, so that these options coincided. There is a similar question about multiplicities. What is important is that you avoid ambiguous situations in which the person using the diagram understands something different from what the writer of the diagram intended. In the draft class diagram for the framework, Figure 16.5, we show only the associations which must exist, and omit multiplicities altogether. For example, because the framework specifies that Game provides a `validate` operation which takes a `Move` as argument and is invoked by `CurrentPosition`, we document the corresponding associations. As before, we omit `Player` from the diagram.

Q: In neither class diagram did we name the associations. Add names or role names, whichever you consider most useful.

Discussion Question 106

What can you say about what operations should be specified by the framework? Add them to the framework class diagram.

Discussion Question 107

Using a general framework may lead you into developing a more complex design than would have been necessary for the particular application. For example, if you were designing just for Noughts and Crosses, you would probably not invent separate classes Square, OXOToken and OXOMove, because the relationship between OXOMove and OXOToken is so close. Consider what you would have done, and what the implications of the differences are. How do you think pitfalls can be avoided?

Here are some leading questions, intended to give you the chance to consider some of the options we rejected (among others).

Discussion Question 108

Why are we talking about tokens at all, rather than generalizing further and talking just about the state of the board? If we must talk about tokens, why is a token an object? Does a token have identity? In all games?

Discussion Question 109

Move was a fairly late addition to our list of classes. Initially we rejected it as a candidate class, on the grounds that it was an Event. Later we added it back, partly because games are described in terms of moves, and to avoid having a move class in our model seemed forced. Consider how you validate a player's (real-life) moves without an explicit Move class. Develop a class model that does not have such a class, and discuss its merits with respect to the one shown here.

Discussion Question 110

At one stage instead of the single class Game we had two classes:

- Play, which recorded any necessary information about past moves when CurrentPosition passed it such information;
- Rules, which validated moves when requested to do so by CurrentPosition, using information from Play, CurrentPosition and Move as required.

Consider the implications. Which solution do you favor?

Discussion Question 111

Our concept of the Player is that this object is essentially data; it has so little behavior that we might possibly choose to implement it as a simple type (say, by using booleans) which could be attributes of tokens and moves. Contrast this with the situation in the previous case study where we used classes that corresponded to actors as the access-control mechanism: for example the Lecturer class provided access to the facilities needed by lecturers. Consider why we have decided not to pursue that approach here.

> **Discussion Question 112**
> There is a two-way association between CurrentPosition and Game, so these classes are tightly coupled and it would not be possible to reuse one without the other. Consider alternative designs, and see whether you think this situation is improvable.

16.4   States

Finally we will consider a state diagram, which might be useful in implementing the operations we have identified. The class with the most obviously interesting state diagram – that is, the one whose behavior will most clearly vary depending on the history of what has been done to the object so far – is CurrentPosition (Figure 16.6) since among its responsibilities are to show the user who is to move, and eventually who won. This immediately gives us three states:

1. A to move
2. B to move
3. Game over.

We have to identify what events cause transitions between these states, and what actions the CurrentPosition object must carry out. When does it move from A to move to B to move? When A has moved, and the move has been validated by the Game, and the Game has told us that B is to move next. To show this we need to use the when form of event (described in Chapter 12), because the event that causes the change of state is actually the *reply* to a message (validate) sent *by* CurrentPosition, not the receipt of a message sent *to* CurrentPosition.

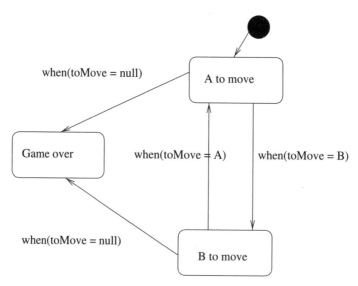

Figure 16.6   State diagram for CurrentPosition.

Discussion Question 113
Recall the discussion in Chapter 11 about the *choice* of the level of abstraction at which to draw the state diagram. Consider alternative versions of this diagram, and discuss their merits. For example (there are others), we have chosen to show a single state Game over, rather than distinguishing between A won, B won and Draw, but it would have been possible to do it the other way. What do you think?

DISCUSSION QUESTIONS

1. Pick your three favorite board games and consider whether they fit into the class of games considered here. If so, analyze how and design an application of the framework for the game. Develop code in a suitable language.

2. Consider the issues that arise in making a distributed version.

3. The company finds that users want to be able to play against the computer, not just against one another. What are the implications? In particular, which object (of an existing or new class) should have responsibility for choosing the computer's moves?

4. Consider the interactions between the objects of the design in this chapter in detail, and consider whether the implementations of the operations obey the Law of Demeter (see Chapter 9). If not, can you find better solutions that do?

5. If you implement the framework and the Noughts and Crosses application, you will probably be irritated by the need to use 'down-casts', for example because the framework specifies that any Game provides a `validate` operation which takes a Move as argument, whereas an OXOGame expects to have to deal with only an OXOMove: that is, a specialization of one class expects to deal with *compatible* specializations of the other classes. Consider the root causes and implications of this problem, and how it might affect your framework design and use.

CHAPTER 17

Discrete event simulation

In this chapter we look at a significant application package, which forms part of an object oriented *Integrated Modeling Support Environment* (IMSE) to support *discrete event simulation* in the *process style*.

An IMSE supports the development of specialized applications called simulation models, which are then used by experimenters, who are also supported by the tool. We will consider how the IMSE supports the development of applications by providing a framework for use by the developer; we will not describe how the interaction between the users and the tool works.

Unlike the case considered in the previous chapter, however, there is a well-developed literature on what classes are needed to support discrete event simulation in the process style. A developer building an IMSE would naturally take advantage of this, so this chapter talks only briefly about identifying classes. We concentrate on the use of UML to understand and document the detailed behavior of a system of classes. Such documentation is particularly important in this case, because a developer who may not be familiar with the conventions of the subject needs to understand how to use effectively the classes provided by the IMSE. The interactions between the objects are necessarily quite subtle, and there are classes with complex (nested) state diagrams, so detailed UML documentation is likely to be useful to a developer. At the end of the chapter we will discuss a simple example of a simulation model which a developer can build using the IMSE.

17.1 Requirements

A *discrete event simulation model* is an executable program which mimics the behavior of a real-world system by following the pattern of events and interactions which take place in that system. Following the conventions of the *process view* of simulation, the models will contain active entities, which correspond to the active parts of the system being modeled, and passive entities, which correspond to resources, queues and other non-active parts of that system. A simulation model must preserve the order of occurrence of events; simulated events in the model must occur in the same order as the real events they simulate.

As we have said, the IMSE must support both the development of discrete event simulation models and their use in experiments.

From the developer's point of view, it can be seen as a specialized CASE tool for developing simulation models. A good IMSE should minimize the amount of work that a developer must do to build a simulation model. For example, although a model will contain different entities, depending on what system it represents, much behavior is common. Therefore the IMSE should include classes that provide as much as possible of the functionality of the active and passive entities. It should also provide facilities for collecting commonly used statistics, and it should handle the scheduling of events and the interactions between entities as generically as possible.

The IMSE must also provide an editor which supports the building of executable models based on this framework, but we do not discuss this here.

From the experimenter's point of view, the tool must support the running of a discrete event simulation model constructed from these reusable features and the collecting of information about what happens as it runs. This information must include a record of the events which occur in the model, known as a trace, and statistical summaries of observations made of important values during the running of a model.

17.1.1 More detailed description

In the following description, noun clauses are underlined in preparation for the identification of candidate objects. A certain amount of preselection has been done, for instance to avoid including obvious actors. The details of how a model is to be run are based on standard mechanisms from discrete event simulation.

Users   There are two kinds of users.

- **Developers** are people who build simulation models and check that they run without errors.
- **Experimenters** have the following goals:

  1. always to watch the unfolding of the events of a model under controlled conditions
  2. sometimes to collect statistics about what happens.

  Both of these goals involve running the simulation model.

Simulation models   The process view divides a modeled system into active entities and passive entities.

The *active entities* represent things in the modeled system which carry out activities, such as workers in a factory. When a real-life worker does something significant which affects other real-life things, the active entity which models that worker causes a <u>simulated event</u> which affects any entities (active or passive) which model those real-life things.

Typical *passive entities* are <u>resources</u>, <u>semaphores</u> and <u>buffers</u>. They represent things in the modeled system which, although they are not active themselves, may affect the behavior of active entities in significant ways. They also observe and report statistics about their state over time.

For instance, the ability of an active entity to carry out some activity often depends on whether a certain amount of some resource is currently available. If the active entity requests an amount that is available, that active entity moves to a state indicating that it is performing the activity and that resource moves to a state where less resource is available for succeeding requests. If the required amount is not available the active entity will have to wait until some other active entity has finished with enough of the resource to allow it to proceed; that is, the active entity becomes *blocked* because of the state of the resource. The average amount of the resource used is typically a statistic of interest.

The behavior of a type of active entity is defined by a sequence of events to be simulated, often called its life cycle. This sequence can include conditional choices and repetitions.

At any point in the simulation, an active entity is in one of three states:

1. active, where it is responding to an event in its life cycle; only one active entity can be in this state at a time and its <u>event time</u> defines the current <u>simulated time</u>;
2. blocked, waiting for a request to be satisfied by a passive entity;
3. waiting for simulated time to reach this object's next event time; in this state it always knows at what simulated time its next simulated event is to be scheduled and what event that will be.

Simulated events arise as messages either from a <u>scheduler</u> which controls the advance in simulated time or from a passive entity whose state has changed due to something like the freeing of a resource by another active entity.

Any simulated event should cause a message to be sent to a trace file, so that an experimenter can follow the detailed internal behavior of the model.

We need to collect <u>statistics</u> by updating information about passive entities and about other values for which information is needed. Examples of values being monitored and their derived statistics are <u>counts</u> of how many times something occurs and the <u>average value over time</u> of something like a queue's length.

The conditions under which a model executes are varied to observe how the system would respond. To make this more flexible, values to be varied are read from an <u>external data set</u>, which is set up before the model is run.

17.2 Outline class model

If you were designing the package with no prior knowledge, the next step would be to find candidate classes, perhaps beginning with the noun clauses underlined in the problem description. As usual, you would make use of CRC cards and/or use case descriptions to evaluate your selection. In fact, as we said, the selection of classes for this kind of application is well understood in the field, so we will not dwell on it. We will, however, consider the class model in more detail later. The high level class diagram is shown in Figure 17.1.

Q: If you know about discrete event simulation, how might random number streams be added to this model?

Q: Is the association `PassiveEntity` updates `Statistic` really aggregation or composition? Justify your answer.

Discussion Question 114

An earlier version of the class model showed `Statistic` and `PassiveEntity` as distinct classes, related in that both supply the interface required by `Report`. In another version, `Statistic` was a generalization of `PassiveEntity`. We have chosen to show an `updates` association, where each `PassiveEntity` makes use of a `Statistic` object. The older variants of this part of the class model are both shown in Figure 17.2. What are the arguments for and against these different ways of modeling the classes?

Discussion Question 115

Try implementing the behavior required for `Report`, `Statistic` and `PassiveEntity` following the three alternatives presented. Which form of design does your implementation language support best?

17.3 Use cases

The developers create models and run them to check for runtime errors.

The experimenters wish to extract information. They execute the models to observe detailed behavior and, optionally, to collect statistics. Before running a model they always set up values in some external dataset to specify the conditions being modeled.

This leads to the use case diagram shown in Figure 17.3.

The three principal use cases are `create model`, `observe behavior` and `collect statistics`. All of these depend on the behavior defined for `run a model`, so a natural way to model this is to make `run a model` a separate internal use case, which both `create model` and `observe behavior` include.

Since `collect statistics` is a variant on `observe behavior`, the former extends the latter.

17.3.1 Summary of `create model`

The actor `Developer` creates an initial executable model, of the sort required by the `run a model` use case, by interaction with the editing functions of the tool. S/he then creates a dataset which allows the model to be run in a controlled manner and checks the model by following the behavior defined in the use case `run a model`. If there are errors when the model is run, the `Developer` modifies the model and runs it again. Once there are no errors the use case is complete.

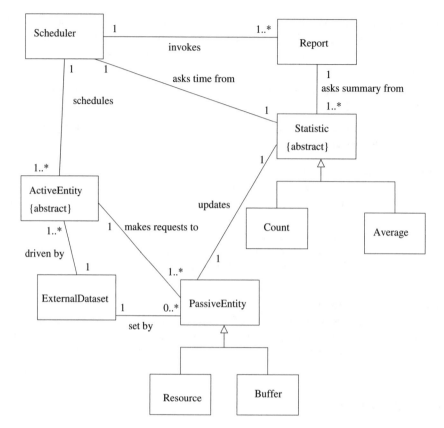

Figure 17.1 Class diagram of discrete event simulation system.

17.3.2 **Summary of** `observe behavior`

The actor `Experimenter` first selects a model. This is assumed already to exist as the output of an earlier instance of the `create model` use case. The `Experimenter` selects or creates an external dataset which holds values describing the conditions for this particular run of the model, such as the amounts of any resources and the durations of any variable delays in the model. The `Experimenter` then follows the behavior in the `run a model` use case and, when the model has run, reads the trace generated to follow the sequence of events.

17.3.3 **Summary of** `collect statistics`

This is a variant on the `observe behavior` use case. Before using the `run a model` use case, the `Experimenter` sets a flag which the model can read when it runs, to say that statistics should be collected and reported by writing them to a file at the end of the run.

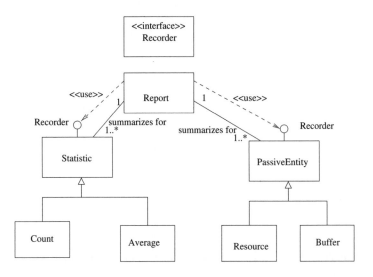

(a) Using an interface to show common behavior

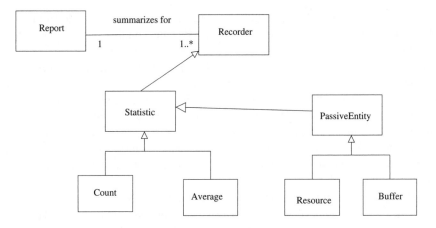

(b) One way to use generalization to show common behavior

Figure 17.2 Some alternatives for classes used in reporting behavior.

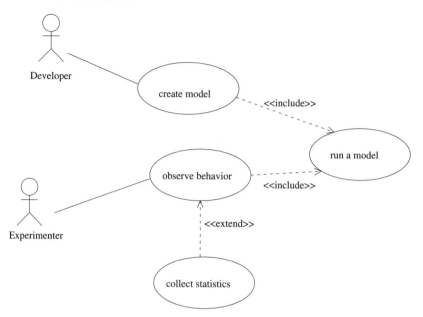

Figure 17.3 Use case diagram of discrete event simulation system.

17.3.4 **Summary of** `run a model`

This use case assumes that the actor initiating it has already selected the model to run and created or selected a matching dataset, which specifies the conditions under which to run the model.

The actor now starts the executable model, which is made up of instances of the objects used to model and observe the system. Each active entity sets itself to an initial simulated event time and to an initial next simulated event, which it reads from the external dataset. Each passive entity reads its initial settings from the same external dataset.

The entities act out the detailed behavior specified in the description of each active entity's life cycle, under the control of the scheduler, which ensures that events occur in the order of their simulated time. Passive entities ensure that constraints on the ability of active entities to proceed are respected.

The occurrence of simulated events causes trace messages to be output.

Where an event changes a value for which a report is required and the statistical collection flag has been set, appropriate information is added to that to be used by the reporting mechanisms.

A runtime error may happen at any point, if the model has errors. This is checked in the `create model` use case and dealt with there. For simplicity, we assume that an `Experimenter` never encounters such errors.

Q: Produce an activity diagram showing the interactions and dependencies among all potential users of the complete system.

Q: How would the use case model be changed if we were to discover that all `Experimenters` always built their own models each each time they wanted to carry out either of their current use cases?

17.4   Standard mechanism for process based simulation

To support the detailed design of our classes, we describe in some detail the mechanism of discrete event simulation which is employed. It is a standard one from the literature on the subject, such as [22].

The model is created as a collection of active entities and passive entities, plus a controlling scheduler and appropriate statistical collection objects. The active entities read in any initial values, such as timings of delays for this run, from the external dataset and enter their waiting state. The input from the external dataset is also used by the passive entities to set their initial values – for instance it specifies an initial amount for each resource.

The active entity with the lowest simulated event time receives a message from the scheduler and enters its active state. This active entity records the event which is being activated, with its event time, in the trace for this run of the model. The event time of the currently enabled active entity always defines the current simulation time.

If the current event involves an interaction with a passive entity – for instance obtaining the use of a resource – the active entity sends an appropriate message to the passive entity. If the message is a request which, depending on the current state of the passive entity, might block the active entity,

1. either the passive entity is updated to show how it satisfied the request – for instance by decrementing the amount available of the resource it represents – and the active entity proceeds,

2. or the active entity waits for the condition to be met, entering a blocked state until the passive entity reschedules it.

The event may also mean that a passive entity must be updated without the possibility of the current active entity being blocked – for instance that a resource is being released. When a passive entity is updated in this way, it must schedule any active entities that are waiting for such a change and who are now able to carry on, setting their next event time to the current simulated time.

When an active entity leaves its active state without being blocked, either it updates its simulated next event time and its next event and returns to its waiting state or it terminates.

The active entity which now has the lowest next event time is moved by a message from the scheduler into its active state.

This pattern is repeated until either there are no unterminated active entities or the simulation time exceeds the simulated period for which the simulation is to run.

If the report flag was set before the model started running, the scheduler will now send a message to the various objects which have been collecting observations requesting them to produce a report of their statistics, either each time a certain interval of simulated time has passed or at the end of the execution of the model. For the sake of presentation, these objects may be collected into related sub-reports and the final output formatted correspondingly.

17.5 Associations and navigability

Which objects will need to know about which others, in other words what are the associations and what are their navigabilities in our class model? We have begun by showing all associations without comment, but as we move to a detailed design, suitable for implementation, we must define and justify their meaning and direction. At the same time we will need to ensure that a way for objects to know about each other is included in their attributes or operations. As we explained in Chapter 6, most associations are one way. Where a two-way association is proposed, it must be justified.

Figure 17.4 shows a more detailed class diagram, which includes attributes and operations to support the associations and their navigability. Notice that, in showing even those attributes whose purpose is to implement associations, we are breaking the rule we made in Chapter 5 and have followed since. We choose to do this, at the expense of making the diagram more complex than it might be, because the mechanisms for implementing the associations are quite subtle and we will want to discuss them in terms of the attributes of the classes.

Scheduler **invokes** Report

- **Direction** One way, from `Scheduler` to `Report`.
- **Meaning** The `Scheduler` is given the responsibility for requesting summaries of their observations from any `Report` objects once the end of the run is reached.
- **Implementation** A `Collection` attribute – `reports` – in `Scheduler`, and an operation – `report()` – in `Report`.

Scheduler **schedules** ActiveEntity

- **Direction** Two way, since the `Scheduler` needs to be able to activate each `ActiveEntity` when its turn comes, while `ActiveEntitys` also need to find the `Scheduler` when they need to rejoin the event list, as we see below.
- **Meaning** The `Scheduler` controls the order of execution of the `ActiveEntitys` to ensure that they always execute in simulated time order.
- **Implementation** A special ordered collection of active entities, `evList : TimeOrderedList`, within `Scheduler`, and an operation `act()` in `ActiveEntity`. An attribute `s : Scheduler` within `ActiveEntity` and an operation – `wait()` – in `Scheduler`. For details see below.

ActiveEntity **driven by** ExternalDataset

- **Direction** One way from `ActiveEntity` to `ExternalDataset`.
- **Meaning** Each `ActiveEntity` reads its initial event time and next event from the one `ExternalDataset`.
- **Implementation** The attribute `input:ExternalDataset` in `ActiveEntity`, and the operation `getValue(): real` in `ExternalDataset`.

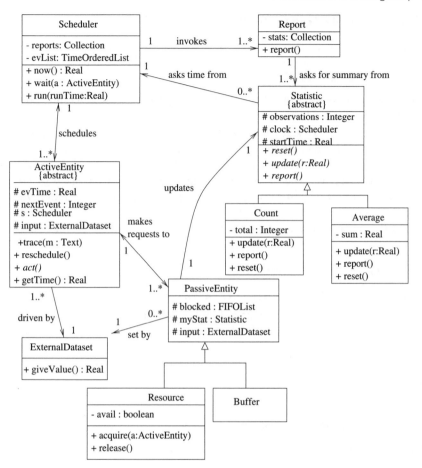

Figure 17.4 Detailed class diagram for a simulation experiment.

PassiveEntity **set by** ExternalDataset

- **Direction**   One way from PassiveEntity to ExternalDataset.
- **Meaning**   Each PassiveEntity reads its initial settings from the one ExternalDataset.
- **Implementation**   The attribute input:ExternalDataset in PassiveEntity, and the operation getValue(): real in ExternalDataset.

PassiveEntity **updates** Statistic

- **Direction**   One way, from PassiveEntity to Statistic.
- **Meaning**   Whenever a request is made to a PassiveEntity it may send an update to its associated Statistic object.
- **Implementation**   The attribute myStat:Statistic in PassiveEntity and the operation update(r:Real) in Statistic.

`ActiveEntity` **makes request to** `PassiveEntity`

- **Direction**   Two way, since the `ActiveEntity` needs to make an initial request to the `PassiveEntity`, while the `PassiveEntity` will need to send back a message when the request has been satisfied.
- **Meaning**   The exact meaning of such a request depends on the specialization of `PassiveEntity` to which it is sent.
- **Implementation**   The `ActiveEntity` to `PassiveEntity` direction is implemented by attributes declared in the specializations of `ActiveEntity` as required (which may refer to `PassiveEntity` objects) and by particular request operations in specializations of `PassiveEntity`. The other direction is implemented by passing of `self` as a parameter with all request messages, by the attribute `blocked` in `PassiveEntity` (which lists the `ActiveEntitys` which are blocked waiting for this `PassiveEntity`) and by the operation `reschedule()` in `ActiveEntity`. See below for examples.

`Report` **asks for summary from** `Statistic`

- **Direction**   One way from `Report` to `Statistic`.
- **Meaning**   When a report is requested by the `Scheduler`, each `Report` object delegates the task of producing individual summaries to appropriate objects which are specializations of `Statistic`.
- **Implementation**   The attribute `stats:Collection` within `Report`, and the operation `report()` within `Statistic`.

`Statistic` **asks time from** `Scheduler`

- **Direction**   One way from `Statistic` to `Scheduler`.
- **Meaning**   Observations need to be recorded along with the time they happen.
- **Implementation**   The attribute `clock:Scheduler` within `Statistic`, which allows a `now()` message to be sent.

> **Discussion Question 116**
> We have not discussed how collection classes are obtained or implemented; for example we gave the class of `Scheduler`'s reports attribute as `Collection` without comment. Suppose that you are implementing this system, in whatever language you use, and investigate the availability of reusable classes which would save you from having to write your own collection classes. How can such classes sensibly be implemented in your language, and what difference does the technique used make to the user of the class? For example, can you make use of the parameterized class construct discussed in Chapter 6?

> **Discussion Question 117**
> There are several circular dependencies in the class diagram shown in Figure 17.4. Identify them, and see what simple changes you could make to the design to eliminate them.

17.6   Classes in detail

We have now documented the static structure of the discrete event simulation package, and have discussed the intended interactions between objects at a high level. Next we should document the main classes in enough detail for a `Developer` to be able to use them to build a model.

We will find state diagrams particularly helpful in capturing the rather complex behavior of this design. We will also find collaboration diagrams useful, since the behavior of the objects involves a lot of interaction between them.

A `Developer` must create a specialized subclass of the abstract class `ActiveEntity`, adding a method to implement the operation `act()`. This method defines the behavior of the particular active entity which the developer wishes to model.

Similarly, a `Developer` may create a specialized subclass of the abstract class `PassiveEntity`. Here, however, two specializations are so common that they are provided in the package. For example, a `Developer` who needs to model a passive entity which behaves like a single discrete resource, which can be used by one active entity at a time, can use the class `Resource` directly rather than having to write more code.

We shall show an example of a simulation model built in this way which involves a specialization of `ActiveEntity` along with some instances of `Resource`.

17.6.1   **Class** Scheduler

There is a single instance of `Scheduler` in a simulation model. It is the first object to receive a message – `run(runLength:Real)` – and the operation which is thus invoked controls the execution of the model.

`Scheduler` has attributes:

- `reports` – the `Collection` of groups of reportable objects
- `evList` – the `TimeOrderedList`, which holds `ActiveEntitys` in the order of their `eventTime`.

It also supports the operations:

- `run(runLength:Real)` – the controlling function of the whole simulation. It takes the first member of `evList` and sends it an `act()` message. It repeats this until the simulation has reached an `ActiveEntity` whose `eventTime` value exceeds `runLength` – the required simulated run length – or until there are no unterminated `ActiveEntitys` left. It now sends `report()` messages to all the `Report` objects in its `reports` collection, asking them to produce reports on any `Statistic` objects they hold.
- `now():Real` – a query function to return the `eventTime` of the current first `ActiveEntity`, which defines the current simulation time. This allows access to this important information without allowing direct access to the list itself.
- `wait(a:ActiveEntity)`, which supports the return to `evList` of `ActiveEntitys` once they have left their active state. It takes a and adds it to `evList` in the appropriate position for a's `evTime`.

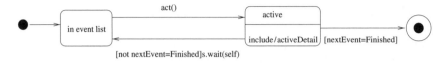

Figure 17.5 State diagram of the generic `ActiveEntity`.

17.6.2 Class `ActiveEntity`

The class `ActiveEntity` has the property `abstract`, since it contains an operation – *act()* – for which no implementation (no method) is provided and which is therefore shown in italics. No instances of `ActiveEntity` can be generated. It can only be used as a generalization and the final simulation model will use specializations where a method for `act()` is provided.

It contains the attributes:

- `s` – the `Scheduler`
- `input` – the `ExternalDataset`
- `eventTime` – the simulated time of its next simulated event
- `nextEv` – a code representing its next simulated event.

These are all shown with a *protected* marker, the # sign. In C++, protected attributes and operations of a class can be accessed from methods of that class or any subclass. This is sometimes a convenient intermediate access restriction, more permissive than private but less permissive than public; however, if you are not using such a language you may regard all protected attributes and operations as having public access, shown with +.

It has the operations:

- `getTime():Real` – a query function, which returns the value of `eventTime`
- `reschedule()` – which will place this `ActiveEntity` in the event list with the current simulation time as its `eventTime`
- *act()* – whose method has to be supplied in any specialization and which defines the simulated behavior of the active components of the system being simulated. The form of this behavior is described below.

States of an `ActiveEntity`   In general, an `ActiveEntity` will follow the simple behavior shown in Figure 17.5. This shows the scheduling behavior of all instances of `ActiveEntity`, which all respond, at this level of abstraction, in equivalent fashion to `act()` messages from the `Scheduler`.

Initially an `ActiveEntity` is in the state in `event list`, which represents its waiting in the `evList` of the `Scheduler`. When it receives an `act()` message, it enters its `active` state. On completion of its active state, it either terminates or sends itself to the `Scheduler`, `s`, in a `wait(self)` message. This causes it to re-enter the event list in the appropriate position.

An `ActiveEntity` has an internal state machine, which is defined to be the state machine called `activeDetail`. This state machine is nested within the `active` state of an `ActiveEntity`, since its name follows the keyword `do` in that state. It represents the specialized detail of `act()` and must be defined by the `Developer` in every specialization of `ActiveEntity` which is to be instantiated in the simulation model.

A typical example is given later in the chapter in Figure 17.7. An `ActiveEntity` always knows its `nextEvent` value and uses this to decide which branch to take each time it enters the `activeDetail` state. Each branch prints an appropriate trace message. After that, behavior depends on the type of event which corresponds to `nextEvent`.

Simulating time delays Some of the transitions merely pass from the start state to the end state, invoking actions and sending messages to other objects. These implement simulated time delays by updating both the next event time (`evTime`) and the event to happen at that time (`nextEvent`).

Simulating requests to `PassiveEntitys` Other transitions send requests to `PassiveEntity` objects. To allow the implementation of blocking, all requests must have the current `ActiveEntity` as a parameter. These transitions all lead to the `blocked` state, which is left when a `reschedule()` message is received from the `PassiveEntity`, indicating that the request can be satisfied.

In the example in Figure 17.7 the `PassiveEntity` is a `Resource`, whose corresponding behavior is explained below.

Q: Use a collaboration diagram to work through the interaction of two `ActiveEntity` objects whose behavior is identical to the one shown but which have different increases in their event times. How many different sequences of tracing messages can be output depending on this combination of event times?

17.6.3 Class `PassiveEntity`

`PassiveEntity` is a class with no operations. It is intended as the generalization of all passive components of a simulation model.

It has the attributes:

- `blocked` – a first-in-first-out list to hold blocked `ActiveEntitys`
- `myStat` – a reference to a suitable specialization of `Statistic`, which can be updated to record changes in the state of this object
- `input` – the `ExternalDataset`, used to set the initial values of this entity, such as the initial amount available in a resource.

Again, the attributes are specified as protected, indicating that they are to be available only to specializations of this class.

Discussion Question 118
Why is it not appropriate to define `PassiveEntity` as having the property `abstract`? Is this sensible?

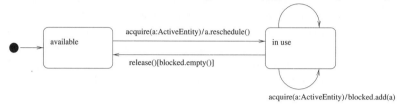

Figure 17.6 State diagram of Resource.

17.6.4 **Class** Resource

Resource is a subclass of PassiveEntity. An object of class Resource represents a thing which can be used as a whole by just one active entity at a time. As well as inheriting the attributes of PassiveEntity, it adds an attribute

- avail – a boolean, which is true if the resource is available for use, and false otherwise.

It also understands the messages

- acquire(a:ActiveEntity) – the request to gain exclusive use of this resource
- release() – the message to say that the resource is free again.

If one ActiveEntity wants to use a Resource when another ActiveEntity is already using it, the message acquire(a:ActiveEntity) will arrive when avail is false. In that case, the Resource adds the active entity a to its (inherited) list blocked. Whenever the Resource becomes free – that is, receives a release() message – it checks to see whether it has any ActiveEntitys in its blocked list; that is, is any active entity waiting to use this resource? If so, it takes the first active entity from the list and sends it the message reschedule() to inform it that the resource is now available.

A side-effect of the need to handle a collection of ActiveEntitys all waiting for the same Resource in a fair way is that what happens when an ActiveEntity wants a Resource when it *is* available is more complex than you might expect. When a Resource receives the message acquire(a:ActiveEntity) while avail is true, it reacts by setting avail to false and sending the message reschedule() to the ActiveEntity. When it receives the reply to reschedule(), it in turn replies to the original message acquire(self). The point is that the signal to the ActiveEntity that the Resource is available is *not* that it receives the reply to the message acquire(self) – this happens quickly whether or not the Resource is available – but that it receives the message reschedule().

We can model this behavior of a Resource using the state diagram shown in Figure 17.6.

Let us consider a simple example of the interaction between an active entity and a passive entity. Suppose that a Developer is modeling two workers who have to share one spanner, which lies on the bench between them. The Developer defines a specialized subclass Worker of ActiveEntity and writes (possibly with help from parts of the CASE tool which we do not discuss) the method act(). Since a Worker needs to use a spanner, there will also be a new attribute spanner in the class Worker. The high level state diagram of the class Worker is the same as for its parent class ActiveEntity, shown in Figure 17.5,

Figure 17.7 `activeDetail` state diagram of class `Worker`.

but the detailed behavior in the nested state diagram `activeDetail` is specific to class `Worker`. We show a possible `activeDetail` in Figure 17.7.

Since the spanner does not have any special behavior of its own, the spanner can be modeled by an instance of class `Resource` whose state diagram was shown in Figure 17.6.

Putting the behaviors together, let's follow what happens when an object `ruth` of class `Worker` wants to use the object `spanner` of class `Resource`, but `jo` is already using it. We haven't given full details of the class `Worker`, but let us assume that `ruth` wanting to use the spanner is modeled by `ruth`'s `nextEvent` being 2 when it receives the `act()` message from the scheduler. According to the state diagram, `ruth`'s `nextEvent` is set to 3, and then `ruth` sends the message `spanner.acquire(ruth)` to `spanner`, entering its `blocked` state. We are assuming that `jo` is using the spanner, so `spanner` is in its `in use` state. According to its state diagram, its reaction to receiving the message is to add `ruth` to its `blocked` list. On receiving the reply to its `spanner.acquire(ruth)` message, `ruth` replies to the message `act()` that it received from the `Scheduler`, so the `Scheduler` will send `act()` to the next `ActiveEntity`.

Eventually (we hope!) `jo` finishes using the spanner and, as part of its reaction to being sent an `act()` message, sends the message `release()` to `spanner`. At this point, according to the state diagram for `Resource`, `spanner` must get the next `ActiveEntity` out of its `blocked` list and send the message `reschedule()` to that `ActiveEntity`. Assuming that `ruth` was the only blocked `ActiveEntity`, the result is that `ruth` receives the message `reschedule()`. According to the `Worker` state diagram, `ruth` sets its `evTime` to `s.now()`, the current simulated time, and then reaches the end state of `activeDetail`. As usual when leaving `activeDetail` with a value of `nextEvent` other than `Finished`, it then sends a `wait(ruth)` message to the `Scheduler`, indicating that it is to rejoin `evList`.

Q: Draw a sequence diagram to illustrate this scenario. You will probably find it helpful to show message return arrows and to use the notation for nested activations.

Q: Go through the slightly simpler interaction in which `ruth` wants to use `spanner` and it is available.

Q: Draw the sequence diagram which shows the interaction of two `Worker` objects which, like the one shown, share a spanner, but have differing patterns of time intervals. How many different sequences of trace messages can be produced in this example?

> **Discussion Question 119**
> We have assumed that a `Resource` models a single item. How could our design be extended to cope with resources where amounts of more than one might be acquired and released?

> **Discussion Question 120**
> Can you describe systematically how to check consistency between state diagrams and interaction diagrams in an example such as this? How much could a CASE tool help, in principle?

17.7 **Class** Report

`Report` is used to provide a grouping of individual statistical reports. Each instance will collect some instances of class `Statistic` together.

This class has an attribute:

- stats – a `Collection` of `Statistic` objects.

It has an operation:

- report() – which is invoked by the `Scheduler` and first prints a heading for this group of summaries and then asks for a summary from each of the `Statistic` objects in stats, by sending a report() message to each in turn.

17.8 **Class** Statistic

`Statistic` has the property abstract, since it has operations for which it does not provide a method. These must be implemented in any specializations.

It provides three attributes, for use in specializations:

- observations – an `Integer` which records how many times the value being observed by this object is updated
- startTime – a `Real` value, which records when the current set of observations began to be collected, in terms of simulated time
- clock – a reference to the `Scheduler`, which allows this object to query the current simulation time, by sending a clock.now() message.

As with some of our other classes, these attributes are specified to be protected, since they are provided only for use in specializations of this class.

It has three operations, all without an implementation and so shown in italics:

- *reset()* – which allows the attributes of the object to be reset to zero at any point. This may be used to limit the period for which statistics are collected
- *report()* – which allows the `Report` object holding this `Statistic` object in its collection to request that it prints out a summary of its observations
- *update(r:Real)* – which allows the value of an observation to be sent to this object, to be included in its report.

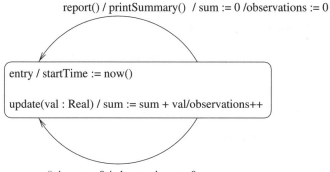

report() / printSummary() / sum := 0 /observations := 0

entry / startTime := now()

update(val : Real) / sum := sum + val/observations++

reset() / sum := 0 / observations := 0

Figure 17.8 State diagram of `Average`.

17.8.1 **Class** Average

`Average` is an example of a specialization of `Statistic`, which in fact we used as an example in Chapter 12. It implements the operations `reset()`, `report()` and `update(r:Real)`, required by its generalization `Statistic`. It also adds the attribute:

- `sum` – a `Real` used to accumulate the sum of its observations' values.

  Its responses to the three messages it can receive are as follows:

- A `reset()` message causes it to set its recording values, `sum` and `observations`, back to zero, and to set `startTime` to the current simulation time, `clock.now()`.
- A `report()` message causes it to print out the average since the last `report()` or `reset()`, and then to behave as though it had received `reset()`.
- An `update(r:Real)` message brings a new observation, in the form of a new value to be included in the average. The attributes `sum` and `observations` must be updated appropriately, but `startTime` is not affected.

A state diagram for this behavior, which we showed in Chapter 12, is reproduced in Figure 17.8.[1]

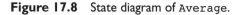

Discussion Question 121
How might you represent this information other than by using a single-state state diagram?

17.9 Building a complete simulation model

A complete discrete event simulation model built using our package will form a collaboration of a number of objects. This must include a single `Scheduler` and one or more

---

[1] We confess that we drew it this way because in Chapter 12 we wanted to demonstrate action sequences appearing on transition arrows – it would probably be clearer to put the resetting of `sum` and `observations` in the `entry` action instead.

instances of specializations of the class `ActiveEntity`. Each of the latter requires a fully defined behavior for the state machine `activeDetail`, following the pattern shown in the example above.

If we assume that a report is to be generated, we must have a `Report` object. Most interesting models will also have one or more instances of specializations of `PassiveEntity` and probably of `Statistic`.

17.10   The dining philosophers

We end this case study with an example based on the dining philosophers model. This famous example has a circle of philosophers who spend their time first thinking great thoughts and then, at varying intervals, eating from a common bowl of spaghetti in the middle of their circle. To eat, each philosopher needs to pick up two forks, one on the philosopher's right, one on the left. A philosopher always tries to pick up the right fork first, then the left. If s/he successfully acquires both forks, s/he spends some time eating before replacing the forks.

This situation was introduced by the famous computer scientist Edsger Dijkstra as an example of a system which could deadlock. It can be described using a discrete event simulation model by defining a new subclass `Philosopher` of `ActiveEntity`, and by modeling each fork as an instance of `Resource`.

The collaboration diagram, Figure 17.9, shows the scenario where `plato` successfully acquires and releases his two forks, and neither `sartre` nor `hegel` is hungry during this period. We are using the instance form of the collaboration diagram, as described in Chapter 8, so only one scenario is shown; we also omit the report related objects for clarity. (They are easy to add: you might like to consider how.)

Q: Draw the sequence diagram which corresponds to Figure 17.9.

Q: Draw the extended model if `marx` decides to join the circle. What does he need to bring with him?

The `activeDetail` state diagram of a `Philosopher` is shown in Figure 17.10.

> **Discussion Question 122**
> Since the actions in our models are all sequential – two actions can never happen at the same time – you might think that the dining philosophers could never get stuck in a deadlock. Deadlock would require that each philosopher had succeeded in picking up his right-hand fork and was waiting for his left-hand fork to be replaced by the philosopher on that side. In fact that can happen here. How, and how can this be fixed?

> **Discussion Question 123**
> Could the simulation system be extended to cope with running the same model several times under varying conditions and collecting the statistics from successive runs as rows in a table of reports? Try to modify this design as little as possible to produce such a system.

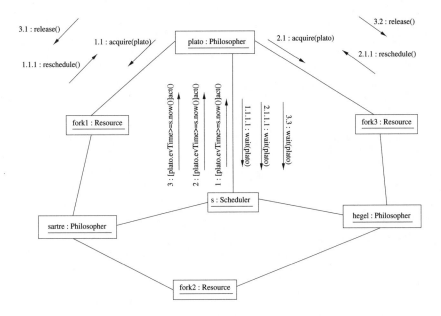

Figure 17.9   Collaboration diagram of the dining philosophers.

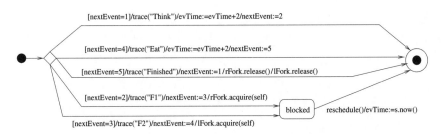

Figure 17.10   `activeDetail` state diagram of class `Philosopher`.

PART IV

Towards practice

Reuse: components, patterns

In this chapter we summarize what the book has said about *reuse*, revisit what Chapter 1 said about components, frameworks and architecture in the light of the rest of the book, and address some non-technical issues which have so far been ignored. So far we have emphasized the reuse of components, but there are several other important kinds of reuse which we consider here. In particular, we will discuss the use of *patterns*; this can be seen as the reuse of good ideas, for example successful designs.

18.1 Practicalities of reuse

In its broadest sense, the term *reuse* covers any situation in which work done for one software project is used to help another.

We will address the questions (some of which we began to tackle as early as Chapter 1):

1. What can be reused, and how?
2. Why reuse?
3. Why is reuse hard?
4. Which components are genuinely reusable?
5. What about building your own components?
6. What difference does object orientation make?

One of our conclusions will be that an organization which wants to achieve high levels of reuse must support the aim by taking seriously the quality of its products and processes, verification, validation and testing, and by having in place the right organizational and procedural structures. These topics are addressed in the remaining two chapters.

18.1.1 What can be reused, and how?

- Architecture, which we considered in Chapter 1, including frameworks

- Code: most obviously components, which we have already started to consider
- Designs, even sections of analysis: see patterns, below
- Documentation: parts of user manuals and development documents tend to be 'boiler plate' text
- Tests: many are standard, e.g. what happens if we run out of memory or disk.

Various other labor-saving techniques are usually not counted as reuse. For example, if a developer gets trained in a new language for one project and the same language is used for the next project, is this reuse? It is one of the beneficial aspects of reusing successful *architecture*, at least: recall that the decision about what language to use can be regarded as an architectural one.

For another example consider tools: that is, code that isn't directly part of the system being built, but which can be used to assist several projects. Test harnesses are a common example.

> **Discussion Question 124**
> What about off-the-shelf tools, such as development environments or bug-tracking systems? Can you think of any other examples of reuse?

Reuse can be achieved in a variety of different ways. Most simply, we can *cut and paste*, that is, simply copy the original artifact. We save the effort of rewriting the reused artifact, but changes to the original do not automatically get propagated to the copy, or vice versa. Sometimes this is sensible, but in many situations it can lead to problems.

> **Discussion Question 125**
> Consider each of the areas of reuse listed above. Is it desirable to keep the two versions in synchrony? Why, or why not?

At present, component reuse is just about the only area in which anything other than cut and paste is regularly done. Even component reuse is in its infancy: it is rare to reuse components which are larger than single classes. Class libraries, however, are commonly used. Although it is clear that it is more beneficial to reuse a component that is larger than one class, a good class library is an important asset. For example, collections of various kinds are sensibly implemented as single classes, and there is no good reason why any developers should have to write their own. Smalltalk and Java have standard libraries, which further increases the benefit. The library may be a commercial product, or a resource which is internal to an organization.

PANEL 18.1 What is a component really? Controversial!

'Component' (and for that matter 'architecture') are words whose meaning varies enormously depending on who's using them.

Let's consider 'component'. The definition we gave in Chapter 1 is one of the more broad. We considered a module to be a component if it was reusable and replaceable; this required it to have a well-defined interface and to be a cohesive abstraction with low coupling with the rest of the system.

Our definition isn't quite the most broad: a few people consider any object – or sometimes, any class – to be a component. This seems to be a waste of a good word – why not just say 'object' or 'class' if that's what is meant? A more interesting candidate is Rational's definition as quoted by Grady Booch [6]:

> A component is a physical and replaceable part of a system that conforms to and provides the realization of a set of interfaces.

Booch clarified that 'replaceable' is intended to mean replaceable at runtime, and this is the major difference from the definition we use in this book. UML's own definition is 'An executable software module with identity and a well-defined interface'.

After much consideration, we prefer to include in our definition modules that can be replaced at maintenance time, without requiring changes to the rest of the system. Both definitions require that a component be pluggable – the only question is *when*?

It's always important to remember that (with any definition) a component does not function in isolation; whether it is replaceable depends on the architecture, not just on the component. (Architecture is itself another controversial term. Some people would separate what we describe here into architecture and *architectural style* [42].)

Here are some more definitions of component:

1. A high-quality type, class or other UML workproduct designed, documented and packaged to be reusable. A component is cohesive and has a stable interface. Components include interfaces; subsystems; use cases, types, actors or classes; and attribute types. Components also include other workproducts, such as templates or test case specifications [30].
2. An encapsulated part of a software system. A component has an interface that provides access to its services. Components serve as building blocks for the structure of a system. On a programming language level components may be represented as modules, classes, objects or a set of related functions [11].
3. A component is an object that lives in the binary world. [5], in explanation of Booch's definition mentioned above.

Discussion Question 126
Consider the definitions and explain the differences between them with the help of examples.

Discussion Question 127
Can a component be reusable without being replaceable, or vice versa? Why?

Discussion Question 128
Is a component something you might instantiate, or something you get after you've instantiated something else? In which case, what is the something else? Consider Booch's statement.

Further reading on components and component based development (aimed at comparatively experienced professionals) includes [45] and [17]. Further reading on architecture includes [42].

18.1.2 Why reuse?

The bottom line is financial, of course. Some of the ways in which achieving high levels of reuse can save a company money are as follows.

- The obvious: developers' time saved on developing the component! Realize that only a small part of this time represents coding. Analysis, design, reviews, documentation, and testing are far more significant overall. Moreover a good solution has to be developed only once, and then it can be used even by people who lack the experience to have developed it themselves.

- Products can be more reliable, because of 'cumulative debugging' of reused components. Someone else has ironed out the problems before you. This saves money by reducing testing, debugging and maintenance effort; it may also result in higher reliability as seen by the customer, which may increase the organization's reputation and hence sales.

- Reduced market cycle time. Faster product development not only saves developers' time, but may also allow the organization to be first to exploit a particular market opportunity – increasing profits.

- Moving to a component based design style in order to achieve high levels of reuse may focus developers' attention on achieving modular designs; so even if in a particular product every module is new, the product may still be easier and cheaper to maintain than in the organization's pre-CBD days.

- Developers may spend less time doing routine tasks, and more on the more interesting and important tasks of making sure that the customers' requirements are met. So staff turnover might be lower, saving money, and quality higher, improving sales. (This point is pure speculation. It assumes that developers would think the change an improvement, which may be wrong given the history of software development; and it probably becomes significant only at higher levels of reuse than organizations commonly achieve today.)

It isn't trivial to achieve these benefits, of course, otherwise we wouldn't still have a software crisis . . . .

18.1.3 Why is reuse hard?

In this subsection let us consider the question from the point of view of the *user* of a component: this is the most important perspective, as we shall argue below. Even when a project has access to a component library, reuse is not automatic. To see why, put yourself in the shoes of the developer searching for a component to fulfill some task, and consider the following questions.

- Even if a suitable component exists, can you find it, and understand its relevance? Once component libraries get bigger than a few hundred things the searching problem is very serious.

Discussion Question 129
How should a component library be arranged and indexed, and what search facilities should be available?

Once you find a candidate component, further questions become relevant:

- Does it do what you want? If you go looking for a component that does a well-specified job, once the design it is supposed to fit into is well under way, the answer is almost certainly not. Ideally you need to go into the problem with a reasonable understanding of what components are available to you, and even be prepared to adapt the requirements to fit the available components. This goes against several decades of software engineering practice: customers and developers may both be unhappy with it. Moreover, it brings us up against the previous point: how do you go into requirements analysis with an understanding of the components available to you if there are many components?

- Do you trust it? Not Invented Here syndrome, the reluctance to use something not developed by oneself or one's colleagues, is easy to laugh at – but if you decide to reuse a component instead of developing a new module, who gets blamed if it doesn't work out?

  It may indeed not work – and even if source is available, if you didn't develop it, it can be harder to debug it than it would have been to develop it in the first place. Or (not so very different) it may work, but not be properly documented, and you may misunderstand it.

Discussion Question 130
What factors influence you, or should, when you decide whether to trust a component?

- A comparatively minor point: you may have to import things you don't need along with the functionality you want to reuse, getting *software bloat*.

Notice that all of these problems (except possibly the first) tend to be more severe the bigger the component – but the main benefits of reuse come from reusing large components.

Q: Why is reusing a large component to do a job more beneficial than reusing several small ones to do the same job?

Discussion Question 131
List the features of good components that help to overcome these problems. Are there relevant features of the organization that uses the component? Of the organization that creates it?

18.1.4   Which components are genuinely reusable?

- A component must be sufficiently general, in a usable way. In fact the mistake of making a component too general, with interfaces which are too large and complex – inventing requirements – is more common than the mistake of making it not general enough. Getting this right simply is hard, and the consequence of getting it wrong in either direction is that the component will not be reused. At least if you didn't put some extra feature in and the component is never reused, you haven't wasted the time it would have taken to add it .... If in doubt, leave it out.

- A component must be properly documented with specification. What form should the documentation take? Components, by definition, realize interfaces and have context dependencies; both aspects should obviously be documented. In a UML-literate environment, the documentation might include, for example, a use case diagram showing the tasks which the component supports. The question of how the detail of the use cases should be recorded is harder, particularly if a use case involves several actors who must behave in a particular way if the component is to perform correctly. Interaction diagrams may help, as may state diagrams, as may English descriptions.

  Actually there is a white box/black box issue here, as in testing. Strictly speaking, users should not need – or perhaps even be permitted – to know how the component is implemented. They should depend only on there being some realization of the interface, provided the context dependencies are satisfied. This suggests, for example, that any interaction diagrams used in the documentation should show the component as a black box, a single subcollaboration that just interacts with actors external to itself. On the other hand, software engineers, being people who understand software design, often find it easier to understand a component from a description of how it works than from a specification of what it does. Provided that the component is sufficiently encapsulated that it is impossible for the user of a component to *rely* on a particular implementation, there may be no harm in using a description of the implementation in the documentation.

> **Discussion Question 132**
> In this case, would the description of the implementation have to be truthful? For example, if the component was later modified in such a way as to outdate the description, but without changing the interface, need the description be updated?

- A component must be thoroughly tested. The consequences of an error in a module are much more severe when the developer of the module is not around to help fix it, and when the module is used in several places. So it's important for components to be *more* thoroughly tested than modules purpose-built for one system.

18.1.5   What about building your own components?

There are some extra risks involved (as well as the extra opportunities) if the organization also develops its own components: these both apply especially to organizations which are starting a reuse program with little experience.

As we have seen, genuine reusable components have characteristics that do not arise by accident. Extra effort may be required to make such a component, compared with the effort required to make a component for one-off use. The component must be documented and tested in a way which does not assume the reader or user is familiar with the assumptions of the system within which the component is being developed, for example. If for any reason 'reusable' components are not reused, the extra effort involved in building them was wasted, and counts against any benefits of successful reuse.

The easiest 'reusable' things to build, and therefore too often the first attempted, are useless because the functionality can be acquired more cheaply by buying it. For example, one of the authors once worked in an organization where someone put a considerable amount of effort into developing a 'reusable' linked list class in C++. Better functionality was available in a commercial C++ class library that the organization bought (belatedly) a few months afterwards.

The moral has to be that a reuse program should concentrate on learning to use components before trying to build them. Not only is building components harder, but there's no point in building them if they won't be used!

> Using components is more important, more beneficial and easier to get right than building them.

Most academic and industrial interest in component based development has focused on developing components, not on using them. This is not surprising: it is a long-established tradition in software that people like to build new things. However, the benefits of CBD arise from using components, while most of the costs arise from building them.

Given that developing reusable products requires extra work, when can the extra work be done? The single main reason why reuse efforts fail is that the answer is often 'it can't' – at least, not without substantial change to the organization. Here are some options (adapted from [23], which in turn cites [28]):

- At the end of the project: but with what resources?
- During the project, so the customer pays for the development of components to be used on the next project (and, presumably, benefits from the development of components on previous projects). This may work until the project gets behind schedule. Since most projects do . . . .
- As time permits, by having two component libraries, one of which is 'ready' components and one of which is 'prototype' components, and gradually moving components from the prototype to the ready library.
- In parallel with mainstream development: have a permanent team to do reuse work. This requires that the organization is willing to fund such a team; and in any case, are its members in a position to do the work, not being the original developers of the components in question?

18.1.6 What difference does object orientation make?

- OO encourages the high cohesion/low coupling style that is anyway good practice. This has been oversold, but is not false.

- Object oriented analysis concentrates on problem domain objects, which are more stable than the functionality of a particular application.

- A related but different point is that problem domain objects, by their nature, frequently recur in different contexts, so they make good reuse candidates. A company can develop a collection of *business objects* reflecting the common entities in its own business.

- In OO reusing a class may not mean putting up with its functionality just as it is: a class can be reused as the base class of a more specialized class. This allows developers to follow the *Open–Closed* rule – that is, to develop classes that are both closed (stable and usable now) and open (extensible later). If we use a notion of component which permits a component to inherit from another – even if the component consists of more than one class – then this advantage can be extended to general components. Unfortunately this form of reuse is not as beneficial as it might seem; and whether it is desirable to allow this kind of reuse of components in general is doubtful (and controversial). The root problem is that inheritance creates tight coupling. For example, as we shall see in the next chapter, a subclass's capabilities must all be tested, even those inherited from a superclass; we do not at present have reliable ways of taking advantage of the fact that the superclass has been carefully tested. So using a component by inheritance is often not as beneficial as using it by composition.

One of the main claims for object orientation is that it enables higher levels of reuse than traditional software development methods. People do quote reuse percentages – sometimes as high as 70% – but beware, these are practically meaningless without a good definition of what's being measured!

18.2 Design patterns

The use of patterns is essentially the reuse of well-established good ideas. A *pattern* is a named, well-understood good solution to a common problem in context.

The idea comes originally from the architect Christopher Alexander, who described and named common architectural problems and discussed solutions to them. For example, he discusses how architecture can support a family with a teenager in the pattern **Teenager's Cottage**. The problem is that a teenager and her/his family need to be supportive of one another, whilst at the same time the teenager becomes more independent; static architecture that keeps the teenager sleeping in a child's bedroom undermines this change. The proposed solution, the 'teenager's cottage', is a place which acts as the teenager's private home. It has its own entrance, but is strongly attached to the main house; it may be part of the main house or, for example, a small building attached by a covered walkway. Alexander's description describes (with diagrams) possible variants on the idea. He discusses the objections that people sometimes have to it – for example, that the cottage will be used for only a few years and will then lie empty – and possible ways round the objections, such as designing the cottage so that it can later be used as a study or workroom. Finally he discusses other patterns which are relevant, for example which may help with the detailed design of the cottage. The full (four-page) description can be found in [18].

Similarly, there are many commonly arising technical problems in software design. Experienced designers recognize them and understand how to solve them. Without patterns, novices have to find solutions from first principles.

> Patterns help novices to learn by example to behave more like experts.

The point is that you get to spend your effort on building the *best* solution, whereas if you have to start from scratch you may have to spend a significant amount of time hunting for any solution at all: and you may not spot disadvantages of a solution until you get bitten by them. Patterns let you stand on the shoulders of giants.

Patterns are by definition not new: they document, at a suitable level of abstraction, designs which are already tried, tested and well understood. A pattern is not likely to be a revelation to an experienced designer. However, a good abstracted description of a solution in context – of a pattern – can be useful even to experts who would essentially have used the pattern anyway. For one thing, this makes it easier to spot improvements and variants: for another, having a name for the pattern, with a commonly agreed meaning, makes it easier to discuss designs.

Rather than giving general instructions about what constitutes good design, a *pattern catalog* documents particular designs that are useful in certain contexts. One of the main challenges for the pattern writer is to get the level of abstraction, at which the pattern is described, right: it must be abstract enough to be applicable to as large a family of situations as possible, but not so abstract as to be platitudinous.

Pattern catalogs have to be easy and quick to refer to. A common format for describing patterns helps. For example a pattern catalog might describe all its patterns using these elements:

- **Name** and possibly aliases. As with classes, the name should be short, but as descriptive as possible.
- **Abstract** A very brief overview of the pattern: not more than about three sentences.
- **Context** A very brief description of the situation in which the problem can arise.
- **Problem** What is the problem that arises in this context? This can usually be explained in terms of (often conflicting) *forces* – things that have to be taken into consideration, such as requirements and constraints.
- **Solution** including explanatory text, models, CRC cards and/or example code as appropriate.
- **Consequences** – good and bad things about what happens if you use the pattern, variants on the pattern, references to other patterns that may be relevant.

The elements aren't always named in this way; for example, [24] lumps context and problems together, while [11] doesn't have a separate consequence section. Opinions run high about whether examples should be included. Alexander's original patterns are comparatively freely written (which is not to say that they are carelessly written: far from it!). There is a name, and a very concise description of the problem, set in boldface, followed by a more detailed discussion of the context, problem, solution and consequences. After this there is the keyword **Therefore**: followed by a very concise, boldface description of the solution. The description of how other patterns are related is split into a brief paragraph at the beginning about what patterns may be implemented using this one, and a brief paragraph at the end about what patterns may be helpful in the implementation of this one.

The extent to which patterns work together varies. As the name suggests, a pattern catalog need be no more than a collection of patterns. Ideally we want a *pattern language*: the difference is that a pattern language describes how the patterns can be used together (the syntax and grammar of the language) rather than just what they are (the words).[1]

In fact the patterns approach is not limited to design. Almost every area of software engineering now has its own patterns; to take a comparatively obscure example, the authors are interested in patterns for reengineering legacy systems. Many patterns describe the process by which something can be done, rather than the artifact which is produced.

Moreover patterns exist at many levels: [11] distinguishes between

- *architectural patterns* (such as layered architecture: this is also an oft-cited example of *architectural style*, and indeed architectural pattern and architectural style are at least near synonyms) at the highest level
- *design patterns* in the middle – Façade, which we'll study, is an example
- *idioms* at the programming level.

Confusingly all three of these levels are included in what most of the patterns community calls *design patterns*; this is to distinguish them from the other large families of patterns such as *process patterns* and *analysis patterns*.

Many books exist on various kinds of patterns. The 'Gang of Four book', [24] is undoubtedly the best known, followed by the 'Siemens book' [11] and [21]. The Web is also an excellent source, and as usual there are links from this book's home page.

> **Discussion Question 133**
> Pick two patterns from books or the Web. What do they have in common and how do they differ?

18.2.1 Example: Façade

The full description of **Façade** can be found in [24]. Here we give just a summary.

- **Name**   Façade
- **Abstract**   Façade defines a clean, high-level interface to a subsystem, hiding its structure to make it easier to use.
- **Context**   Building easy-to-use subsystems.
- **Problem**   If a subsystem consists of many related classes, each providing part of the subsystem's functionality, clients of the subsystem have to understand the structure of the subsystem in order to use it effectively. This increases the burden on the developers of clients. It also increases the coupling in the system: changes to the structure of the subsystem may require changes to the clients.

---

[1] However, understanding the interactions between patterns is not easy. Beware: some so-called pattern languages are really just pattern catalogs with some limited cross-referencing.

- **Solution**   Add a new Façade class which provides a single unified interface to the subsystem. An object of this class (the Façade) accepts messages asking for any functionality of the subsystem. It knows the structure of the subsystem, and forwards the messages to the appropriate object. The classes in the subsystem do not depend on the Façade: for example, no object inside the subsystem keeps a reference to it.

- **Consequences**   Clients can avoid depending on the structure of the subsystem, though they may be permitted to access the subsystem's classes directly if need be. As a variant, the Façade class may be the only publicly accessible class in the subsystem: in this case clients *cannot* depend on the structure of the subsystem. The subsystem becomes easier for clients to use, and the subsystem can be maintained with less impact on the clients. This is particularly useful when subsystems are layered: each layer can have a façade providing access to its functionality.

Discussion Question 134
What is the relevance of Façade to components?

18.2.2   UML and patterns

UML is useful in two different ways in connection with patterns. Firstly, it can be used to help communicate the patterns. The existing patterns books each use their own notation, usually some form of OMT-like class diagram and sequence diagrams like UML's. In future we may expect pattern catalogs to describe patterns using UML, removing the language barrier imposed by the need to understand different notations in different books.

Secondly, UML makes it easy to record how patterns are used in a design. Provided that the reader is familiar with the pattern, this makes it easier for someone reading a UML diagram to understand how it works. It also makes it less likely that someone modifying the design will accidentally modify the design out of the pattern without understanding that they're doing so.

In an object oriented system, a design using a pattern will have a family of objects each playing a role described in the pattern; that is, interacting in the way described in the pattern. For example, a design which uses Façade will have a subsystem[2] containing an object which acts as the Façade to the subsystem; that is, it receives messages for the subsystem and passes them on to the correct objects. Its class has an interface which includes operations for all the subsystem's functionality, and there are associations between the class of the Façade object and the class of each relevant subsystem object, navigable from the Façade class to the subsystem class but not the other way.

This is starting to sound like a *collaboration*, which as we saw in Chapter 9 is UML's term for a family of related object roles. In fact, the object roles in a collaboration define the exact class of each participating object, which is too specific for describing patterns. We know that in each design that uses the Façade pattern there is a class that acts as a Façade, but of course what that class is varies from system to system. So in fact the structure of a pattern is described by a *parameterized collaboration*. This is a template with slots for

---

[2]   strictly, in UML terms, subsystem instance.

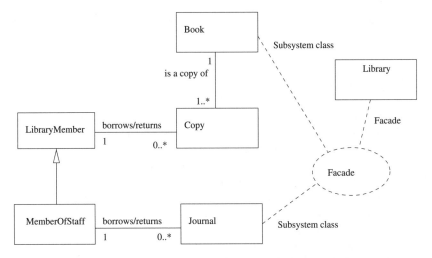

Figure 18.1 The Façade pattern applied to the library.

classes; when you plug in specific classes, you get a collaboration. (It's the same idea as parameterized classes, which were mentioned in Chapter 6.)[3]

The parameterized collaboration representing the structure of a pattern can be shown on a class diagram as a dotted oval, with dotted lines joining it to the class rectangles which represent the classes which are the parameters. The lines are labeled by role names. For example, suppose that in a future iteration of the Library case study of Chapter 3 it turns out to be necessary to provide other library systems with access to information about which books and journals the library has. We would like to allow external systems to access the library system through a clean interface that allowed them access to the information they need about books and journals, but not to information which is of no interest to them. If we decide to use the Façade pattern we could notate it as in Figure 18.1. Notice that we have chosen to omit the associations between the Façade class `Library` and the subsystem classes `Book` and `Journal`, because they can be deduced from knowing the pattern, and including them would clutter the diagram.

Q: What would be in the interface of class `Library`?

If you do use patterns, by name without explaining them, as part of your design, it is of course important to have an agreed 'vocabulary' of patterns which can be used in this way! This might be agreed at the team level or the organization level. Probably you would name one or two pattern catalogs whose patterns could be used without description: one would almost certainly be [24], which already gets used in this way. Possibly an organization might build up its own collection of patterns as well as agreeing on standard ones: but we have a suspicion that the need to do this might be a sign that the patterns are being described at too low a level of abstraction. We doubt that genuinely commonly occurring design problems

---

[3] Though since a pattern can involve an indeterminate number of classes – as Façade does, since there can be any number of subsystem classes – it's not immediately obvious how to make this informally clear idea precise.

are really domain-specific. This really remains to be seen: the use of patterns in software is young.

18.3 Frameworks

In Chapter 4 we described a *framework* as 'a reusable chunk of architecture'. Now let's be a little more precise. We won't be very much more precise because – you guessed it – the exact meaning of the term is still rather fluid.

A framework is rather like the structural part of a pattern, only bigger. It describes how a collection of objects work together, usually by defining classes which will be subclassed when the framework is applied, and describing the collaborations between the objects. To use a framework you implement the variable parts of the framework, for example by subclassing from what is provided. Some of the classes in a framework are normally abstract: that is, you have to create a subclass before you can use the framework.

The games framework in Chapter 16 is a small example. Developing frameworks is very hard, and we do not claim to be expert: send us your improvements to that framework! The arguments for buying a framework if possible, rather than developing it, are even more compelling than the same argument for buying components.

It has been convincingly argued (for example, by the frameworks expert Don Roberts: see the links from the book's home page) that reuse of frameworks is the key to establishing reuse in object oriented systems.

SUMMARY

We discussed reuse, covering what can be reused and the practical problems in getting a reuse program established. As a special case, we considered patterns, which can be seen as the reuse of expertise. Many of the difficulties in achieving a high level of reuse, especially by building components in-house, stem from the need for reused artifacts to have high quality and for the organization to support the work needed to build and to use them. In the next chapters we consider these questions more generally.

Discussion Question 135

It often happens that when one object changes state, one or more other objects need to know about it, so that their states remain consistent. For example, one or more elements of a user interface may need to show the correct version of some data in an object; perhaps several client user interfaces must show up-to-date versions of a share price, for example. Consider how this can be arranged. Then investigate the Observer pattern, also known as Publisher–Subscriber, which describes how to keep some (subscriber) objects up to date when another object (the publisher) changes. This is in both [24] and [11], and there are also Web sources available from this book's home page.

CHAPTER 19

Product quality: verification, validation, testing

This chapter returns to the question of what a high-quality system is. We suggest that to build high-quality systems an organization needs both techniques that focus on the quality of the product, and techniques that focus on the quality of the process.

In the remainder of the chapter we consider product-focused techniques for ensuring that a software system has high quality. Often considered together as 'VV&T', verification, validation and testing do not fall into the same category. Verification is the process of making sure that we have *built the product right*, that is, that it meets its stated requirements. Validation is the process of making sure that we have *built the right product*, that is, that the product is fit for its purpose, even in ways which may not have been captured by the stated requirements. The main way to ensure both of these things is to try the system out and look for problems of either kind: that is, to test it. In the next sections we consider how testing and other techniques can be used for verification and for validation.

We will try to bring out what's special about VV&T for projects that follow an iterative, architecture-centric, component-based process, as recommended for use with UML. As always, what we say is independent of which particular such process is used.

19.1 Quality review

Discussion Question 136
What does 'high quality' mean in other areas of life?

Recall that the high-level definition of software quality is that a system has high quality if it meets the customer's requirements: in Chapter 1 we gave a short classification of what this means.

Q: Review that classification, and consider what if anything needs to be added.

In order to ensure that these requirements are met, we may require some attributes which the user doesn't directly care about but which contribute to things the customer does care about: for example, we want the system to have high testability, so that the developers can practically ensure that there are few bugs; and we want it to be highly maintainable so that it is possible to respond promptly and helpfully to bug reports and change requests. Notice that these are not aspects of quality in themselves. For example, if we knew for sure that a system would only be used once and that there would never be any bug reports or change requests, we might not care whether it was maintainable.[1]

Terminology   In software as elsewhere it has become conventional to use 'quality' as a synonym for 'high quality'.

19.2   How can high quality be achieved?

There are two orthogonal ways of approaching this question: in practice one needs to combine the approaches.

19.2.1   Focus on the product

Examine the product, and the products of intermediate stages of the development process, to see whether quality standards are being met. The examination can take the form of *verification*, checking whether the product has the characteristics that we know it should have; or *validation*, checking that it does the job it is supposed to do. We will examine techniques for both sorts of examination, the most important of which is *testing*.

19.2.2   Focus on the process

We may take the view that focusing on the product alone is not enough. For example, if our tests repeatedly find similar faults in different products, we will of course want to find out how to prevent the same faults occurring in future products. We have already argued in Chapter 4 that an iterative process with evaluation at every stage is essential. Chapter 20 discusses how *quality assurance* can help, both by controlling the process which is followed on each project, and by improving the process itself.

19.2.3   Further reading

There are many resources that deal with software quality on the Web and elsewhere. Some links are collected on this book's home page. In particular, the SQM Web site contains

---

[1]   In the authors' experience, though, it is dangerous to believe anyone when they say that software will be short-lived. Successful software tends to live longer than anyone expects – hence the Millennium Bug!

a number of short, accessible articles on software quality which are well worth browsing. Particularly relevant to this chapter is [9], which goes into more detail than we have here about the factors that may be important. There are many specialist books on software quality: one popular one is [26].

19.3   Verification

Verification always involves the testing of one explicit thing (the product) against another (the specification). However, the identity of the product and the specification can vary. The most obvious example is when we test the code (or more accurately, the running system) against the requirements specification, and we'll consider this in more detail later in the chapter. In the context of a UML development we may also, for example, split that check up into stages:

1. Verify that the use cases described in the UML model satisfy the requirements described in the requirements specification (if that isn't just a collection of use case descriptions).
2. Verify that the classes are capable of providing the use cases.
3. Verify that the code corresponds to the classes in the design.

Of course in an iterative development these checks will be done for each iteration.

Certain 'sanity' checks are also usually considered as part of verification. For example, we assume that all projects have as part of their requirements that the code they produce should compile cleanly, and should run without errors. (By 'error' we mean unexpected behavior which cannot be explained by the program responding correctly to exceptional circumstances or user error. Admittedly without further explanation this is a fuzzy concept: we have in mind that the program should not have segmentation faults, Message Not Understood errors or other such 'definitely bad' properties.) UML models produced as part of a project should be syntactically correct and should be consistent, in the sense that there should always be *some* program that is described by the model (otherwise some later verification task is bound to fail!). Verification, then, includes the task of checking such sanity conditions.

Apart from testing code, how can such checks be done? At the most informal end, a developer may read the two models, documents or source files and check in his or her head that there is an appropriate correspondence. At the most formal end, we might produce a proof that the two models, documents or source files correspond. This is rarely done in practice, and it makes sense only if both of the things being compared are themselves formally well-understood objects, with a well-defined *semantics*, that is, meaning. UML itself does not (yet) have a formal semantics, so completely formal verification against a UML model is not (yet) possible even in principle. In practice given the state of the art, formal verifications tend to be very time consuming and therefore very expensive, so that even where they are practicable they tend to be done only for safety-critical systems.

Let us consider some techniques in between these two extremes. The most ubiquitous is the use of a compiler! The fact that the code compiles without error is itself verification of one of the sanity checks we mentioned. Rather similarly, a UML modeling tool will enable the developers to exclude some other routine errors such as writing syntactically incorrect

UML models. It may help in the process of checking consistency between the various UML models, enabling problems to be found at the modeling stage that might otherwise not become apparent until implementation of the relevant iteration. Some tools are able to generate code from UML models, and vice versa. This makes it easier to maintain consistency between the UML models and the code, which increases the likely usefulness of testing UML models.

Toward the other end of the human/tool spectrum we may consider ways of improving on the 'developer looks at the two models' way of finding inconsistencies and errors. The simplest is to have a developer other than the one who developed the two stages check them for consistency. A checklist can help the developer remember to check for the most common sources of problems. Another is to have reviews of some kind. Reviews, like testing, contribute to both verification and validation, so we will consider them after discussing validation.

19.4 Validation

Verification is the easy part of the job of ensuring that the product has high quality. It is definite: you know what you are trying to check. Validation is harder because you do not know exactly what you're looking for: you are looking for anything that might make the product less useful to the customer than it should be. To do validation effectively really requires customer involvement. It is possible to try to perform some validation by having a developer imagine being the customer; but the worst errors are caused by failures of communication between the customer and the developer about what is wanted.

Of course it is desirable to find problems and misunderstandings as soon as possible: this, as we have already discussed in Chapter 4, is the main reason for having an iterative development process. There are various ways in which the customer can be involved. The simplest is that the customer should need to sign certain documents, for example the specifications of what functionality is to be provided in each iteration. The problem with this approach is that it is difficult to criticize a system which is described in words. All too often, the customer only realizes that they haven't got what they wanted only when faced with a running system that is wrong. The greater the uncertainty about the requirements, the better the arguments for having short iterations to provide feedback as early as possible. At the beginning of a project or of a high-risk iteration it may be worthwhile to build a *throwaway prototype* solely for the purpose of checking that there is a common understanding about the requirements.

19.4.1 Usability

A high quality system must not only provide the right functionality, it must provide it in a way which its users can effectively use. For example, users must be able to find out how to carry out a task, carry it out quickly and without too much stress, and recover from errors. Yet this aspect of software is often neglected. In part this is because it's hard for developers to believe that there can be problems with the usability of their software so serious as to reduce customers' satisfaction with the system. There are two main reasons why this is so:

1. If you understand how something can be done, it is practically impossible to put yourself in the position of someone who does not understand it. Real users will make mistakes that would never occur to the developers, however conscientiously they tried to imagine possible problems.

2. Only rarely are software developers typical of the users of a system! Software developers are, for example, much more competent and confident using strange computer programs than the typical user of almost any system.

So you can't assess your system's usability yourself, and your colleagues can help marginally if at all. Two other resources that may be available are an expert in usability, and real users. Ideally you use both, in an iterative cycle involving investigating what changes might make the system more usable (expert involvement can help a great deal here), making the change and testing to see whether the change really did help. This *usability testing* may involve, for example, asking users to do a task with the system, and observing what problems they have.

Thomas Landauer's highly readable book *The Trouble with Computers* [33] goes into this question in depth, and proposes *user centered design* as a solution. Part of what he proposes is a task-based approach to requirements capture, taking into account the different perspectives of different users. The strength of capturing requirements using use cases is exactly this. Landauer also emphasizes that a small amount of well-directed work can bring a large benefit: for example, he estimates that a single day of usability testing can result in a 25% improvement in the work efficiency of a typical system (that is, in the amount of work users get done in a given time).

> **Discussion Question 137**
> The easiest thing to do with barely usable software is just to document all its foibles in the user manual. To what extent is this a solution?

19.5   Testing

Testing contributes to both verification and validation, probably more to the former. Readers are probably familiar with the basic ideas and kinds of testing: we will summarize briefly, before discussing the special features of object oriented projects. Testing can be carried out on many different artifacts, including not only running systems but also designs and parts of systems. It has three major aims:

- to help you find the bugs[2]
- to convince the customer that there are no (important) bugs
- to provide information that will help with system evolution. For example, the testing process can help to gather information about future requirements and priorities, as well as information about present performance which may only have been estimated before.

The first aim is of course the most crucial, and leads directly to the conclusion:

---

[2] 'bug' here includes all defects, of whatever kind.

> A successful test is one that finds a bug.

It's easy to make the system pass all its tests – just use an inadequate test suite. It is not easy to eliminate all bugs.

Different kinds of testing can help to eliminate different kinds of defect:

- **Usability testing** tests that the system will be easy to use effectively. This may include testing the whole system, some part of it, or its documentation.
- **Module (or unit) testing** tests the individual modules of the system; in an OO development, as we shall see, this normally means the classes.
- **Integration testing** tests that the parts of the system at some level work together correctly: for example, that the objects involved in a collaboration work together as planned, or that components and frameworks really do plug together as they should.
- **System testing** tests that the system meets its requirements, both functional and non-functional.
- **Acceptance testing** is usually performed by the customer, or some independent group representing the customer; it validates that the system is really fit for purpose.
- **Performance testing** may happen at any level (module, integration, or system testing) to check that the system's performance is or will be satisfactory.
- **Stress testing** is a kind of performance testing that puts the system under greater loads than will normally be expected, to check that it degrades gracefully rather than failing catastrophically.
- **Regression testing** tests that those features of a system which worked before a modification still work after it. The tests carried out are some of those carried out previously: unit tests for any affected units, integration tests for any subsystem which includes a modified unit, and some or all of the whole-system tests (usability, system, acceptance, performance and stress tests).

These categories are not mutually exclusive, and the boundaries are not always clear: the most variable aspect is what's covered by integration testing. Should it include all testing of a subsystem or multi-class component, for example, or should it check only that all use of interfaces is syntactically correct? The distinction is not important provided that all kinds of tests are done under some heading!

19.5.1 Choosing and carrying out tests

Tests can be broadly classified as

- black box (the tests are chosen by looking at the *specification* of the thing to be tested), or
- white box (the tests are chosen by looking at the *structure* of the thing to be tested).

Which aspects of a thing is it most important to test? In [38], N.H. Petschenik identified three facts about which kinds of testing are important in ensuring that the customer experiences the software as having high quality:

- It is more important to test what the whole system does than to test its components.

- It is more important to check that the system can still do the things it could do before, than to check that new features work.
- It is more important to test typical cases than boundary value cases.

Q: Why? Do these statements seem counterintuitive?

Since it is essential to retest existing functionality when changes are made – that is, to do *regression testing* – tests have to be:

- repeatable
- documented (both the tests and the results)
- precise
- done on configuration-controlled software.

In iterative projects, especially, the same functionality may have to be retested many times; so some kind of automation of the testing process is a necessity. Specialist testing tools exist that can also generate many test cases automatically. However, a simple Perl script [51] (or even more primitive scripts, such as DOS batch files) can help considerably with

- running a set of tests
- recording what tests were done, on what configuration, and with what results
- comparing the results with what was expected.

It is important to remember, of course, that automation cannot compensate for poor test planning.

When should the test specification for an artifact, which describes what tests should be done and what results are acceptable, be written? The short answer is 'as early as possible, but no earlier'. The test specification can be written at the same time and with the same level of detail as the corresponding requirements specification; but it is futile to suppose that you can write tests for something if you do not yet understand what it is supposed to do!

The reason for writing the test specification as early as possible is that it helps to ensure that the requirements are clearly understood, and that they are highly testable. Requirements may be written in numbered sentences, and a table can record which test (or tests) checks which requirement (or requirements). Thinking about how a requirement can be tested is often a good way to pin down what the requirement really is.

It is sometimes advocated that acceptance tests and their results should be precisely defined at the beginning of a project, and that the developers should be contractually bound to produce a system which passes these tests. The idea is that this benefits both the customer, who does not have to accept an incorrect or incomplete system, and the developer, who knows from the beginning exactly what is required. The problem with this approach is that it can easily fail the 'but no earlier' test, if detailed tests are written when only the outline requirements are known. Capturing requirements using use cases can help to ensure that tests are written at the right level, because the scenarios in the use case describe the requirements and also serve as an obvious source of test cases. A good way to keep clear of premature design is to concentrate on what changes occur between the beginning and end of a scenario: for example, how does an actor benefit?

In an iterative development it is often useful to write the tests, which the result of the iteration should pass, at the beginning of the iteration: one of the benefits of the iterative approach is that this is likely to be possible, even if the requirements on later iterations are not yet completely understood.

But that's not the whole story. It's very hard to describe complex tests properly, or to define the right ones – but some bugs show up only if you do a complex sequence of things. How can such bugs be caught?

- By writing well-modularized and module-tested software so that this is less likely to happen in the first place!
- By having someone testing software with the aim of breaking it, however sneakily.

That is, although precise, short, documented tests are essential, they are not sufficient.

DeMarco and Lister in [14] describe IBM's Black Team, which was a team of particularly fiendish testers who delighted in finding bugs in software. Of course, the team was a great success for IBM – if the team found the bugs the customer didn't!

This kind of testing is particularly important for graphical user interfaces, which are hard to test systematically. It's practically impossible to automate testing of a GUI without a special tool, and even with one it isn't easy. Moreover, a high proportion of the problems with user interfaces are failures either of usability – and usability testing cannot be automated! – or of behaviors which are required of every user interface irrespective of the underlying system ('sanity conditions'). For example, each button should have a label (or some other visual indicator) to show what effect pressing it will have, and clicking it should not hang the application.

> **Discussion Question 138**
>
> What other sanity conditions are there? How, if at all, should the requirement that a user interface be sane, in the senses you consider, be documented in the requirements specification? How can the interface best be tested?

19.5.2 Special problems of OO

There are three main extra problems at the unit testing level.

Unit test what?   The unit of test has to be (at least[3]) the class, and a class is harder to test than a function. The reason is that an object has state, on which its behavior may depend, so testing each method in isolation might miss bugs caused by one method changing an object's state to something that exposed a bug in another method.

State diagrams expose the problem as well as suggesting a way of tackling it. As explained in Chapter 11, an object moves between two states of a state diagram when its full state, the values of all its attributes, changes in a way that may qualitatively affect its behavior. So at the least, an object must be tested in every state. Testing an object in a state ought to include checking all the ways in which the object might leave that state; so in fact every *transition* of a state diagram should be tested.

---

[3]   The commonest view is that the unit of test is the class, but some experts – Martin Fowler, in [20] for example – say that they normally prefer to unit test a package containing a related family of classes.

Discussion Question 139
Is this sufficient? If not, can you formulate a better rule?

> Classes with complex state diagrams are hard to understand and to test – try to avoid designing such classes.

Encapsulation   In Chapter 1 we claimed that encapsulation was important precisely because it decreased the chances of bugs being introduced by ill-understood interactions between components. This is true, but it can also make testing an encapsulated component difficult. For example, to test whether an object has made a transition from one state to another, you need to be able to tell what state the object is in, which should probably be encapsulated information, not available to the outside world. One solution is for each class to provide a method, to be used *only* during testing, that reports all of an object's state.

Discussion Question 140
If there are state-reporting methods, how can you be confident that they themselves are correct?

Inheritance and polymorphism   When a subclass extends a thoroughly tested class by overriding some of its methods, what tests of the new subclass are necessary? You might hope it would be enough to test the overridden methods; but unfortunately because of dynamic binding this is not the case. Suppose the subclass D overrides method foo(), but not method bar(), of the superclass G. The results of sending bar() to an object of class D could still be different from the results of sending it to an object of class G. For example, the implementation of bar() could involve the sending of the message foo() to the object itself. If the object has class D, then D's new implementation of foo() will be used. If this has different behavior from G's foo(), a knock-on effect could be that D's bar() behaves differently from G's bar() as well – even though the code for D's bar() method is identical to G's! So to be safe all of a subclass's capabilities have to be tested, even those which are inherited from the superclass.

Q: Write classes D and G with methods foo() and bar() that behave as described above.

Discussion Question 141
Does the problem still arise when a subclass only adds new operations, without overriding any methods?

Inheritance-based polymorphism adds an extra layer of complication. When an object of class A interacts with an object of class B, it may in fact be interacting with an object of any subclass of B – which may not even have been invented when class A is tested!

Discussion Question 142
How can this problem be dealt with in practice?

> A class is tightly coupled with its superclasses, which creates difficulties for testing. Use inheritance only when its advantages outweigh the disadvantages.

Of course, because the state dependency is in objects, which have well-defined interfaces, we hope to save effort at integration and system testing, and to win overall. But this isn't automatic in object oriented programs. The architecture of a system has a major effect on its testability.

Testing aims to expose imperfections in systems, of whatever kind; yet imperfect systems frequently pass their tests and are released to users. Why?

19.5.3 Why is testing so often done badly?

- It's *very very boring*, especially the documentation of the whole process. Automation may help; but there is still a substantial amount of work to be done to document how the system must be set up for testing and what tests must be done. This is important in order to ensure that tests are repeatable. This is an area where a streamlined quality management system (see Chapter 20) is essential: boring tasks are tolerable provided that it's clear they are important, but can be extremely demoralizing if they seem to be bureaucracy.

- It's very expensive, in time and hence money. (Testing time may exceed 50% of project time: 30% is about average.) The alternative – not testing thoroughly – may be worse, but the cost may not show up until later, when the complaints start arising . . . .

- Testing is often planned mostly for the end of the project, and gets squeezed by deadline pressure. This is an argument in favor of an iterative process in which integration happens frequently; testing is spread through the development cycle and is less likely to get squeezed.

- Customers may pressure developers to deliver on time and untested, rather than late and tested.

Discussion Question 143
What should you do?

Discussion Question 144
What are the special problems of verifying systems involving concurrency? How can they be tackled?

In the next section we examine another family of techniques, complementary to testing.

19.6 Reviews and inspections

Reviews and inspections of various sorts can contribute both to verification and to validation, probably more to the latter.

A review, inspection or walkthrough is essentially a meeting which attempts to find problems with some product of the development process: this could be code or design, for example. They are sometimes known as a group as Formal Technical Reviews (FTRs).[4] The *Fagan inspection* [19] is probably the best known.

FTRs vary widely in their process and degree of formality, but usually have the following properties:

1. The participants are peers (not manager and subordinates) and include the main Author of the thing being reviewed, someone designated as Moderator, and someone (the Scribe) to record the meeting's findings.

2. The artifact to be reviewed is made available to the participants in advance, and they study it before the meeting. The main areas of concern are identified before the meeting. Usually the artifact must satisfy some entry criteria to be considered ready for inspection: for example, if it is code it may be required to compile without errors or warnings.

3. The meeting follows some predefined agenda, and delivers a record of the defects found, with some kind of analysis of them. This might have to say how serious the defect is or what its root cause is, for example.

4. The meeting does not discuss how to remedy the defects.

5. There is some predefined follow-up procedure, often just between the Moderator and the Author, to check that the defects have been addressed. (Not necessarily fixed: some defects may be considered too minor to be worth fixing.)

For example, a relatively informal *design review* of a UML class model for an iteration of development which is supposed to deliver some use cases might involve a group of four to seven people in a room for an hour or two. The Author, the main developer of the UML model, may be asked to explain how the UML model provides the functionality of the use cases, with the other participants asking questions and trying to expose possible problems. The Moderator makes sure that the meeting stays on track and does not, for example, deviate into on-the-spot design to fix the defects. The Scribe records the problems that the meeting finds, and whether they are minor, moderate or serious. After the meeting, the Author is given a copy of the defect list, and reconsiders the design with colleagues. Some time (usually not more than a week) later there is a follow-up meeting between the Author and the Moderator to check that the defects have been considered, and fixed where appropriate.

In a *code review*, as the name suggests, a similar process is carried out with respect to code.

19.6.1   Problems of FTRs

It is more than 20 years since Fagan inspections were first described, and plenty of authorities say that they can be cost-effective for finding defects, especially design defects. Yet FTRs are nowhere near as ubiquitous as testing, and if anything they are less common in projects that follow a modern iterative process than in those following the waterfall model. Why? A newsgroup discussion led by Bill Brykczynski on the subject is well worth reading (there's a link from the book's home page). Basically, problems seem to fall into two categories:

---

[4] 'Formal' here is being contrasted with an informal impromptu chat over coffee – nothing to do with formal specification!

1. An FTR, which after all aims to find defects in an artifact, can easily feel like an attack on the developers of the artifact.
2. FTRs are very time-consuming, especially when they review inadequately documented code. Worse, FTRs sometimes produce long lists of trivial defects, whilst missing more fundamental problems with the artifact.

Discussion Question 145

As the Moderator of an inspection, how can you influence its success?

Discussion Question 146

What advantages do code reviews have over code testing? What disadvantages?

Discussion Question 147

What might be suitable entry criteria for a design document?

Discussion Question 148

Some organizations invite a customer representative to design reviews. What advantages and disadvantages does this have? What factors influence whether it is a good idea?

SUMMARY

This chapter considered product-focused techniques for improving quality, after briefly returning to the question of what quality of software is. It classified product quality improvement activities into verification (checking whether we're building the product right) and validation (checking whether we're building the right product). It considered techniques for verification ranging from informal human checks, perhaps aided by a list of things to check, through to formal proof. An important part of validation is usability analysis, which requires the involvement of users. Testing is useful both for verification and for validation; we discussed the special needs of object oriented systems. Formal technical reviews, too, are useful in both areas. However, we suggested that focusing on the product might not be sufficient; in the next chapter we consider process-focused approaches to ensuring high quality.

CHAPTER 20

Process quality: management, teams, QA

In this final chapter we consider the contribution made to the quality of systems by the organizations which build them and the quality assurance processes of these organizations. We start off with the management, leadership and teamwork, because these are the most important determinants of success and failure. We go on to consider what is meant by *quality assurance* in the context of the kind of project we are considering, and to discuss the role of a *quality management system*.

20.1   Management

Two types of management are relevant to software:

- people management
- project management.

Both kinds of management can be seen in two ways, between which there is a tension.

Management as enabling activity   The most important function of the manager of a task is to enable the people doing the task to get on with the job. The ideal manager minimizes, removes or ideally prevents the appearance of obstacles including risks – such as missing information, inadequate training or equipment – and other destructive influences, such as unrealistic schedules and mindless bureaucracy. The manager may remove such an obstacle by making the necessary arguments to make it go away, and if necessary by doing the dirty work him or herself.[1]

---

[1]   See *The Dilbert Principle* [1] p. 233.

Management as (financial) control   Perhaps a more common view of management is that managers control what happens, with the main aim of maximizing the financial success of the organization. According to this view, building high quality products, making a positive social contribution, ensuring the happiness of customers or employees are all at best secondary aims: if they matter at all, it's because they indirectly further the financial goal.

Discussion Question 149

Can you make an argument that the financial consequences of the failure of a safety-critical system are sufficient to make avoiding such a failure an important goal even if financial success is considered the single high-level aim? Do you believe it?

20.1.1   Project management

A project manager has overall responsibility for the success of the project. The manager's responsibilities include:

- analyzing and controlling risk
- liaising with the customer or with other parts of the organization
- defining lines of communication (between teams on the project, and between people and the customer)
- making sure appropriate people are selected for the project, and that they are appropriately trained
- producing a plan for the project, including a schedule, a cost estimate and a quality plan
- assigning tasks (among teams on a large project, to individual people on a small one)
- measuring the progress of the project
- making sure appropriate components, tools and techniques are used
- keeping the project on track, and taking action to limit damage if it slips
- ensuring that any contractual obligations such as adherence to standards are fulfilled
- making sure that the project implements improvements suggested by previous projects' experience and that this project's experience is fed back into the organization's other projects.

Of course this does not mean that the manager personally does all of these tasks.

Discussion Question 150

Is anything missing?

Discussion Question 151

One classification of the tasks of a project manager [46] is that they are:

- planning
- organizing
- staffing
- monitoring
- controlling
- innovating
- representing

Are the tasks listed above and any others you found covered by this classification? Is anything missing?

20.1.2 Estimating an iterative project

An organization which switches to an iterative development process from a traditional waterfall process has to build up new expertise for estimating, planning and scheduling. For example, in an iterative project there aren't automatically milestones like 'the end of analysis' which can be used to measure a project's progress. An appropriate milestone might be the delivery of an iteration containing particular functionality, for example. In Chapter 7 we mentioned Kent Beck's *planning game* as a technique for estimating a project from the use cases: that is, the units of time that go into the schedule are the times taken for each use case (including design, test and documentation time for the use case), rather than being the phases of the project (all the design, all the documentation, etc.). We get back the ability to build up a schedule from more understandable and estimatable parts, which helps avoiding making unrealistically optimistic (or pessimistic!) estimates.

Recall (from Chapter 1) that the *average* large project takes 50% longer than it is scheduled to. Even though this statistic hides many projects that do deliver on time or ahead of time, this is an appalling state of affairs. Why is estimation so hard to get right? The principal reason is of course lack of information on which to base the estimate; this applies particularly to large, one-off systems built to meet the needs of the customer's particular set of problems. The project schedule is normally set long before anyone has a really detailed understanding of the requirements of the project. So the schedule is done on the basis of a 'best guess' at the requirements, and the real requirements are found as the project proceeds. In addition, requirements (even the 'ideal' ones which may or may not be known!) are not static. The needs of the customer change. If a project lasts several years, the nature of the problem to be solved may be very different at the end of the project than at the beginning.

But hang on a moment. We've explained that estimating is hard to do: but if this was all there was to it, wouldn't we expect projects to deliver massively ahead of schedule as often as they deliver massively behind schedule? They do not: estimates are usually (not always) too optimistic, rather than too pessimistic. There is enormous pressure to come up with an estimate which is acceptable to the customer (or the marketing department, or another part of the organization which is acting as the customer). One of the most difficult tasks of a project manager is to defend the project schedule even if it unpopular with the customer: see [35] on this.

> The fact that projects often slip is not an excuse for complacency. Every slip is a failure.

Discussion Question 152

Take a critical look at the statistics involved in measuring the success of project estimation: do some back-of-envelope calculations along the lines of 'If there are 100 projects and 50 of them deliver in half the time planned ...' and see what you get for the mean slip. Is this the right statistic to be looking at? Suppose you are a project manager deciding what statistics your organization will use in order to measure how good or bad its estimation practices are, and to track whether changes to your process are improvements or not. What measurements should you collect, and what statistics will be most useful?

Discussion Question 153

Research one or more estimation models and tools, such as COCOMO. What might be the benefits of using such a model or tool? (Consider social effects, as well as technical ones.) Will it suit an iterative process? Are there any disadvantages?

Discussion Question 154

What aspects of human psychology may affect estimation? You may find Mark Paulk's paper [37] interesting.

20.1.3 Managing component based development

Part of the project manager's responsibility is to enable the developers to make the best possible use of available components. This may include authorizing the investigation and purchase of component libraries, liaising with other parts of the organization about possible reuse, and (perhaps most importantly) making sure that the project has mechanisms in place to ensure effective internal reuse. This can be difficult in a use case driven project; it is easy for different teams, charged with implementing different use cases, to reimplement much of the same functionality because it occurs in several use cases and has not been identified as common. Solution techniques include understanding enough about what teams are doing to put teams in touch with one another when commonalities appear; and at a technical level, making *appropriate* use of the ≪include≫ relationship when the use case model is developed.

We have said that the development process needs to be *architecture-centric*. Somebody has to champion the architecture: James Coplien's *Organizational Patterns* (see the book's Web page) suggest that in order to ensure coherence of the architecture of a system, there should be a single architect, but that the architecture should be reviewed by other people. The manager does not have to be the architect, indeed usually will not be, but does need to ensure that somebody takes responsibility for the architecture and that the project team accepts it.

Q: Why should the architecture be reviewed?

The project manager must also ensure that the project fulfills whatever responsibilities it has to the organization's component-building strategy; for example, that potential components are identified, documented, tested and placed in the component library.

> **Discussion Question 155**
> Under which of the headings we gave in subsection 20.1.1 do these responsibilities of a project manager fall?

20.1.4   People management

Normally each employee will have a personal manager. This may be the same person as the project manager, but (especially in a large organization) may not be. Whereas you may have a different project manager for each project, a personal manager (sometimes called a line manager) will have a long-term involvement. His or her job is to make sure your career is progressing, that you are getting appropriate training, that your performance is satisfactory, etc. He or she probably also has a role in deciding what projects to assign you to. The term *matrix management* is sometimes used for a situation in which it's normal to have two different people managing your project and managing you: the idea is that one defines which row of a matrix you're in and the other defines which column you're in.

The main argument for having two separate people as project manager and personal manager is that there's a conflict of interests between the roles, since the project manager has the immediate project's best interests at heart, whereas the personal manager is aiming to further the long-term interests of the company by making best use of people and enabling them to develop their skills. On the other hand, a structure in which people have several managers with different responsibilities needs careful definition if it is not to result in confusion; and neither manager will know the employee's work as well as a single manager would.

> **Discussion Question 156**
> Does a line manager need to behave differently depending on whether the organization uses the kind of development process we consider here, or a traditional waterfall method? If so, how?

> **Discussion Question 157**
> What are the characteristics of a good manager? Does this differ according to whether you consider project or people management? If so, how?

20.2   Teams

> **Discussion Question 158**
> Consider teams you've been part of. To what extent were they successful teams? What factors influenced this?

What makes a successful team? A partial answer is that its members:

- have an appropriate balance of personal characteristics. For example, the team needs people (perhaps different people) who are good at

  — seeing the customer's point of view
  — coming up with ideas
  — finding the flaws in ideas
  — helping the team stay focused on the task
  — making sure everyone's voice is heard;

- have an appropriate balance of skills for the task;
- are people who get on with one another: at least, they have a reasonable level of trust in and respect for one another;
- are part of a basically happy and successful wider organization.

Success builds on success. For example, the more successful a team the more likely it is to have low turnover, which is likely to lead to further success . . . .

At the lowest level teams normally have between three and eight people: this is small enough to keep communication problems under control, though of course the size depends on the project. Each team should have a clearly defined task, otherwise the burdens of communicating with other teams will be overwhelming. There will usually be a team manager: this may be a member of the team so designated for one project only, or it may be a separate job title for a managerial person. The team manager will have the main responsibility for managing interactions with other teams. On a large project there might be a hierarchy with groups of teams forming sub-projects under a sub-project manager and so on. Managing communications in such a project is very hard, and failure to do so is one of the main reasons why projects fail. There are various approaches to tackling this. At one extreme, a large project may try to keep all interaction between people on different teams to managed pathways: you talk to your team manager who talks to your sub-project manager who talks to another sub-project manager who talks to a team manager on that sub-project who . . . . At the other extreme, a project may try to keep all possible channels of communication open, for example by having regular project meetings to which everyone involved in the project is invited. (If we knew that one of these worked better than the other, we might have less of a software crisis than we do!) Note, however, that having a known structure to allow communication to happen is more important than what that structure is.

Individual roles within a team may be well defined or not, depending on the process being followed.

There's also a wider concept of teamwork involving a whole company 'pulling together' – this is more nebulous, but depends on factors such as the developers feeling valued by the organization, and everybody being committed to a common goal.

20.3 Leadership

Leadership is often confused with management (not least by managers!) but the functions are essentially different, and need not be taken by the same people; indeed it's possible to argue that they shouldn't be.[2]

So what's the difference? It's hard to characterize, but the best we've come up with is the following:

A manager is a smoother-down and a leader is a shaker-up.

A leader is a person who knows where they're going and has ideas about how to get there: a vision person. Leaders may concentrate on the most important goals to such an extent that they lose sight of more peripheral issues altogether. They aren't easily sidetracked, or indeed diverted from their course in any way. As you see, any of these characteristics can be strengths or weaknesses, and which each one is in any circumstance may well depend on whether the observer agrees with the leader or not!

Discussion Question 159
An alternative characterization of the difference (which Stephen Covey eloquently explains in [12], where he attributes it to 'both Peter Drucker and Warren Bennis') is 'Management is doing things right; leadership is doing the right things'. This is structurally similar to the standard characterization of the difference between verification and validation, which we discussed in Chapter 19. Can you make connections between the four topics?

Management skills can (to some extent at least) be learned, and someone who's a good manager will probably be competent at managing any task which they understand well enough. It's not so clear that leadership skills can be learned. It's certainly possible for someone to be a good leader for one task, and quite unable to lead another, since a personal commitment to the task is important. On the other hand, it's not essential for leadership to come always from the same person, even within a task. Since a large part of good management is about understanding lines of communication, we don't think it's possible to distribute management in the same way. One may argue that in making appointments into a hierarchy one should look primarily for good management skills, and let leadership arise where it will; this is one of the justifications for matrix management.

Discussion Question 160
Can someone simultaneously lead and manage?

Discussion Question 161
What makes a good leader?

Discussion Question 162
Do you think you are more likely to make a good manager, or a good leader?

Discussion Question 163
Consider some people in authority over you. Are they good managers? Good leaders? What would the ideal person for the job be like?

---

[2] The authors have several times observed apparently successful situations where the X is a leader whilst the Deputy X is a manager: it would be interesting to see how common this is.

> **Discussion Question 164**
> What personal qualities and skills does the project's architect need?

20.3.1 Reform of development process

Any major change in the way an organization operates, including a change to a new development culture, needs a champion to lead the reform. Changes such as moving to iterative development, instituting a reuse program, or adopting object orientation, are examples. It is equally necessary that the reform should be supported by good management; if either management or leadership is lacking, the reform can be expected to fail.

20.4 Quality assurance

Quality assurance is the process of

- convincing oneself and one's customer that any product delivered will have high quality;
- providing a basis for continuous improvement.

This is done by monitoring and improving the *process* of developing software with the aim of increasing the chances that people following the process will produce high quality software.[3]

An organization will normally have a *quality management system* (QMS: the document is sometimes called a quality assurance manual, or similar). This specifies what structures and processes the organization has for ensuring that each project follows an appropriate quality process, and that the process is continually improved using experience from previous projects. For example, the QMS may specify that each project should have a *quality plan* and define what should be covered in it. The quality plan is normally part of the overall project plan, and prescribes aspects of the way the project will be run which are intended to ensure high quality. It may define, for example, what design documents are to be produced and how they are to be reviewed. The QMS also specifies what *quality audits* the organization carries out to make sure that a project's quality plan is adhered to, and specifies how improvements are proposed, validated and rolled out.

> **Discussion Question 165**
> Try to get access to a real QMS (e.g. from the book's home page) and study it.

One way for an organization to increase its confidence that its quality control is adequate, is to acquire a quality certification such as ISO9001/BS5750 or TickIt. Usually several project audits are carried out by external bodies before the certificate is awarded. In some contexts, particularly development for defense or other government organizations and of safety-critical systems, adherence to particular standards, or a particular certification, is required, either legally or contractually.

---

[3] QA is sometimes – by CMM, for example – used in a more restrictive sense including only the monitoring part of this definition, in which case the term *process improvement* may be used for the rest.

Discussion Question 166
Research two or more quality standards; compare and contrast them.

The most important aspect of quality assurance, however, is that by documenting and measuring what is done and how well it works, it provides a basis for continuous improvement of the process of producing software, with the aim of achieving a continually improving level of quality in the product. If you're aware of what was done differently in a particularly successful project, and you have a way of rolling out changes to a whole organization, you can spread successful innovations throughout an organization. Unfortunately, many quality systems actually work against this aim, by making it difficult and bureaucratic to change processes, even where people agree that the change is for the better: see Panel 20.1 'Quality assurance: the case against'.

International and US companies often classify the process they follow by claiming to be at 'CMM level *n*' for *n* between 1 and 5. This refers to the *Capability Maturity Model* developed at CMU's SEI, which also provides a framework for *process improvement*. In brief, the idea is to improve the quality of the software development process by:

- documenting the way work is performed
- measuring its performance
- using data for controlling the performance
- planning based on historical performance
- training people.

CMM has five levels, from the Level 1, Initial, where process is *ad hoc* and projects succeed through 'individual heroism', through to Level 5, Optimizing, where the organization makes quantitative measurements of its projects and makes use of those measurements to tune the process. Level 3, Defined, corresponds roughly to ISO9001; the organization has a well-defined process, but does not necessarily support it with quantitative measurements.

Discussion Question 167
What kinds of quantitative measurements are relevant, and how? Investigate metrics, using whatever resources are available (as usual, this book's home page is a starting point). What qualities must a metric have in order to be useful?

Discussion Question 168
What are the differences between a suitable QMS for safety-critical projects and for mainstream projects?

20.4.1 Quality assurance for iterative projects

Iterative projects present challenges for a quality assurance system because, for example, the documentation produced will exist in many different versions at different times of the project. Having a document reviewed and signed by an appropriate person may be seen as less significant when the document will be changed again the next week. A QMS for an iterative project will probably define what has to be done before an iteration can be released to the customer, for example, rather than specifying what has to be done before the end of the analysis phase of a waterfall process.

20.4.2 Total Quality Management

TQM works on the basis that the quality of a product is affected more strongly by the commitment to high quality of the people involved in producing the product, than by how carefully people follow an approved process. Ken Croucher writes in [13] that 'Quality is achieved by making unlimited numbers of trivial improvements'. The idea of TQM is that it is part of everybody's job to contribute improvements.

Supporting this view, TQM also involves improving the quality of people to match the needs of the projects they work on. Taking notice of training needs is a vital part of adopting TQM.

Discussion Question 169

What is the relationship between TQM and a formal quality assurance system? Are they in conflict, or can they support one another? How?

PANEL 20.1 Quality assurance: the case against

In universities, and in some industrial contexts, we are used to seeing formalized quality assurance, ISO9001 registration, high CMM levels, etc., sold as unequivocally Good Things.[4]

So why aren't all organizations ISO9001 registered? Are their managers just stupid?

Of course not. Some of the arguments that can be made against such registrations are as follows.

- The costs involved outweigh the benefits. This is the crux of the matter. Increasing the amount of documentation you produce and the number of meetings you have is expensive: and the introduction of a QMS almost always causes these effects. The benefit is supposed to be improved quality of products, and hence enough financial benefit to outweigh the cost. However, great care is needed to make sure that every aspect of the QA process pays for itself.
- Documenting the process that must be followed makes the project inflexible: it cannot react properly to particular circumstances.
- It discourages people from thinking. If a QMS lays down the process you are supposed to follow to achieve high quality products, there is a temptation to give up thinking independently about how to do that, and instead rely solely on the QMS. This doesn't work.
- It demoralizes the best staff. Writing documentation and having meetings is less interesting than developing software. And introducing a QMS often seems to involve writing documents that nobody ever uses and having pointless meetings.
- Controlling what must be done actually stifles innovation, because if you want to do anything different you have to write it into the quality plan and get it approved.

The only hope is that these are criticisms of *bad* quality assurance, not of quality assurance *per se*.

---

[4] Except, tellingly, that people aren't always so keen on QA as applied to their own activities . . . .

> **Discussion Question 170**
> (How) can a quality assurance process avoid the problems above?

Quality assurance is intended to assure high quality. If some activity doesn't contribute to raising quality, why are you doing it?

Of course there may be valid answers to this rhetorical question: the commonest is 'Because our customer will only deal with ISO9001 registered suppliers'. Even here, though, there is usually no reason to continue with practices which aren't useful. Standards are intended to be sufficiently flexible that they should be a help and not a hindrance.

> **Discussion Question 171**
> Is it true that some kinds of organizations or projects (for example, very small ones, or those with very experienced staff) will not benefit from the introduction of a QMS, however sane? If so, which organizations or projects fall into this category?

> **Discussion Question 172**
> Is it fair to lump process improvement frameworks like CMM together with ISO9001 in this context? Or do these problems arise only if you concentrate on monitoring process without improving it?

> **Discussion Question 173**
> What are the interactions between quality culture and reuse? You should consider possible ill effects of an organization's QA system on its reuse program, as well as the beneficial effects. (You might like to consult Martin Griss' paper – [27] – or see the book's home page – which addresses the relationship between CMM and reuse.)

20.5 Further reading

There is a *huge* amount of further reading available on the subjects in this chapter, including on the Web. As usual, there are some starting points on the book's home page.

SUMMARY

In this final chapter we considered the contribution made to the quality of systems by the organizations which build them and the quality assurance processes of these organizations. We discussed management, leadership, teams, organizations and quality assurance. We emphasized that quality and quality assurance are different but related things. Of course they are essentially bound up with all sorts of other properties of an organization and the software it produces.

DISCUSSION QUESTIONS

These final questions invite you to consider how you personally feel about some of the issues we've discussed. There are, of course, no right and wrong answers!

1. Would you prefer to work in a situation where you will have a great deal of autonomy and responsibility for dealing with customers directly; or would you prefer to concentrate on solving well-defined technical problems, leaving interfacing with the customer to others?

2. Promotion: in some organizations being promoted necessarily involves taking on more management responsibilities. In others, there is a 'technical track' such that it is possible to be promoted into a position as 'technical expert' available for consultation in your area of expertise, without moving into management.

3. Most management structures will include the idea that a given team has a 'team leader'. In some cases, the team leader will be someone with a different job title from the rest of the team and particular experience or expertise in management; that is, you have to have a formal promotion before you can be a team leader, and from then on you will (almost) always lead the team on which you work. In other organizations, anyone, however recently appointed, can act as team leader for a project. In the latter case the decision might be made on the basis of such factors as the person's experience in the technical or business field. Which do you think is best, or which would you prefer?

4. Would you prefer to work on a large project or a small one?

5. Would you prefer to be involved in development of new products or in maintenance of existing products?

6. Should your company frequently employ contractors to balance out peaks and troughs of work? What about specialist consultants? What should its attitude be towards subcontracting out parts of its work? Which parts? For example, should it contract out the boring routine parts, or should it contract out the difficult parts to specialists?

7. Would you prefer to be involved with products which are well understood, where the challenges are to do with producing exactly the right variant of a basically well-understood thing? Or would you prefer to work on something technically innovative, where the challenge is to make the thing work at all, and where this may prove impossible?

8. Would you prefer to work in an organization which has a certification such as BS5750/ISO9001, or in one which does not?

9. Would you prefer to work in the IT division of a larger organization, satisfying the IT needs of that organization? Or would you prefer to work for a specialist software company that bids for contracts from outside? Or for one whose business is selling 'off the shelf' software?

Bibliography

[1] Scott Adams. *The Dilbert Principle*. New York: Harper Collins, 1996.

[2] K. Beck and W. Cunningham. 'A laboratory for teaching object oriented thinking'. *ACM SIGPLAN Notices*, 24(10): 1–6, October 1989.

[3] Kent Beck. *Smalltalk Best Practice Patterns*. Englewood Cliffs, NJ: Prentice Hall, 1996.

[4] Barry W. Boehm. A spiral model of software development and enhancement. *IEEE Computer*, 21(5): 61–72, 1988.

[5] Grady Booch. Component ware chat hosted by Grady Booch transcript. `http://www.rational.com/connection/chats/docs/cwchat.html`.

[6] Grady Booch. Rational's definition of component. Posting to comp.object, May 11th, 1998.

[7] Grady Booch. *Object Oriented Design with Applications*. Benjamin/Cummings series in Ada and software engineering. Menlo Park, CA: Benjamin/Cummings Pub. Co., 1991.

[8] Donald G. Firesmith, Brian Henderson-Sellers, and Ian Graham. *The OPEN Modelling Language (OML) Reference Model*. Englewood Cliffs, NJ: Prentice Hall, 1998.

[9] John Brinkworth. What is a high quality software system? *SQM 27*, 1995.

[10] Frederick P. Brooks. *The Mythical Man-Month*. Reading, MA: Addison-Wesley, 1975/1995.

[11] Frank Buschmann, Regine Meunier, Hans Rohnert, Peter Sommerlad, and Michael Stad. *Pattern-Oriented Software Architecture – A System of Patterns*. New York: John Wiley, 1996.

[12] Stephen R. Covey. *The Seven Habits of Highly Effective People*. New York: Simon & Schuster, 1992.

[13] Ken Croucher. Co-existence of TQM and quality management systems. *SQM*, 8, 1991.

[14] Tom DeMarco and Timothy Lister. *Peopleware: Productive Projects and Teams*. New York: Dorset House, 1987.

[15] E. W. Dijkstra. Goto statement considered harmful. *Communications of the ACM*, 11: 147–148, 1968.

[16] Alan Dix, Janet Finlay, Gregory Abowd, and Russell Beale. *Human–Computer Interaction*. Englewood Cliffs, NJ: Prentice Hall, 1993.

[17] Desmond D'Souza and Alan Cameron Wills. *Catalysis: Objects, Frameworks and Components in UML*. Reading, MA: Addison-Wesley, 1998.

[18] Christopher Alexander *et al*. *A Pattern Language*. Oxford: OUP, 1977.

[19] M. E. Fagan. Design and code inspection to reduce errors in program development. *IBM Systems Journal*, pp. 182–211, 1976.

[20] M. Fowler and K. Scott. *UML Distilled: Applying the Standard Object Modeling Language*. Reading, MA: Addison-Wesley, 1997.

[21] Martin Fowler. *Analysis Patterns: Reusable Objects Models*. Reading, MA: Addison-Wesley, 1997.

[22] W. R. Franta. *A Process View of Simulation*. Amsterdam: North-Holland, 1977.

[23] Bruce F. Webster. *Pitfalls of Object-Oriented Development*. Foster City, CA: M & T Books, 1995.

[24] Erich Gamma, Richard Helm, Ralph Johnson, and John Vlissides. *Design Patterns*. Reading, MA: Addison Wesley, 1995.

[25] W. Wayt Gibbs. Software's chronic crisis. *Scientific American (International Edition)*, pp. 72–81, September 1994.

[26] Alan Gillies. *Software Quality: Theory and Management*. Florence, KY: International Thomson, 1997.

[27] Martin L. Griss. CMM as a framework for adopting systematic reuse. *Object Magazine*, 10, 1998.

[28] B. Henderson-Sellers and Y. R. Pant. Adopting the reuse mindset throughout the lifecycle. *Object Magazine* 3(4), Nov/Dec, 1993.

[29] I. Jacobson, M. Christenson, P. Jonsson, and G. Oevergaard. *Object-Oriented Software Engineering: A Use Case Driven Approach*. Harlow: Addison-Wesley, 1992.

[30] I. Jacobson, M. Griss, and P. Jonsson. *Software Reuse: Architecture, Process and Organization for Business Success*. Harlow: Addison-Wesley, 1997.

[31] Setrag Khoshafian. *Object-Oriented Databases*. Wiley, New York, 1993.

[32] Philippe B. Kruchten. The $4 + 1$ view model of architecture. *IEEE Software*, 12(6): 42–50, November 1995.

[33] Thomas K. Landauer. *The Trouble with Computers: Usefulness, Usability and Productivity*. Cambridge, MA: MIT Press, 1996.

[34] Karl J. Lieberherr and Ian Holland. Formulations and benefits of the Law of Demeter. *ACM SIGPLAN Notices*, 24(3): 67–78, March 1989.

[35] Steve McConnell. Best practices: How to defend an unpopular schedule. *IEEE Software*, 13(3): 118–120, May 1996.

[36] B. Meyer. *Object-Oriented Software Construction*. New York: Prentice Hall, 1989.

[37] Mark C. Paulk. The rational planning of (software) projects. SEI Report 1995.

[38] Nathan H. Petschenik. Practical priorities in system testing. *IEEE Software*, 2(5): 18–23, September 1985.

[39] James Newkirk and Robert C. Martin. A case study of OOD and reuse in C++. *ROAD*, 1995.

[40] Robert Harper, Robin Milner, Mads Tofte, and David MacQueen. *The Definition of Standard ML (Revised)*. Cambridge, MA: MIT Press, 1997.

[41] J. Rumbaugh, M. Blaha, W. Premerlani, F. Eddy, and W. Lorensen. *Object-Oriented Modelling and Design*. Englewood Cliffs, NJ: Prentice-Hall, 1991

[42] M. Shaw and D. Garlan. *Software Architecture. Perspectives on an Emerging Discipline*. Englewood Cliffs, NJ: Prentice-Hall, 1996.

[43] S. Shlaer and S. J. Mellor. *Object-Oriented Systems Analysis – Modelling the World in Data*. Computing Series, Englewood Cliffs, NJ: Yourdon Press, 1988.

[44] I. Sommerville and P. Sawyer. *Requirements Engineering*. Chichester: Wiley, 1997.

[45] Clemens Szyperski. *Component Software*. Harlow: Addison-Wesley, 1997.

[46] The Course Team. *M355, Topics in Software Engineering*. The Open University, Milton Keynes, UK, 1995.

[47] The Course Team. *M868, Object Oriented Software Technology*. The Open University, Milton Keynes, UK, 1995.

[48] Harold Thimbleby. *User Interface Design*. Reading, MA: Addison-Wesley (ACM Press), 1990.

[49] *UML Notation Guide version 1.3*, OMG ad/99-06-08 (Part 3) 1999.

[50] *UML Semantics version 1.3*, OMG ad/99-06-08 (Part 2) 1999.

[51] Larry Wall and Randal L. Schwartz. *Programming Perl*. O'Reilly & Associates, Inc., 1992.

[52] Jos Warmer and Anneke Kleppe. *The Object Constraint Language*. Addison-Wesley, 1999.

Index

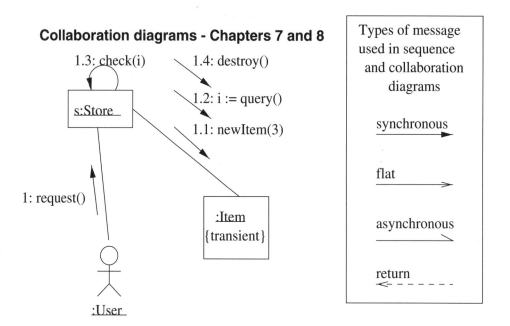

Collaboration diagrams - Chapters 7 and 8

1.3: check(i)   1.4: destroy()

1.2: i := query()

s:Store

1.1: newItem(3)

1: request()

:Item
{transient}

:User

Types of message
used in sequence
and collaboration
diagrams

synchronous

flat

asynchronous

return

State diagrams - Chapters 11 and 12

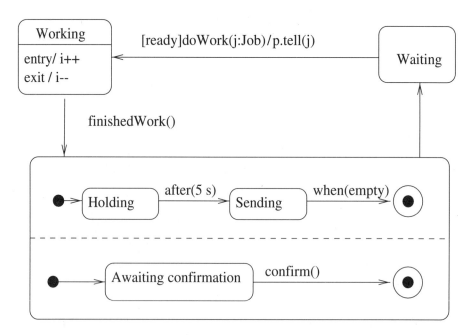

Working

entry/ i++
exit / i--

[ready]doWork(j:Job)/p.tell(j)

Waiting

finishedWork()

Holding   after(5 s)   Sending   when(empty)

Awaiting confirmation   confirm()

Nested concurrent state diagram